TRADING FATE

How a Little-Known Company Stopped British Columbia from Becoming an American State

GRAEME MENZIES

Heritage House Publishing Company Ltd.
heritagehouse.ca

Cataloguing information available from Library and Archives Canada
978-1-77203-548-3 (paperback)
978-1-77203-549-0 (e-book)

Edited by Marial Shea
Proofread by Audrey McClellan
Index by Audrey McClellan
Cover and interior book design by Setareh Ashrafologhalai
Cover image: *Many canoes accompany'd us* by Mark Richard Myers.
Maps by Eric Leinberger, unless otherwise credited

The interior of this book was produced on 100% post-consumer recycled paper, processed chlorine free, and printed with vegetable-based inks.

Heritage House gratefully acknowledges that the land on which we live and work is within the traditional territories of the lək̓ʷəŋən (Esquimalt and Songhees), Malahat, Pacheedaht, Scia'new, T'Sou-ke, and W̱SÁNEĆ (Pauquachin, Tsartlip, Tsawout, Tseycum) Peoples.

We acknowledge the financial support of the Government of Canada through the Canada Book Fund (CBF) and the Canada Council for the Arts, and the Province of British Columbia through the British Columbia Arts Council and the Book Publishing Tax Credit.

29 28 27 26 25 1 2 3 4 5

Printed in Canada

To ordinary people,
and uncommon events

CONTENTS

PART THREE The 1800s

PART FOUR Counterfactual Canada

PREFACE

WHEN I began writing this book I had no idea the United States would start a trade war with Canada and float the idea of making it the fifty-first state, just as the book was about to go to press. My goal was simply to present a west coast perspective of the Canadian origin story.

I wanted to show, contrary to the many oversimplified histories that suggest both countries were created virtually overnight—in the US with a Declaration of Independence in 1776, and in Canada with a conference in 1867—that the true backstory is much more complex and also much more interesting. I also wanted to show that, while heroic personalities like Sir John A. Macdonald and George Washington certainly played their part in big events on the eastern side of the continent, there were many other less well-known personalities making history on the west coast and with equal impact. Key among these was a brief and now mostly overlooked incident at King George's Sound (Nootka Sound), involving ordinary people seldom heard of, which saved British Columbia and stopped Canada from becoming America.

This story unfolds in four parts. The first part covers events in the 1700s, and the third covers those in the 1800s. Between these two centuries is an important second part, which reviews the earliest known encounters between Europeans and west coast Indigenous Peoples. The fourth and final part of the book imagines how the history of British Columbia, and Canada, might have unfolded had the King George's Sound Company never existed.

I have tried to include as many original sources as possible, and have presented the reader with the authentic texts wherever practical. There is one drawback to using 200-year-old texts, however: Spelling and punctuation were varied and inconsistent back then. Readers will find that Nootka is also spelled Nutca, Nutka, and Nuca. I have taken some small liberties, such as changing an "f" to an "s" or adding the occasional comma or period, to make sure authenticity is not provided at the cost of clarity. Those changes have been put in square brackets. For the most part, currency values are in their original form (Spanish dollars, American dollars, British pounds) and unconverted to present-day values.

I hope that by the end of the book readers will have gained a deeper appreciation for the reality behind the common history of two of the continent's countries, and will have enjoyed reading the tales of history's less celebrated characters.

With regard to events of the present day, readers may rightly conclude from this book that the recent tensions between Canada and the United States are not really anything new. America's desire for continental domination goes back a long time and continues to unfold. The popular narrative today, as before, remains focused on the east and on the big personalities in Ottawa and Washington. But if there is a lesson to this book, it is that the fate of nations is as likely to be shaped by common people, tangled up in unforeseen and unscripted events in some remote area of the country, as by the powerful policymakers at the centre of the drama.

GRAEME MENZIES

Vancouver, Canada

PART ONE

The 1700s

1

AMERICA, 1776

WE CANNOT understand how British Columbia was saved, and Canada stopped, from becoming a part of the United States of America without first having some appreciation for how absurd an idea that initially was.

Today, we think of the United States as a big and powerful country. And so we should: it has the largest economy—and defence spending—in the world. We know its independence movement was fuelled by various taxation and policy grievances and by the output of intellectuals stimulated by the Age of Enlightenment. Its political discourse was shaped by people like David Hume, Edmund Burke, Benjamin Franklin, and Thomas Jefferson, with exciting ideas about governance, justice, rights, property, and so on. Thomas Paine, for example, an emigrant to America from England, became one of the best-known of these thinkers when he published his pamphlet *Common Sense* in 1776. The work, which advocated American independence, proved a major intellectual stimulus to the colonies' secession from Britain. These people were intellectual giants.

Despite the magnitude of this intellectual thought, however, at the end of the Revolutionary War in 1783, the United States of America was a small country. In fact, it was hardly a country at all. The thirteen colonies whose representatives had signed the Declaration of Independence in Pennsylvania seven years earlier held an impressive total population of 2.5 million people (half of whom were slaves),[1] but they were spread over a region of more than a million square kilometres, giving a population density of about two-and-a-half people for every square kilometre. Philadelphia, the city where the declaration was signed and the largest city in the American colonies, was home to some 40,000 people, big by North American standards of the day but falling far short of European cities like Paris (about 500,000) or London (over 750,000). The new republic's second-largest city, New York, was home to just 25,000 persons.[2]

The newly formed US, affirmed in the Treaty of Paris in September of 1783, was small in other ways too. Despite having just won a war, it had no military to speak of. The feisty and effective Continental Army that George Washington led, with help from France and Spain, melted away to nothing when he disbanded it in November of 1783. The following year Congress, skeptical of governments with permanent armies, rejected his appeal for a force of around two thousand troops and authorized a new professional standing army of just seven hundred men. In comparison, the British army was about fifty times that size, the French army had about 160,000 men, and the Austrians about 150,000.[3]

The new republic's navy was also comparatively insignificant. While their wartime Continental Navy had scraped together a handful of schooners and brigs to harass and disrupt Britain's Royal Navy, it was the French and Spanish ships that did the heavy lifting for the revolutionaries' battles at sea. As Washington expressed so clearly in a letter to his comrade the French aristocrat Lafayette in 1781, "As certain as night succeeds the day, that without a decisive naval force we can do nothing definitive," and further that "no land force can [act] decisively unless it is accompanied by a maritime superiority."[4] He was absolutely right, and perhaps no better example of this truism exists in the American context than the 1781 Battle of Chesapeake. This match between twenty-four French ships and nineteen British ships near the mouth of Chesapeake Bay—the entrance to the estuary leading to Yorktown—was critical to Washington's success there. Without the French ships blocking access to the British, the British would have either reinforced the troops of General Cornwallis or evacuated them and prevented their surrender to Washington. As it was, the blockade enabled Washington's Continental Army to prevail, Cornwallis was unable to hold out longer, and the Battle of Yorktown is remembered now as a decisive battle that led to ultimate victory for the revolutionaries. But it was the French navy, not the American, that won the day.

A follow-up naval conflict between the French and British navies, the Battle of the Saintes, occurred the following year, and though it had no immediate tactical impact on any land-based operation, it deprived the revolutionaries of any possibility of repeating the success of Chesapeake and helped bring peace negotiations to a quick resolution. In this case, the battle in the Caribbean Sea was a match between thirty French ships and thirty-six British ships (and zero American ships). The conflict saw the British suffer fewer than a thousand dead or wounded while the French lost about three thousand, dead or wounded, with another five thousand captured. The human loss for France was substantial, and so was the loss of treasure: all the surviving French vessels were confiscated by the British navy, along with twenty-six chests of gold and silver that were aboard the French admiral's flagship.

Washington knew that without a navy—the French navy—there was little more to be accomplished with his army, and the peace negotiators in Paris were motivated to draw the conflict to its conclusion. When that came to pass, the Continental Navy, like its Army, was disbanded, having served its purpose. The new republic could not afford, and would not authorize, a professional navy until ten years later, in 1794, when it approved construction of just six frigates, mostly for the purpose of protecting trade ships from pirates. Meanwhile, the European forces continued to dominate the world's oceans. The Royal Navy at this time had about 127 battleships and carriers (and growing),[5] while the French and Spanish navies each had about forty-five ships-of-the-line,[6] and Russia and Denmark had thirty-four and twenty-one, respectively.[7]

The United States' economic size was also small at this time, and somewhat unstable. The thirteen colonies were barely coordinated, with each managing its budgets and trade relationships separately and using different currencies. In 1789, the colonies had only three banks, the oldest just eight years old. Financial markets crashed in 1791 and again in 1792.[8]

The new republic had gained control over an impressive export commodity—tobacco—worth an average annual value of about £750,000. But this compared poorly to Britain's sugar exports from its Caribbean colonies, worth nearly six times that amount.[9] Britain had other sources of trade around the world as well, including spices, tea, and other goods from India and China.

During the wartime period of 1774 to 1781, the colonies' economy, once generating a per-person GDP higher than that enjoyed in Britain, declined by 15 percent as production and exports were reduced and disrupted.[10] The immediate post-revolution economy was no better, with both high inflation and huge debt. In the words of James Madison of Virginia, writing to Richard Henry Lee in 1785: "We have lost by the Revolution our trade with the West Indies, the only one which yielded us a favorable balance, without having gained new channels to compensate it." And, "In every point of view indeed the trade of this Country is in a deplorable Condition. A comparison of current prices here with those in the Northern States, either at this time or at any time since the peace, will shew that the loss direct on our produce & indirect on our imports, is not less than 50 Per Ct."[11]

Exodus

An exodus of human talent following the war was not helpful to the new country either. Some estimates peg the total number of refugees at about eighty thousand people.

Among the thousands of refugees leaving the new republic was a young Black man, Harry Washington. Born in West Africa around 1740 and sold into slavery, he was purchased by George Washington to labour on his Virginia plantation in 1763. Along with several thousand other Black men in his circumstances, Harry Washington had thrown his lot in with the British during the war and served in New York and with the Ethiopian Regiment created by Lord Dunmore, the last loyal governor of Virginia. In 1775, with rebellion brewing, Dunmore had declared martial law in Virginia. He called all loyal subjects to arms and declared all indentured servants and slaves free if they joined the British forces:

> I do require every Person capable of bearing Arms to resort to his MAJESTY'S STANDARD, or be looked upon as Traitors to his MAJESTY'S Crown and Government, and thereby become liable to the Penalty the Law inflicts upon such Offences; such as forfeiture of Life, confiscation of Lands, &c. &c. And I do hereby farther declare all indentured Servants, Negroes, or others, (appertaining to Rebels,) free that are able and willing to bear Arms, they joining his MAJESTY'S Troops as soon as may be, for the more speedily reducing this Colony to a proper Sense of their Duty, to his MAJESTY'S Crown and Dignity.[12]

Harry's association with the US's first president is exceptional, but his story is far from unique. During the war many thousands of slaves—perhaps as many as 100,000[13]—fought with the British and otherwise escaped from their owners and southern plantations, causing material and economic damage to the nascent republic. South Carolina lost about 30 percent of its slave population during the revolution. When the British evacuated Savannah, Georgia, and Charleston, South Carolina, at the end of the war, an estimated 10,000 Black people "accompanied them."[14] Many slaves and free Black people also escaped from New England and New York.

Immediately after the war, Harry Washington was among some 4,000 Black loyalists who fled to safe harbour (literally and figuratively) in Halifax, Nova Scotia. In a very short time, Birchtown, Nova Scotia, became the largest settlement of free Black people outside of Africa.[15]

But many whites fled too. Some were motivated by firm loyalty to the Crown, while others may have held views similar to those of Boston clergyman Mather Byles who, when asked why he didn't support the revolution, notably quipped,

"Which is better—to be ruled by one tyrant three thousand miles away or by three thousand tyrants one mile away?"[16]

Among the refugees were some leading intellectuals: There was a brain drain as well as a labour drain. Two examples are Charles Inglis and Myles Cooper, prominent loyalists in New York City. Cooper was an Anglican priest and president of King's College (its name "decolonized" in 1784 and renamed Columbia College, now Columbia University) and Inglis was the Anglican rector of Trinity Church. The college had been founded in 1754 under royal charter of King George II and was located a short walk from the church, established about sixty years earlier, in 1696. Given the close proximity of their workplaces, and the shared loyalties and views regarding the revolution, it was only natural these men of letters would become close friends and share a great deal of correspondence. Inglis became an active participant in what was later known as the "pamphlet war," often sending drafts to his learned friend Cooper for review before publication.

Inglis's pamphlet *The True Interest of America Impartially Stated* was a direct response to Thomas Paine's more widely known pro-revolution pamphlet *Common Sense*. In that small but influential publication, Inglis outlined the need to patch up differences with Great Britain and end the war quickly, forecasting the challenges and burdens of continued conflict. But a key section explains the moral and ethical conflict torturing loyal subjects at that time:

> What a horrid situation would thousands be reduced to who have taken the oath of allegiance to the King: yet contrary to their oath, as well as inclination, must be compelled to renounce that allegiance, or abandon all their property in America! How many thousands more would be reduced to a

> similar situation; who, although they took not that oath, yet would think it inconsistent with their duty and a good conscience to renounce their Sovereign; I dare say these will appear trifling difficulties to our author [Thomas Paine]; but whatever he may think, there are thousands and thousands who would sooner lose all they had in the world, nay life itself, than thus wound their conscience.[17]

Inglis was firm in his views and did not shrink from making them known. In 1777, when the City of New York was under control of the revolutionaries, General George Washington attended one of Inglis's church services and was shocked that Inglis prayed aloud for the King.

After the war, feeling no longer welcome and determined to walk the talk regarding their convictions, Inglis and his entire congregation moved to Nova Scotia.[18] Inglis became the Church of England's first bishop in North America, based in Halifax, and is buried there in the crypt at St. Paul's Cathedral.

Myles Cooper was also known to take pen to paper and, with Church of England priest Thomas Bradbury Chandler, wrote the dreadfully long-titled essay "A friendly address to all reasonable Americans, on the subject of our political confusions: in which the necessary consequences of violently opposing the King's troops, and of a general non-importation are fairly stated." In this address, Cooper leaned heavily on themes of respect and duty, and was dismissive of the fuss revolutionaries were making about the taxation of tea:

> If the supreme power of any kingdom or state, through want of due information or attention, should adopt measures that are wrong or oppressive, the subjects may complain and remonstrate against them in a respectful manner; but they are bound, by the laws of Heaven and Earth, not to

> behave undutifully, much more not to behave insolently and rebelliously.
>
> But consider; wherein have they been arbitrary, and in what do you suffer? Why, it seems, a duty of three pence a pound, has been laid, by Parliament, upon their teas exported to America; and we cannot purchase the tea, without paying the duty. But if this may be called a burden, so may the weight of an atom on the shoulders of a giant: Besides, this burden may be easily avoided; for we have no occasion to purchase the tea, and unless we purchase it, we are under no obligations to pay the duty.

Cooper's open and strong resistance to the revolutionary forces made him a target of death threats; he was eventually forced out of his home by a mob in the middle of the night. After sheltering at a friend's (possibly Inglis's) house, he made his way to the harbour and took passage on a British warship, making his way to Edinburgh.

The examples of Cooper and Inglis underline the sense of loyalty, duty, and propriety that weighed heavily on the minds of many Americans, along with concerns about the economy, trade, and governance. When the war was over, and the revolutionaries ultimately successful, many people rejoiced at their newfound independence. But many thousands of others—slaves and intellectuals alike—moved away.

Boxed In

The one bright light for the revolutionaries was that the republic had gained some territory to the west, making the Mississippi River its westernmost border. But aside from that, the new country was geographically surrounded and boxed in by Great Britain, France, and Spain. Territory to the north of the thirteen colonies was held by Britain; to the immediate south were the Spanish territories of Florida; to the west of the Mississippi River, both France and Spain claimed the Territory of Louisiana at different times; to the southwest, and as far west as the Pacific coast, Spain again claimed possession.

All of this is to say that the US, in its sovereign infancy, was not a political or economic threat to anyone. Yes, they had won their independence from a mighty global power, but everyone knew their victory was thanks largely to help from another mighty global power: France. Having done their duty to their ally, France had moved on to other things after the American Revolution—like having its own revolution, which, ironically, began in part because of debts the kingdom had racked up fighting the British on behalf of the Americans. Spain, another global power, had also been on the revolutionaries' side in the war and, like France, was largely content to carry on with its own affairs after the war concluded.

The British territory to the north, British North America, included the provinces of Quebec and Nova Scotia, the colony of St. John's Island (in 1799 renamed Prince Edward Island), Newfoundland, and the Hudson's Bay Company territories (also known as Rupert's Land). The colonies of New Brunswick and Cape Breton Island were carved out of Nova Scotia the year after the Treaty of Paris to help manage the number of loyalists relocating to the region.

The east coast of North America at the end of the 1700s was well defined and charted, both geographically and politically. There was no reason for anyone to expect that the United States would ever try, or even have the capability, to swallow up the entire continent.

They didn't even really know where the west coast of the continent was.

2

COOK AND THE WEST COAST OF AMERICA

AT THE END of the American Revolution, the west coast of America was up for grabs as far as the European powers were concerned. This would be a surprise—in time a harsh one indeed—for the Indigenous Peoples who had lived there for millennia. But for the most part, neither the Europeans in Europe nor those who had settled along the east coast of the American continent centuries earlier had more than the foggiest idea of where, exactly, the west coast was. Continental maps of the era portrayed the general outline of the western side of the continent, without the detail of the well-charted east coast, which had been sailed repeatedly by hundreds of ships over the previous century and more.

That was all about to change.

At the same time as delegates to Philadelphia were signing the Declaration of Independence, Captain James Cook was in Portsmouth, England, preparing to start his third voyage around the world. This journey would take him to the northern Pacific west coast and would kickstart a whole new wave of exploration, and also conflict: internationally between

European powers, locally with Indigenous Peoples, and, later, between subjects of Britain and citizens of the United States of America. Cook, forty-eight years old at this time, had been in the Royal Navy for nineteen years and had gained a reputation for being an outstanding marine navigator, surveyor, cartographer, and astronomer. While serving in eastern North America during the Seven Years War (1756–1763) and afterward, he had created hydrographic surveys and charts for the St. Lawrence River and the coasts of Newfoundland and Nova Scotia. He was supremely qualified for the job.

Since Cook's voyages were initially commissioned by the Royal Society as scientific missions, he received advice, referred to as "hints," from the society's president, James Douglas, fourteenth Earl of Morton. Anticipating that Cook would encounter Indigenous Peoples on his voyages, the Scottish Lord Morton wrote in August 1768 that Cook should check the petulance of his sailors and restrain the wanton use of firearms, warning that "shedding the blood of those people is a crime of the highest nature: They are human creatures, the work of the same omnipotent Author, equally under his care with the most polished European; perhaps being less offensive, more entitled to his favor." He added, significantly, that "they are the natural, and in the strictest sense of the word, the legal possessors of the several Regions they inhabit. No European Nation has a right to occupy any part of their country, or settle among them without their voluntary consent. Conquest over such people can give no just title; because they could never be the Aggressors."[1]

But before reviewing Cook's important third voyage, which is so critical to our story about the development of the Pacific coast of North America, it is useful to quickly review the first two. Those previous voyages shaped the attitudes and experiences of many important characters we will encounter later in our story, and help us understand the general attitudes and experiences of the generation that first encountered new lands and people at this moment in history.

The First Voyage

Cook's first voyage around the world took three years and began in 1768—the same year Great Britain responded to revolutionary agitators by deploying troops to Boston. Cook's ship, like himself, had modest but sturdy origins: It was a four-year-old merchant collier from North Yorkshire. Purchased by the Royal Navy, the *Earl of Pembroke* was refitted for adventure and survival at the River Thames's bustling Deptford docks, emerging anew as the adventure-ready bark HMS *Endeavour*. The forty-year-old Cook had a complement of ninety-four people on his ship, including seventy-three sailors, twelve armed Royal Marines, and nine supernumeraries—a scientist, artists, a naturalist, and servants.

The scientist was thirty-four-year-old astronomer Charles Green. Like Cook, Green had been appointed to the voyage by the Royal Society, a key sponsor of the mission, along with the Royal Navy. Green's task was to observe the transit of Venus (its movement directly between the Earth and the sun) in Tahiti, so that the Society could better measure the distance between the Earth and the sun, and thus help determine the size of the solar system.

The theory was that by noting the start and stop times of the transit from various locations on Earth, astronomers could calculate the distance to Venus using the principles of parallax—something akin to stereoscopic vision. By obtaining measurements from various places (in this case the hard-to-reach and faraway south Pacific), the distance to Venus could be accurately determined and then, using complex mathematical equations, the scale of the rest of the solar system could be revealed.

Green was paid two hundred guineas for his role in this groundbreaking scientific effort, and Cook was paid one hundred guineas as an observer, no doubt in recognition of his talents as an accomplished navigator, but perhaps also to ensure he did everything possible to make sure Green was able to achieve his goal.[2] If Cook failed to get them to Tahiti on time, the next opportunity would not occur until 1874. In support of this mission, the ship carried the very latest technological innovations among its cargo: four telescopes, two clocks, and an astronomical quadrant.

Cook also carried secret sealed instructions from the Admiralty, a co-sponsor of the voyages, which were not to be opened until after the Venus mission had been completed. These instructions told him to find, if possible, a rumoured southern continent—Terra Australis (meaning "southern land")—and to chart its coast, bays, and harbours along with noting all manner of wildlife: birds, fish, animals. He was also told: "You are likewise to observe the Genius, Temper, Disposition and Number of the Natives, if there be any and endeavour by all proper means to cultivate a Friendship and Alliance with them, making them presents of such Trifles as they may Value inviting them to Traffick, and Shewing them every kind of Civility and Regard; taking Care however not to suffer yourself to be surprized by them, but to be always upon your guard against any Accidents."[3]

Both of these tasks were carried out to the best of his ability, but not with absolute success. The transit of Venus was observed in June 1769, and the east and northeast coasts of Australia were charted in August of 1770. But Cook did not chart enough of the eastern coast to know whether Terra

Australis was an island or a continent. Likewise, Green's astronomical observations were marred by atmospheric interference, rendering the data less than precise. The voyage did not end well for Green personally either. On the way home, he first suffered from scurvy and then, in his weakened state, contracted dysentery. On January 29, 1771, Cook wrote rather matter-of-factly, and perhaps with a touch of resentment, that Green had died:

> Very variable weather; sometimes squally, with rain, other times little wind and calms. In the Night died Mr. Charles Green, who was sent out by the Royal Society to observe the Transit of Venus. He had long been in a bad state of health, which he took no care to repair, but, on the contrary, lived in such a manner as greatly promoted the disorders he had had long upon him; this brought on the Flux, which put a period to his life.[4]

Perhaps the most interesting and influential person sailing along with Cook on his first voyage was the aristocrat and botanist Joseph Banks. Just twenty-five years old when he stepped aboard HMS *Endeavour* and joined its mission, Banks was a triple threat: adventurous, intelligent, and stinking rich.

Cushioned by an annual income of £5,000 (enough to buy and equip a ship like *Endeavour* twice over), Banks brought along with him a personal secretary, two artists, four servants, and two greyhound dogs. Aside from his onshore expeditions in Rio de Janeiro (where he was among the first to describe for science the bougainvillea plant[5]), Tahiti, and the east coast of Australia, Banks was most enraptured by the six months he spent with Cook in New Zealand. In addition to his many botanical explorations and discoveries, and the astronomical work on the transit of Venus, he was fascinated by the

Indigenous Peoples' use of a hand-held weapon he called a "patoo patoo" (known today as a Māori patu ōnewa). So fascinated, in fact, that he would commission a number of brass versions to be cast in London for Cook to take on subsequent voyages as gifts he could offer to various Pacific Indigenous kings, chiefs, and statesmen—much like the fancy presentation swords that were exchanged between dignitaries in European courts at this time.

Without diminishing Banks's personal achievements on the botanical aspects of *Endeavour*'s mission, it should be noted that he also brought with him the accomplished Swedish naturalist Daniel Solander. When the duo returned from Cook's first voyage in 1771, they brought home 30,000 plant specimens and almost as many tales of adventure and discovery. In almost no time at all, the energetic, wealthy, and charismatic Banks became the most popular and celebrated botanist in Great Britain, a sought-after speaker whose status as botanical advisor to King George III was permanently cemented. And, as we shall see later, he played a critically important role in launching the King George's Sound Company.

Although forty members of the crew died during Cook's first voyage, mostly from malaria and dysentery like astronomer Charles Green,[6] the mission was considered a success. It was also a matter of some discretion if not outright secrecy. Britain had invested heavily in both blood and treasure to advance celestial navigational technology and to gain knowledge of the resources and peoples of the Pacific; it did not want that knowledge to fall into the hands of France, Spain, or any other commercial power. To maintain this secrecy, Cook's instructions included confiscation of all journals and log books:

> Upon your Arrival in England you are immediately to repair to this Office in order to lay before us a full account of your Proceedings in the whole Course of your Voyage; taking care before you leave the Vessel to demand from the Officers and Petty Officers the Log Books and Journals they may have Kept, and to seal them up for our inspection and enjoining them, and the whole Crew, not to divulge where they have been until they shall have Permission so to do.[7]

This would become standard operating procedure for voyages of this nature.

The Second Voyage

Almost exactly a year after the first mission ended (July 16, 1771), Cook set sail from Portsmouth on his second voyage to the Pacific (departing July 13, 1772). This time he was to focus almost exclusively on the search for that southern continent rumoured, but not proven, to exist. Having proved his mettle on his previous voyage, bringing back volumes of new charts, data, artefacts, and insights, Cook was rewarded and entrusted with a new ship: HMS *Resolution.* Not only that, he was also provided with the support of a companion ship under command of thirty-five-year-old naval officer Tobias Furneaux: HMS *Adventure.*

HMS *Resolution*, like the *Endeavour*, started life as a collier and was refitted at Deptford for scientific exploration and adventure. The original name, *Marquis of Granby*, was changed to HMS *Resolution* after a decision to name the ship after the British explorer Francis Drake was rejected. It was thought, with good reason, that naming a ship after Drake might aggravate and provoke Spain unnecessarily. The Spanish remembered Drake not only as Queen Elizabeth's sharpest weapon against her mortal enemy, King Philip II of Spain, but also as a skilled and successful pirate. In 1578 he had sailed into the Pacific through the Strait of Magellan and surprised Spanish ships so full of treasure that it took his crew three days to transfer bullion from one captured ship to their own (one contemporary estimated that the plunder lugged home by the *Golden Hind* would be enough to pay for seven years of war against the very Spaniards from whom it was stolen).[8]

HMS *Adventure* was a slightly smaller ship, technically a bark (whereas HMS *Resolution* was a sloop); like many other ships outfitted for voyages of this nature, it had started life as a collier. It was a sturdy ship, ready for hard work. Its commander, Furneaux, was an experienced navigator and had recently circumnavigated the globe on a different Admiralty mission a couple of years earlier, becoming the first European known to have set foot on Tahiti.

Cook's second mission, as before, was scientific. On board were the latest navigational tools, including a state-of-the-art John Harrison chronometer that made it possible to calculate longitude with more ease and accuracy than the lunar distances method used previously. So precious and precise, the tool was accompanied by two caretakers: astronomers William Wales (who had observed the transit of Venus from Hudson Bay in 1769) and William Bayly (who had observed it from Norway). Aside from field-testing this groundbreaking navigational technology, the main task of the voyage was to find Terra Australis. The Admiralty's instructions directed Cook to search for "that Southern Continent which has so much engaged the attention of Geographers & former Navigators." We know now that there is no southern continent—but that is thanks directly to Cook's many attempts to find it, crossing the Antarctic Circle three times and making long circuits around the South Pacific in the effort. In the course of fulfilling this assignment, Cook took his ship farther south than anyone was known to have been before, charted new islands in the South Pacific, and by process of elimination confidently put to bed the idea of a lost continent.

Along with astronomer William Wales, the crew of HMS *Resolution* included artist William Hodges, gardener Francis Masson, naturalists Johann Reinhold Forster and Johann George Forster, and two characters we will read about later: nineteen-year-old midshipman James Colnett and fifteen-year-old able seaman George Vancouver. Among HMS *Adventure*'s crew, in addition to astronomer William Bayly, was another noteworthy character we'll learn more about later: eighteen-year-old able seaman Richard Hergest.

Fewer died on the second voyage than the first. Only four of HMS *Resolution*'s 120 souls failed to make it home. Those sailing with Furneaux were less lucky: thirteen of HMS *Adventure*'s complement of eighty persons died during the mission, ten of them from an unfortunate and violent confrontation with Indigenous people at Wharehunga Bay, New Zealand, which also left two Māori dead. The Admiralty's admonition to "be upon your guard against any Accidents" with the Indigenous Peoples had been well placed, but proved impossible to uphold at all times.

With two voyages of discovery completed, returning with ships and crew mostly intact, and with the most accurate and precise navigational charts available, Cook was by this time the supreme explorer and navigator of his time. As he wrote in his journals:

> I had now made the circuit of the Southern Ocean in a high Latitude and traversed it in such a manner as to leave not

> the least room for the Possibility of there being a continent, unless near the Pole and out of the reach of Navigation; by twice visiting the Pacific Tropical Sea, I had not only settled the situation of some old discoveries but made there many new ones and left, I conceive, very little to be done even in that part. Thus I flatter myself that the intention of the Voyage has in every respect been fully Answered, the Southern Hemisphere sufficiently explored and a final end put to the searching after a Southern Continent, which has at times engrossed the attention of some of the Maritime Powers for near two Centuries past and the Geographers of all ages.[9]

The Third Voyage

By the time Cook was assigned his third mission around the world, he was acknowledged as a champion of exploration and science; to use a contemporary reference, he was the Neil Armstrong of his time. Indeed, he had become legendary for his territorial and scientific discovery, exploration of strange new worlds, and search for new life and civilizations. His promise to not only go "farther than any man has been before me, but as far as I think it is possible for a man to go" would eventually inspire twentieth-century TV producer Gene Rodenberry's *Star Trek* series. Rodenberry's bold Captain James Kirk, along with his science and medical officers, engineer, and anonymous ill-fated red-shirted marines, who promised to "go where no man has gone before," owes a debt of gratitude to Captain James Cook.

King George III personally presented Cook with his commission to the higher rank of post-captain. The Royal Society made him a Fellow.

To those who read of his exploits, and especially to those who sailed with him, Cook was a living legend. His third mission promised to be extraordinary. The goal was the discovery—or disproval—of the Northwest Passage. Finding a direct route from the Atlantic to the Pacific would be a game-changer. Instead of sailing to Asian markets via lengthy and dangerous routes past Cape Horn, Chile, or Cape of Good Hope, South Africa, British ships could sail directly across British North America. The Hudson's Bay Company, which had been exporting fur from North America to Europe via a network of waterways since it was established in 1670, was among the most prepared commercial enterprises to benefit, but there were others ready to pounce.

For the assignment, Cook would continue on the *Resolution*. His companion ship this time was HMS *Discovery*, under command of thirty-one-year-old Charles Clerke, a veteran of Cook's first and second voyages. Among the noteworthy crew joining Cook on the *Resolution*, in addition to the usual variety of scientists, was his new Sailing Master, the twenty-two-year-old Royal Navy officer William Bligh. Perhaps as a consequence of his tutelage under Cook, Bligh would later gain fame not only for the mutiny on his ship, HMS *Bounty,* but for safely navigating his exiled team of loyal officers to safety, covering 7,000 kilometres in an open launch with no charts and only a compass, quadrant, and pocket watch for navigation.

Richard Hergest, who had served as an able seaman on the second voyage, returned as a midshipman on the *Resolution*. Likewise, George Vancouver, now aged nineteen, signed on for another voyage and was assigned to the *Discovery* as a midshipman. Joining him on the *Discovery* were Cook newcomers George Dixon and Nathaniel Portlock. Dixon was an armourer and skilled mechanic. Portlock joined the *Discovery* as its master's mate. The experiences these four characters had with Cook, and the skills they learned on this voyage, would shape the rest of their lives and the future of North America.

The ships left Plymouth in July of 1776. Cook's instructions were lengthy and detailed, including the following direction specifically about the Northwest Passage:

> Upon your arrival on the coast of New Albion [the west coast of North America], you are to put into the first convenient port, to recruit your wood and water and procure refreshments, and then to proceed northward along the coast as far as the latitude of 65°, or farther, if you are not obstructed by lands or ice, taking care not to lose any time in exploring rivers or inlets, or upon any other account, until you get into the before-mentioned latitude of 65°, where we could wish you to arrive in the month of June next. When you get that length, you are very carefully to search for and to explore such rivers or inlets as may appear to be of a considerable extent, and pointing towards Hudson's or Baffin's Bay; and if, from you[r] own observations, or from any information you may receive from the natives (who, there is reason to believe, are the same race of people, and speak the same language of which you are furnished with a vocabulary, as the Esquimaux) there shall appear to be a certainty or even a probability of a water passage into the aforementioned bays, or either of them, you are in such case to use your utmost endeavours to pass through with one or both of the sloops, unless you shall be of opinion that the passage may be effected with more certainty, or with greater probability, by smaller vessels; in which case you are to set up the frames of one or both the small vessels with which you are provided; and when they are put

> together, and are properly fitted, stored, and victualled, you are to dispatch one or both of them, under the care of proper officers, with a sufficient number of petty officers, men, and boats, in order to attempt the said passage; with such instructions for their rejoining you, if they should fail, or for their further proceedings if they should succeed in the attempt, as you shall judge most proper.[10]

In addition to the frames for the smaller vessels, and everything else required on a long mission like this, Joseph Banks made sure his friend Charles Clerke, commander of HMS *Discovery*, had with him a number of the brass "patoo patoos" he commissioned to be cast at a foundry in London from samples he brought back with him from the first voyage, for Clerke to distribute as gifts to Indigenous people. Banks theorized that Indigenous people would be more appreciative of a gift that copied their own precious items than of the usual European gift items like hats, beads, nails, and mirrors.

The two ships followed a southerly route to the Cape of Good Hope, then east toward New Zealand. Heading northeast from there, the expedition discovered what we now call the Hawaiian Islands, making contact with the Indigenous Peoples of Kauai in January of 1778. Despite a tragic early incident that cost one islander his life—a warrior who took some iron from the ship by force was shot and killed—the remaining encounters were positive. "In the course of my several voyages," wrote Cook on January 20, 1778, "I never before met with the natives of any place so much astonished, as these people were, upon entering a ship. Their eyes were continually flying from object to object . . . strongly marking to us, that, till now, they had never been visited by Europeans, nor been acquainted with any of our commodities except iron."[11]

The ships stayed for two weeks and Cook named the islands the Sandwich Islands after his patron, John Montagu, First Lord of the Admiralty and the fourth Earl of Sandwich.[12]

Leaving Hawaii in early February, the two ships sailed northeast to the west coast of North America. In early March 1778 Cook sighted the continent near Cape Blanco, the second most westerly point of that part of the American coast. Cook would have known that this location (about 100 kilometres north of the present border between California and Oregon) was about as far north as Sir Francis Drake had indisputably sailed up the coast in 1759.

In an account of the voyage attributed to John Rickman, a second lieutenant on the HMS *Discovery*, the arrival was celebrated with a feast of rats: "This day the gentlemen in the gun room dined on a fricassee of rats, which they account a venison feast, and it was a high treat to the sailors, whenever they could be lucky enough to catch a number sufficient to make a meal."[13]

Cook likely did not know that Spanish explorer Juan Francisco de la Bodega y Quadra had visited and named the point Cabo Diligensias in 1775, though he may have known that Spanish explorer Martín de Aguilar had been here in 1603. In any case, his instructions had advised him "not to touch upon any part of the Spanish dominions on the western continent of America, unless driven thither by some unavoidable accident."[14] Accordingly, Cook soon left and began heading north, toward the fabled Northwest Passage and away from Spanish eyes and sensibilities.

Frustrated by poor weather that inhibited visual contact between HMS *Discovery* and the coastline, Cook and HMS *Resolution* unfortunately sailed right past the mouth of the Columbia River about 380 kilometres north of Cape Blanco.

In time, others would discover that, through its network of tributaries, the river would facilitate the transport of goods from here to Hudson Bay (and vice versa). But, in Cook's defence, his instructions had been specific: "proceed northward along the coast as far as the latitude of 65°... taking care not to lose any time in exploring rivers or inlets, or upon any other account, until you get into the before-mentioned latitude of 65°."[15]

It is a further irony, and also a pity, that Cook—the first to circumnavigate New Zealand—also sailed past and failed to investigate the Strait of Juan de Fuca. Poor visibility has often been given as the excuse for this oversight, but it may also be that he was following his instructions adamantly. Had he taken the time to investigate, he may have been the first to circumnavigate what we now call Vancouver Island.

However, battered and tired from a long voyage from Hawaii, an inhospitable coast, and poor weather, Cook proceeded north without delay and finally found a safe and pleasant harbour at a place he later named King George's Sound, now known as Nootka Sound. In the words of Lieutenant Rickman, "We were now so far advanced to the northward and eastward as to be far beyond the limits of European Geography, and to have reached that void space in our maps, which is marked as a country unknown."[16]

What the journals of Cook, Rickman, and others on his ships would ultimately report about King George's Sound when they returned to England two years later, in October 1780, would titillate and entice the minds of commercial traders and—as often happens when trade precedes diplomacy—would lead to conflict, disrupt Indigenous society, and shape international borders.

3

KING GEORGE'S SOUND

THE VOYAGE from Hawaii, and the recent inhospitality of the weather, had left Cook's crew and ships in need of refreshment and repair. King George's Sound was the perfect place for both. The five weeks he spent there were recorded in journals and later reported very favourably. According to Rickman, the harbour was safe and allowed ships to get close enough to shore that fresh water and other goods could be transported easily. It was, he wrote, "a cove the most convenient that could be wished, the entrance of which was about two cables length, bounded by high land on each [s]ide, and furnished with wood and water (now much wanted) so conveniently situated, that both could be taken on board at less than a cable's length from the shore."[1]

The harbour into which Cook had sailed his research ship was new to him but very familiar to the local Mowachaht Nuu-chah-nulth people. Known to them as Yuquot, it had been a focus of seasonal activity for them for perhaps four thousand years. A few hundred people lived in the nearest village, in lodges made from cedar wood, but hundreds more lived in other villages nearby, bringing the total local Indigenous population to about twenty-five hundred. In the summer months the area was used for herring fishing and whale hunting; in the winter months the people moved to the islets nearby and shifted their attention to salmon fishing.[2]

Not knowing otherwise, everyone sailing with Cook assumed this harbour was on the west coast of the American continent (not on an island) and consequently believed the harbour at Nootka was of the type and location that had the potential to turn into a major port such as those found at Macao, Boston, Halifax, Cape of Good Hope and—a century later—like those of Los Angeles, San Francisco, Seattle, and Vancouver.

Not only was the harbour the most convenient that could be wished for from a seafaring point of view, Cook was happy to discover that the Indigenous people were friendly and cooperative. Those who greeted Cook's two ships vastly outnumbered the crew, but Rickman wrote that they were not nearly as frightening as the Māori they had encountered in New Zealand: "When they saw our distress, and that we only meant to repair our ships, so far from giving us any disturbance, they gave every assistance in their power; they supplied us regularly with fish, and, when they found that our men liked their oil, they brought it in bladders, and exchanged it for whatever they pleased to give for it."[3]

Rickman made other observations about the local people that would soon encourage other Europeans to visit Nootka for trade purposes. His reviews were exemplary: "The Indians behaved peaceably and apparently with much friendship. They brought after a short acquaintance, a great variety of valuable skins, such as beaver, foxes, racoons, squirrels, rein-deer, bears, and several others, with which we were but little acquainted, but what they chiefly desired in exchange, were cutlery wares of all sorts, edge-tools, copper, pewter, iron, brass, or any kind of metal with the use of which they were not unacquainted." He added: "They brought, besides skins, great quantities of fish, with plenty of game, which we purchased of them for glass bowls, looking glasses, nails, hatchets, or whatever utensils or toys were either useful or ornamental." In case there were any doubt of his sentiments, he concluded: "During our stay here . . . no people could be more obliging; they were ready to accompany the gentlemen, who delighted in shooting, in their excursions, and to show them the different devices they made use of to catch and to kill their game; they sold them their masks, their calls, and their gins, and made no secret of their methods of curing the skins, with which they carried on a traffic with occasional visitors; in short, a more open and communicative people does not live under the sun."[4]

In the weeks he was there, Cook took advantage of the well-protected harbour, the bountiful resources, and the friendly Indigenous people to repair his ships, refresh his supplies, make some astronomical observations, and conduct trade. His interest in fur was practical: they were heading north after all and, as he and veterans of his previous voyages knew, the weather would get freezing cold. They needed fur to keep themselves warm. On April 26, now loaded with furs and food, and in good health, the two ships went on to explore the northwest coastline further, looking in vain for a Northwest Passage. Heading north from King George's Sound, they made Prince William Sound, Alaska, by mid-May and Cook Inlet, Alaska, by the end of the month. From there the two ships continued along a northeastern route, reaching the Aleutian Islands by the end of June and crossing the Bering Strait by early August. In October they met with Russian fur traders in Unalaska. While they met more Indigenous

Peoples, and conducted more trade for fur and other items, the passage to the Atlantic could not be found. By January of the following year (1779) they were ready to head south for the winter, and a course was set for Hawaii.

Unfortunately, Hawaii is where the voyage ended for Cook. In an event that has been well-documented elsewhere, Cook was struck down on the beach of Kealakekua Bay, clubbed and then stabbed to death. The melee on the beach cost four marines who were with Cook their lives, and some sixteen Indigenous warriors were also killed. Confusion and retribution followed in the hours afterward. Lieutenant Bligh led an assault on the Kealakekua village on the southern shore. Midshipman Richard Hergest, shaken by Cook's death, attempted to exact revenge by shooting Koa, the high priest present at the murder, but was foiled when his pistol misfired. Impressionable midshipman George Vancouver was forever scarred by the incident, and on his subsequent missions to the Pacific he would enforce very strict rules limiting interactions between his crew and any Indigenous persons encountered.

The next day Clerke, who had taken over command of HMS *Resolution*, demanded the return of Cook's body and was horrified to receive only pieces of it. Days later additional bones were delivered to him, with gifts of peace, and Clerke had Cook buried at sea on February 22. The rest of the year was spent attempting to fulfill their mission, searching in vain for the Northwest Passage. In December, ten months after Cook's death, they made a final stop in Macao before beginning their return voyage to England. To their amazement, the amount of money they received for their sea otter pelts in Macao was astronomical.

When at long last HMS *Resolution* and HMS *Discovery* returned to the Thames, in October of 1780, news of Cook's death had preceded them. Their arrival home was a sensation, as was news of their voyage—particularly the reports of business opportunity for those wishing to profit from the fur trade. Cook's words from his journal were carefully scrutinized and duly noted: "There is no doubt," he had written about the King George's Sound area, "but a very beneficial fur trade might be carried on with the inhabitants of this vast coast." He observed that fur skins "are not a scarce article in the country."[5]

Though word of Cook's death was what caught the attention and the imagination of the general public, keen businessmen were more interested in the news of the fur trade. It was as true then as it is today that those who are the first to enter a market are usually the ones who will profit most from it and ultimately capture it. So there were several ambitious men of enterprise who wasted no time heading for Nootka.

First Movers

The earliest to move were those closest to the action—the merchants and traders based at the factories in China and India. These "factories" were not the kind we think of today, where products are manufactured. They were more like trade offices with warehouse capacity. The Canton Factories were the only official place for Western ships to conduct trade with China. At the time of our story—from the mid-1700s to the mid-1800s—they consisted of thirteen houses, the main ones being British, Dutch, Swedish, Austrian, French, Spanish, Danish, and American. In India, there were many factories at many locations. The first factories established by Britain's East India Company were in the cities of Masulipatnam, on the east coast, and Surat, on the west coast, but by the time of our story they had many factories along the coast in cities that remain key trade centres to this day.

In addition to well-known trade companies like the East India Company (est. 1600), there were others competing for trade, such as the Dutch East India Company (est. 1602), the Danish East India Company (1616), the Portuguese East India Company (1628), the Danish West India Company (1671), and the Swedish East India Company (1731). All of these commercial enterprises enjoyed some sort of official licensing and sanctioning from their home countries and contributed not just to the wealth of their owners and shareholders but also to their countries. There were also smaller bit players, some risk-taking adventurers, a few bold entrepreneurs, and others who operated between the margins of officialdom and piracy.

An experienced veteran of these factories and trade companies was a little-known British wine merchant named William Bolts. Born in Amsterdam to English parents, he had moved to Portugal before he was twenty to work in the diamond trade; by the time he was twenty-one he had moved to Bengal and was working for the East India Company. After several years learning the ins and outs of international trade, and eventually falling out with the East India Company, he undertook a number of ventures for the Austrian government and, sailing under their flag, had conducted trade between Austria, India, Africa, and China. It was through his agent at Canton (present-day Guangzhou), John Reid—a Scotsman who had become an Austrian subject in order to act as an agent for the Austrian East India Company—that he heard about HMS *Resolution* and HMS *Discovery*'s fur-selling experience there at the end of 1779. And what he heard through the grapevine would have been a version of what HMS *Discovery*'s commander James King later published for the record:

> One of our seamen sold his stock, alone, for eight hundred dollars; and a few prime skins, which were clean, and had been well preserved, were sold for one hundred and twenty each. The whole amount of the value, in specie and goods, that was got for the furs, in both ships, I am confident, did not fall short of two thousand pounds sterling.[6]

Receiving this intelligence months before the ships returned to London, Bolts knew he had a first-mover advantage and he acted quickly to secure it. He was first to buy a ship for the purpose of sailing to King George's Sound, buying it just a year after the *Resolution* and *Discovery* had returned to London, and two years before Cook's journals were published. Then he recruited four veterans of the Cook mission, including George Dixon, to sail with him. But he needed financial and political backing before he could go any further. Having burned bridges with the East India Company, he turned in May of 1782 to Austrian Emperor Joseph II and pitched him on the idea. It was a golden opportunity, he said, to repeat what the British had done: circumnavigate the globe on a mission of discovery and trade. The emperor was intrigued and supportive, but ultimately didn't bite. Bolts then pitched the project, with Joseph II's approval, to Catherine II of Russia. Striking out again, he pitched it to Ferdinand IV of Italy. Finally, now three years later, he tried Louis XVI of France. But, again, no deal. They all appreciated the business case, but ultimately were more interested in the affairs of continental Europe than the barely charted, unknown coast of the Pacific Northwest.

Unfortunately, like many visionaries, Bolts never quite got his plans off the ground. Had he succeeded with the Austrian emperor, he would have arrived in the King George's Sound area by 1783 and captured the market. But it was not to be and his dreams faded away. Instead, the first trader to actually get there was James Hanna, dispatched from Canton in April 1785.

Like Bolts, Hanna was an experienced businessman with a series of contacts who gathered all the latest intelligence months before it reached the higher-ups in London, Paris, or Vienna. He had one clear advantage over Bolts, however: his financial backers were more imaginative and more dependable. Hanna's main backer was John Henry Cox, a merchant who lived in China and explicitly understood the business opportunity. Cox was also a business partner of John Reid and, like Reid, had heard the tales of the *Resolution* and *Discovery*'s near-accidental fur fortune. He wasted no time assisting Hanna in his venture. The *Sea Otter*, a small snow (so named because its rigging included a type of mast called a "snow mast"), was put under Hanna's command, and by August he and his crew of twenty people were buying fur in King George's Sound. By December 1785 they were back in Macao with 560 sea otter pelts, which they were able to sell for just over twenty thousand Spanish dollars.[7]

It would take a year before the news of Hanna's financial success was reported in the London newspapers, on September 21, 1786, but the reports when they arrived were electrifying:

> The *Sea Otter*, Capt. Hannah, is arrived from King George's Sound, on the West coast of America, after one of the most prosperous voyages, perhaps, ever made in so short a time... you will be astonished when I tell you, that the whole out-fit,

> with the vessel, did not cost them 1,000l. and though she was not more than one month on the coast, the furs she collected were sold at Canton for upwards of 30,000l. Had they had goods to have bartered, and had been two or three months more on the coast, Captain Hannah assured me he could have collected above 100,000l. of furs.[8]

Based on this initial success, Hanna was funded for a second trip. This time he was given command of a ship twice as large. Also named *Sea Otter,* the ship left Macao in May of 1786 and arrived at King George's Sound that August.

While these China-based merchants were clearly the first to cash in on the fur trade, their enterprising colleagues in India were not far behind. In December 1785, at just about the same time as Hanna was arriving back in China from his successful first trade mission, thirty-three-year-old James Charles Stuart Strange began his voyage toward King George's Sound from Bombay. He had two new ships under his overall command: the *Captain Cook* and the *Experiment*. Born in Scotland's remote Orkney Islands, Strange—as his full name hints—was a godson to Bonnie Prince Charlie; he was well connected with traders in the East India Company and received their tacit approval to attempt the mission. He had obtained support from forty-year-old Bombay merchant David Scott, also born in Scotland, who helped Strange purchase the two ships privately. Strange's main ship, the *Captain Cook*, was twice the size of Hanna's *Sea Otter* and, combined with the *Experiment,* had the capacity to bring back three or four times as many furs as Hanna had. Arriving at his destination in July, and receiving a warm welcome from the Indigenous people there, he called the harbour "Friendly Cove."

The age-old saying that timing is everything was proven true once again that summer. Hanna arrived at King George's

Sound for his second fur-buying frenzy one month after Strange. He then discovered, to his great dismay and disappointment, that Strange had scooped up most of the available merchandise. Hanna was able to purchase only fifty pelts.

Meares

Around the same time, a couple of other ships sailed to the area, though they did not trade specifically at King George's Sound. The most notable of these, for reasons that will become clear later, was the voyage from Calcutta by thirty-year-old adventurer John Meares. Coming from Ireland, Meares arrived in Calcutta toward the end of 1785 and, despite having no previous experience as a trader, almost immediately got involved with the Bengal Fur Company. The owners of this venture are now familiar names to our narrative: John Henry Cox and John Reid. Through their connections and affiliations with the Austrian East India Company, the British East India Company, and their own side ventures and deals, the two were working all the angles to maximize opportunities to profit from the trade between China, India, and Europe. When Meares arrived on the scene, full of gusto and with no experience as a trader or any familiarity with the Pacific Ocean, they wasted little time fixing him up with a trade mission to the Pacific Northwest.

In February 1786, Meares sailed from Calcutta in command of the snow *Nootka,* together with a companion vessel, the sloop *Sea Otter,* under William Tipping. Their mission was to sail north toward Russia and then northeast toward Alaska, gather furs, and return to China. The two ships separated, with Tipping making it to Prince William Sound, Alaska, by

September. There he met, quite by accident, James Strange. The two commanders and their crews visited and exchanged information for a couple of days and then went their separate ways: Strange back to China, and Tipping to oblivion. He was never seen again.

Meares arrived at Prince William Sound a couple of weeks later, unaware of Tipping's fate. After seven months at sea, and with the fur-trading season coming to a close, Meares made the rather foolish decision—the kind novice adventurers sometimes make—to winter in Prince William Sound rather than sail south to Hawaii. With the help of local Indigenous guides, Meares sailed his ship to a safe harbour. But while the harbour provided protection from ocean waves, he was about to learn a hard lesson about winters in Alaska. By November his ship was iced in and unable to move. By December the crew was running short of food and hitting the rum to alleviate the pain of hunger and scurvy. By May, twenty-three men—half the crew—were dead: starved and frozen.

To Meares's great good fortune, rescue arrived shortly thereafter. Other fur traders arrived on the scene and fixed him up, feeding his crew and repairing his ship, so that by June he was able to leave Prince William Sound and head back to China.

As Meares was limping away from the Pacific Northwest, a third trader was arriving at Nootka: twenty-eight-year-old Charles Barkley, at sea since the age of eleven, pulled into the harbour with his unlicensed ship, *Imperial Eagle*. Arriving in June 1787, the 400-ton ship was the largest to ever enter the main harbour of Friendly Cove.

While these unlicensed get-rich-quick traders can be credited with making the first moves toward capturing the fur market, a more thoughtful—and perhaps even more ambitious—man was making bigger plans in London. His name was Richard Etches, and the company he was creating was, aptly, called the King George's Sound Company.

4

THE KING GEORGE'S SOUND COMPANY

RICHARD CADMAN Etches, son of a wine merchant in the English town of Ashbourne, halfway between Manchester and London, was an independent and enterprising soul. Not much is known of his youth except that he left Ashbourne as a young man and by 1775, age twenty-two, he had started his own business as a wine and brandy merchant in London. He was thrilled to be operating in this vibrant, bustling city where business was brisk and life full of excitement.

When Etches arrived in London, it was a city of nearly a million people at a time when all of Great Britain held just eight million people. The city was the centre not only of political power but also of financial power. The port of London dominated overseas trade; the volume of overseas trade and the tonnage of shipping were so great that they surpassed all other British ports combined. Within twenty years of Etches entering the fray, 65 percent of all imported goods to England, and exports from England, would arrive or leave through London. In a typical year, the Thames would see somewhere between two and three thousand ships transporting their cargo—linens from Ireland; wine, oil, soap, and olives from Italy; sugar and rum from the West Indies; tea and spices from the East Indies; fur, timber, and hemp for rope from Russia and the Baltic; tobacco from America—and London was gaining recognition as the busiest port in the world.

The evidence of Etches's success in this busy and competitive arena is revealed in a newspaper advertisement he ran in November 1775 promising his customers "a large assortment of the very best cognac brandy, Jamaica rum, hollands geneva [an early type of gin, imported from the Netherlands], compounds, and all sorts of foreign wines... equal in strength and flavour to any sold in London."[1] It is possible Captain Cook saw the ad, having returned to London from his second voyage around the world that very same month. Who knows, maybe he was even a customer.

For the next few years, Etches worked diligently to build his business and expand his social connections within the city. His enterprise, first located on Watling Street, not far from St. Paul's Cathedral, eventually settled at 38 Fenchurch Street, a short walk northwest from the Tower of London and just 400 metres north of the mighty River Thames. He prospered enough that he soon had a trading ship of his own serving ports in France, Denmark, and Holland. By 1779, he expanded from wine to tea, forming a partnership with established tea merchant Robert Hanning Brooks.

Just months after forming this partnership, Etches undoubtedly read the January 11, 1780, edition of the *London Gazette,* which reported news from the Admiralty Office that Cook and four of his marines had been violently killed the previous February. The news was sensational and ubiquitous. Every society in every era has its heroes, and Cook was among the most iconic in his time; his was a celebrity death. The news stories and conversation in the local coffee houses would have turned Etches's calculating and imaginative mind to the Pacific once again—to its great unknown threats, risks, and its untapped business possibilities.

The sensational news of Cook's death brought new attention to all of his voyages and made the conclusion of his third voyage particularly poignant. When HMS *Resolution* and HMS *Discovery* finally returned to London in October of 1780, the thirst for tales of their adventures and discoveries was insatiable. It would be some time before an official account was released but, as had happened in Canton and Calcutta, those who were in the trade business had ways to gather intelligence quickly. Etches undoubtedly heard, through his network, the rumours about Cook's crew making handsome profits from the furs they sold in Macao and began to consider expanding his business from wine and tea to fur. But he was not as impulsive (or as reckless) as some of the other traders we read about in the previous chapter. He was not the sort of adventurer who set sail himself, seeking a quick payoff. He was the sort who stayed in London and dreamed the big dream while making methodical plans for a long-term play.

Banks and Company

For the next three years, Etches continued to develop his wine and tea business, grow his business and social network, and keep his ear to the ground, constantly gathering information about new opportunities. Among the relationships he cultivated was one with Joseph Banks, the wealthy botanist, who, after travelling with Cook on his first voyage a decade earlier, had become the most celebrated and influential botanist-adventurer in the country. Shortly after Banks's return from that first voyage, King George III had made him advisor for his

Gardens at Kew, an extensive private garden that was a centre of scientific and intellectual advancement. A few years later, Banks became president of the Royal Society, and around the time Etches was getting to know him, in 1781, he became "Sir" Joseph Banks. He was an important person to know.

But Etches waited for the official account of Cook's voyages to be published, in 1783, before he started to articulate his plans. And they would be big plans indeed, far grander than anything being dreamed up by Hanna, Strange, or any of the others who were at that very moment getting their ships ready to sail on the other side of the globe. Etches imagined a trading company that would, in time, rival the East India Company or the Hudson's Bay Company. It would be named after the body of water near Nootka that Cook had charted in 1778: the King George's Sound Company. Not only would the company conduct trade in the King George's Sound area; it would also establish a factory (trade office) there.

The concept was grand, but not impossible to achieve. Etches was ambitious and connected, and far more successful when appealing to his patrons than William Bolts had ever been. For one thing, he was a skilled businessman and entrepreneur. He had keen insights and knew how to make a persuasive business case. For another, he could pitch his ideas to someone who had been to the Pacific and understood what he was talking about: Joseph Banks. The fact that Banks had not been to King George's Sound did not matter. What mattered was that he had sailed the Pacific with Cook and understood the vast size and potential of what was yet to be discovered.

King George III was a far more global visionary than most other European monarchs; it was entirely in character, therefore, that, when informed of Banks's plan, he was sympathetic to it. Despite his less than favourable political experiences with the revolutionaries on the east coast of North America, the king was highly informed and interested in the affairs and various qualities of that continent and personally vested in the development of British North America. His interests were multidisciplinary: he was an enthusiastic scientist who had built the world's largest telescope for astronomer William Herschel, and his enthusiasm for gardens and agriculture earned him the endearing nickname "Farmer George" (he occasionally hid his knowledge behind the pseudonym "Ralph Robinson" when submitting articles to the *Annals of Agriculture*, edited by noted agriculturalist Arthur Young). His desire to see the west coast of the continent explored, charted, and fully botanized was genuine, even if he also appreciated the geopolitical advantages.

The King George's Sound Company (KGSC) envisaged by Etches would not be the first to respond to Cook's report of fur-trade opportunities on the Pacific Northwest coast, but it would be the most substantial and consequential of the several traders who sought commercial enterprise there. Following his March 1785 meeting with Banks at his Soho digs (Banks was now well established among the leaders of scientific, commercial, and political activity in London), Etches began to transform his vision into reality. With Banks's offer of help, and an endorsement from the King achieved through him, they agreed on a goal to raise £200,000 in capital. Etches then moved to put the company's legal framework in place.

A licence was obtained from the South Sea Company "with full liberty to make discoveries, to erect factories, and to prosecute other commercial objects" along the west coast of North America.[2] Another licence was granted by the directors of the East India Company's Committee of Correspondence, allowing the KGSC to legally trade its cargoes at the factories in China.

Etches then took great care to recruit the best possible men to fulfill the mission: skilled, reliable, professional, and proven. To command the first pair of trade ships, he selected familiar names from the Cook expeditions: Nathaniel Portlock, who had served on both HMS *Resolution* and HMS *Discovery*, was given command of the 320-ton KGSC *King George*. George Dixon, who had been with Cook on HMS *Discovery*, was given command of the smaller 200-ton KGSC *Queen Charlotte*. The crew capacities for the two ships were fifty-nine and thirty-three respectively.

Portlock and Dixon were also made partners in the company and thus fully vested in its commercial success. Other investors included Etches's brother John Cadman Etches, two of his relatives—both named William Etches—his tea company partner John Hanning, a merchant from Hampshire named Nathaniel Gilmour, and a tea dealer in London named Mary Camilla Brook.

The two ships were named at a commissioning ceremony that same year, attended in person by Banks and other dignitaries and supporters, including Lord Mulgrave, a Royal Navy veteran of the American Revolutionary War and now one of the Lords of the Admiralty. The Prime Minister's Secretary to the Treasury, Mr. George Rose, and his junior Secretary to the Treasury, Mr. Thomas Steele, also attended the ceremony at Deptford, along with the president of the Royal Society at that time, Sir John Pringle. Mr. Rose named KGSC *King George* (after George III) as the lead ship. Sir John Pringle named KGSC *Queen Charlotte* (after George III's wife).[3]

A second pair of ships would be launched the following year, in 1786, with KGSC *Prince of Wales* the lead ship and KGSC *Princess Royal* the smaller partner. And again Etches would choose his leadership crew wisely, with command of KGSC *Prince of Wales* going to James Colnett, who had served with Cook on HMS *Resolution* and was a Royal Navy veteran of the American Revolutionary War. Among his crew would be two other characters of note we'll read more about later: twenty-seven-year-old ship's mate James Johnstone, veteran of both the Battle of Chesapeake and the Battle of the Saintes; and Archibald Menzies, a Royal Navy surgeon and protégé of Joseph Banks, and also a veteran of the Battle of the Saintes. Etches would assign his brother, John Cadman Etches, to sail on the second mission as the company's representative. Charles Duncan, an experienced Royal Navy officer and veteran of the American Revolutionary War, would take command of KGSC *Princess Royal.*

By Trade We Prosper

For the King George's Sound Company motto, Etches and partners chose the phrase *Commercio liberali crescimus* ("By trade we prosper"), no doubt reflecting the degree to which Adam Smith's seminal 1776 work, *The Wealth of Nations*, had been embraced by civic, business, and political leaders of the time.

Etches had laid out his ambitious goals for the mission in a September 1785 mandate letter to Portlock, explaining that he was not simply to buy furs on the Pacific Northwest coast and sell them in China. He was also required to establish friendly relationships with the Indigenous Peoples and purchase land from them in order that a permanent trading base could be established. He wrote:

> On your arrival at the North West coast you are to make the first convenient port you can endeavour to cultivate friendship with the natives for the purpose of trade using items to barter and to give presents.

You are required to traffic with them with that liberality, integrity and generosity as shall imprint on their minds the true character of a British merchant.

Although furs are the main item of traffic you are to enquire, particularly at King George's Sound, about copper, and whatever other articles of commerce there are to be met with and for future trade you are to establish such factories as you shall see necessary and confident with the safety of such settlers, and your ship's company King George's Sound looks the most ideal but you must use your discretion. You are to purchase a tract of land from the natives as you see best suited for trading and security paying them in the most liberal and friendly manner for the same.

You are to give them [the workers and factory hands] every assistance to erect a log house and / or such other buildings as shall appear necessary for their residence and for carrying on a traffic with the natives.

You are to leave them such quantities of provisions and other articles of convenience, for the purpose of carrying on a trade.

Always have our motto in your mind "Commercio liberali crescimus."

You are particularly ordered while you remain at the cape or any other place you touch at, to refresh your ship's companies, before entering the Pacific Ocean and to put your vessels in the best possible state of defence. That you keep proper discipline among your people [crew] and wherever you touch to act with the utmost prudence and caution.

On your arrival at Canton, should the ships be ordered to Europe on the East India Company's account and you have established any factories in the course of your voyage

> you are to, in that case, purchase a vessel to return to the said factories.
>
> You are also requested to take a draft or sketch of any place you may discover and if such ports have not before been visited by other nations you are to take possession with the consent of the natives, which you will attempt to gain by making them presents (the light horsemen's caps will be a good emblem of your having been among them) in the name of the King of Great Britain; and set up such marks and inscriptions as you will give testimony of such parts having been taken possession of by His Majesty's subjects.[4]

In a postscript reminiscent of the orders given to Cook years earlier, Etches reminded Portlock and Dixon to keep all the intelligence gathered from their mission top secret.

It should be noted that while Etches was a visionary and full of hope for success, he was not without detractors. The success of his venture was not by any means guaranteed. As he was issuing his letters to Portlock and Dixon, the *Daily Universal Register* of September 24, 1785, carried an ominous article that commented sourly:

> The project of establishing colonies on the North West parts of America, though it seems at present to be the favourite topic of the people of England, must be considered indeed as truly chimerical. In arriving at this remote part, and returning back, a voyage of more than the circumnavigation of the globe must be made, and without numerous colonies, that country could not ever be cultivated, or its trade worth pursuing ... The Russians are the only people that can form settlements in these quarters, and derive essential benefit from the same. As to the sea

otter skins that abound in these parts, they may indeed turn out to great profit, but they could not possibly be procured in such abundance, as to compensate the risk and expense of such voyage.

But Etches pressed on anyway.

5

VOYAGES OF THE KING GEORGE'S SOUND COMPANY

PORTLOCK AND DIXON set sail from Deptford the last day of August 1785. Despite all that had been done to prepare them for success, and all the good wishes and intentions, their voyage would be a disappointment. Richard Etches would later write to Banks of the duo's "misconduct, disobedience of their instructions, pusillanimity" and "waste of the property committed to their care."[1] The main problem was Portlock's failure to buy land at Nootka and establish a physical presence there for the company. Why he failed to follow through on that aspect of the mission remains a mystery.

But the two captains did achieve some of their trade goals and, more important to our story, they established an official British commercial presence along the northwest coast of North America. A year after leaving Deptford, they arrived at Nootka in September 1786, via Hawaii and a few other stops along the way, and made contact with the Indigenous Peoples there and elsewhere along the coast, buying fur, building relationships, and waving the company flag. They sailed back to Hawaii for the winter, then returned to Nootka the following spring, arriving in July 1787 and carrying on as before, reinforcing a trade presence for the KGSC.

Another important accomplishment, though an accidental one, was their rescue of John Meares. It was Dixon who found Meares frozen in the ice in June of 1787 (see page 41), and it was Portlock who resupplied Meares and repaired his ship for the journey back to Macao (after chastising him for trading in the area without a licence). Had they not arrived on the scene at that time, Meares might not have survived and would probably have disappeared from the history books just as surely and silently as his partner, William Tipping, had disappeared from the cold waters of the north Pacific months before.

While simply visiting Nootka and rescuing Meares were achievements that ranked on the low end of Etches's expectations, subsequent events would prove their consequence to the tide of history.

The second pair of KGSC ships sent to the area by Etches built on this initial success and would also, unwittingly, play their part in the history of empires. Colnett and Duncan set sail from Deptford in September 1786 and arrived at Nootka in July 1787, ambitiously shaving three months off Portlock and Dixon's travel time. It was unfortunate they did not shave four months off, since they were met not by their KGSC colleagues, but by Charles Barkley, captain of the *Imperial Eagle*, flying the Austrian flag. To their dismay, Barkley and his seventeen-year-old wife, Frances—who would soon become the first woman to sail around the world—had been at Nootka for several weeks and bought up the best of the furs.[2]

Had Portlock established a factory there the previous fall, all the goods would have been in the hands of the KGSC. As it was, everything was stuffed in the belly of the *Imperial Eagle*.

Despite this initial commercial setback at Nootka, Colnett and Duncan continued the work of Portlock and Dixon, establishing a trading presence and cordial relationships along the Pacific Northwest coast from present-day Washington to Alaska. They met Dixon by chance the next month, and he encouraged them to seek Indigenous fur traders in the Queen Charlotte Islands (Haida Gwaii). It was in this area that their Banks-appointed botanist, Archibald Menzies, encountered one of the brass "patoo patoos" that Banks had provided to Charles Clerke, commander of HMS *Discovery*, eleven years earlier. Menzies wrote to Banks to let him know of the discovery:

> On the west coast of America, in a remote corner inland, the natives had a short warlike weapon of solid brass, somewhat in the shape of a New Zealand pata-patos, about fifteen inches long. It had a short handle, with a round knob at the end; and the blade was of an oval form, thick in the middle but becoming thinner towards the edges, and embellished on one side with an escutcheon, inscribing Jos. Banks, Esq. The natives put a high value on it; they would not part with it for considerable offers. The inscription, and escutcheonal embellishments, were nearly worn off by their great attention in keeping it clean... To commemorate this discovery I have given your name to a cluster of islands, round where we were then at anchor.[3]

Etches was wise to include Menzies on the mission. His observations about the plants and people of the area were of more interest to Banks and King George III than the trade in furs. Including Menzies on the mission helped Etches maintain the support of his most important patrons. While Menzies made ethnographic notes and gathered botanical samples, Colnett, Duncan, Portlock, and Dixon continued sailing around the west coast gathering furs.

Eventually, Portlock and Dixon headed to Canton to cash in at the factories there. They arrived in late November 1787, sold what they could, and set sail back home to England.[4]

Colnett and Duncan did not end their mission quite so complacently. Colnett was determined to follow through on Richard Etches's instructions; the fact that Richard's brother John was sailing with him no doubt helped to steel his resolve. So when they completed their first season of gathering furs and arrived at the Canton markets in late November 1788, they determined that only one ship should head home with the fur profits, cargo from China, and botanical samples for Banks and George III. The other ship would sail back to Nootka, gather more fur, and establish the company's much-desired factory. Accordingly, Colnett transferred command of KGSC *Prince of Wales* to ship's mate James Johnstone and sent him home to London with Duncan, John Etches, and Menzies.[5] Colnett then took command of KGSC *Princess Royal*.

But Colnett would not be making a solo trip back to Nootka. When arriving in Canton, he and John Etches had discovered that the rascal John Meares had arrived just a few months earlier and was still determined to prosper as a fur trader. Meares may have lost his partner, William Tipping, and the entire crew of the *Sea Otter*, along with half his own crew, and he may have promised Portlock he wouldn't continue to trade on the west coast without a licence, but Etches and Colnett discovered he was indefatigable. In 1788, he had launched a new expedition with two vessels and more false papers. Sailing under the Portuguese flag, he had given the vessels Portuguese names (even though they were British ships): the *Felice Adventurero*, which Meares captained himself, and the *Iphigenia Nubiana*, under command of a new partner, William Douglas. The two had sailed from China in January 1788 and arrived at Nootka Sound in May. There, they had built a small 40-ton schooner named the *North West America*—the first non-Indigenous craft ever made there—and spent that summer trading for furs all along the coast. Meares had sailed as far south as the Columbia River, but unfortunately, like Cook before him, failed to explore it.

Meares even claimed he had done what Portlock had failed to do: purchase land on the shore of Friendly Cove in Nootka Sound for the purpose of establishing a more permanent, physical, base of operations.

What happened next was reported later, in an account to George III, as follows:

> Mr. John Etches and captain Mears fortunately meeting at Canton in 1788, and being fully sensible of the necessity of enlarging their capital, to secure the commerce to the British nation, and to render abortive the feeble attempts of some foreign rivals, agreed to form a joint concern and co-partnership, and to equip two more ships that season from Canton, with additional mechanics, artificers, and others, to reinforce the establishment at Nootka.[6]

Which is a fancy way of saying they decided they could do better together than as competitors. Besides which, it was becoming clear that others—American traders—were beginning to sniff out the opportunities in Nootka. The Boston trading ships *Columbia Rediviva* and *Lady Washington* had arrived in Nootka in September 1788.

Merger with Meares

Joining forces was a wise move for Etches and Meares. Colnett summarized the situation in his journal:

> It was thought advisable by both parties to form a Junction of trade under the British Flag, each flattering himself [that] from the knowledge acquired by their Commanders of the Coast, [of the] dispositions of the natives, and articles coveted by them in Trade, [we] would soon expel all other adventurers, and enable us to make returns adequate to [meet] expenses of outfit which none of our former Voyages had done.[7]

And so, John Etches and John Meares signed a deal in Macao to form a new partnership called the Associated Merchants of London and India Trading to the Northwest Coast of America. They agreed that Etches would manage affairs from London while Meares managed business affairs in China. The merger between the two companies was signed and sealed on January 23, 1789, and, grandfathered by the agreements negotiated for the King George's Sound Company, was licensed by the South Sea Company and the East India Company.

It was agreed that Colnett would be put in overall command of their small flotilla of ships, to set sail for Nootka in the spring. He took personal command of the recently purchased 120-ton *Argonaut*, William Douglas the *Iphigenia*, and Thomas Hudson the *Princess Royal*. The Nootka-built schooner *North West America* was waiting for them there, and would be under the command of Robert Funter, one of Meares's officers. Colnett brought with him a team of twenty-nine Chinese carpenters, blacksmiths, bricklayers, and masons to help build a permanent trading base in Nootka.[8] He also brought a prefabricated keel and frame for a 93-foot, 200-ton vessel to be constructed at Nootka. Soon they would have everything Richard Etches had first envisaged: a licensed trading company, five ships, and a permanent "bricks-and-mortar" factory at Nootka.

It had taken nearly five years, but all the pieces were now coming together.

Except that, actually, their carefully constructed plans were about to fall apart.

When Colnett and the *Argonaut* arrived at Nootka in July 1789, he found the twenty-six-gun Spanish frigate *Princesa* waiting for him. Its commander, forty-seven-year-old Esteban José Martínez, had been dispatched from his base in San Blas, Mexico, to enforce Spain's claims to the entire west coast of the continent. He was backed up by a smaller ship, the *San Carlos*, under command of Gonzalo López de Haro, and had been there since May.

In the eight weeks between Martínez's arrival and Colnett's, Martínez had turned everything upside down. He had captured the *Iphigenia*, arrested its crew, and confiscated all its stores, using their supplies and resources, as well as his own, to build Fort San Miguel at the entrance to Friendly Cove. Complete with military barracks, powder storeroom, and ten artillery cannons, the new fort made Friendly Cove seem a lot less friendly. After some negotiation, Martínez eventually agreed to let the *Iphigenia* go. He had been confused by its Portuguese name and British crew (and Douglas had not yet been informed by Colnett that he was now part of a new British company), but he was prepared to go along with the notion that it was a Portuguese ship and let them go on their way, grateful for their liberty, and with a stern warning not to infringe on Spanish territory again.

Just days after the *Iphigenia* departed, the *North West America* arrived. Funter received the same treatment as Douglas—his furs were confiscated and his crew arrested—with the additional insult of having his ship permanently confiscated and renamed the *Santa Gertrudis la Magna*. He was also reprimanded by Martínez for being on Spanish territory.

Thomas Hudson and the *Princess Royal* were the third of the amalgamated KGSC–Associated Merchants fleet to arrive on the scene, in mid-June. Martínez allowed the ship to conduct repairs and replenish supplies, but sent them packing after two weeks, with a warning to Hudson that if he were to conduct any fur trading anywhere south of Prince William Sound, Alaska (2,000 kilometres north of Nootka), his ship would be confiscated.

Almost immediately after Hudson left Nootka (to conduct trade all along the northern coast, in defiance of Martínez's instructions), Colnett arrived. Having not had a chance to speak directly with Captains Douglas, Funter, or Hudson, he was completely unprepared for what happened next. He expected to meet all three of them at Meares's base. Instead, as he anchored outside the harbour, he was received by the Spaniard Martínez, accompanied by the *Lady Washington*'s American captain Robert Gray. Surprised but not yet alarmed, Colnett accepted Martínez's offer of a tow into harbour and joined both captains below deck for hospitality and refreshments. When he next went back on deck, he discovered that the *Argonaut* had been made fast to another American ship, John Kendrick's *Columbia Rediviva*, and the Spanish ship *Princesa*. The *San Carlos* had sixteen guns trained on him. Meares's modest base was dwarfed by the new Spanish fort. Not at all what he had expected.

Colnett understood that not only was he cornered, he was also captured. After a heated conversation—some might say argument—about his right to trade and build a factory in the area, Colnett was stripped of his sword and arrested at gunpoint. Martínez calculated that it was too risky to let the hot-headed British captain sail away, as he had allowed the others. Since he didn't want to shoot him on the spot, he sent him back to San Blas as a prisoner to be dealt with by the authorities there.

From the early months of 1789, John Meares in China and John Etches in London had assumed that all was going well with their new venture. Not until Douglas arrived back in Macao in early October did Meares have the first inkling that all was not going to plan. The American captain Robert Gray arrived the next month on the *Lady Washington*, bringing a cargo of fur and the disenfranchised crew of the *North West America*, including deposed captain Funter. Listening intently to the testimony of the three captains and various crew, Meares was able to stitch together a full picture of what had transpired. Alarmed by what he learned, and eager to recoup his losses, he made immediate plans to travel to London and left in December.

Meares arrived in London in mid-April of 1790 to an unsettled and evolving geopolitical environment. France was in full revolution, the Bastille having been stormed the previous July. Thomas Paine, who we recall published *Common Sense* in America during its revolution fifteen years earlier, had moved to France to join the movement and was working on his book *The Rights of Man*, which would be published the following year. The year before, philosopher Jeremy Bentham had coined the phrase "international law" when he published his work *An Introduction to the Principles of Morals and Legislation*. Political leaders influenced by these ideas and those of others like Adam Smith were carefully weighing issues around trade and conflict.

Meares's experiences and colourful stories from the remote northwest coast of America fell on attentive ears.

His four-month voyage to London had given Meares plenty of time to digest what had happened and to strategize his next steps. Giving up, as we have seen already, was not in his nature. He had been crafty and loose with the truth when operating as an unlicensed trader. Now, with powerful business partners operating under the full licence of the South Sea Company and the East India Company, and with the support of connected influencers like Joseph Banks, Lord Mulgrave of the Admiralty, George Rose and Thomas Steele of the Pitt government, and even George III himself, he was prepared to pull every lever and ring every bell to turn the situation around.

Insult to the British Nation

He immediately prepared an account of events, titled *Mr. Meares Memorial*, which he had printed and distributed weeks after his return. Key among his claims was that he had not only purchased land directly from the Mowachaht Chief Maquinna, but he had also "built a House for his occasional Residence, as well as for the more convenient Pursuit of his Trade with the Natives, and hoisted the British Colours thereon." The latter was somewhat improbable, given he had not yet made his business deal with John Etches and was trading illegally with ships flying the Portuguese colours—but it was not impossible. In any case, throwing an insult to the flag into the mix of legitimate injuries was a good way to motivate the British government to take action.

John Etches joined the lobbying and publicity campaign. Writing under the pseudonym "Argonaut," he published a document, addressed to the King, titled *An Authentic Statement of All the Facts Relative to Nootka Sound*. The account was based on what he had learned from Meares and, through him, from others who had been at Nootka when his ships and personnel encountered Martínez. The *Statement* underscored

Meares's claims that the licensed British company had established a presence, including structures, at Nootka long before the Spanish. He wrote: "Everything that commercial genius, with human prudence, could devise, was established on the most regular and permanent footing, at an immense expense. The infant colony was in the most flourishing and prosperous state, and presented to the proprietors a certainty of being rewarded with ample fortunes, when the arrival of the Spanish fleet put an end, for the present, to all their hopes."[9]

Pressing further, the *Statement* reminded readers of Spain's role in the American Revolutionary War and—like Meares's account—emphasized how the British flag had been insulted: "An American brig, lying in the Sound, was not molested; and, to aggravate the insult to the British nation, several days after the captivity of Capt. Colnet, the anniversary of the American Independence was commemorated with every demonstration of joy; the English flag, which till then had been flying on board the *Argonaut*, was hauled down, and the Spanish flag hoisted to complete the celebration and triumph of the day."[10] The publication noted both Spain's "insidious and mercenary conspiracy in the assistance of our revolted American colonies," and its clear desire to dismember the British Empire.[11]

Through the *Statement*, Etches also made appeals to common sense, noting that Nootka was a hundred leagues north of established Spanish settlements. He also made appeals to history, noting that Drake had discovered the area first (in 1579), and that all the subsequent efforts to seriously develop the area (not just to trade there, but to chart its coast and establish diplomatic relations with its people) had been achieved by Cook and other British envoys.

Finally, he attempted to raise every reader's blood pressure by pointing out how insatiable and unreasonable the

Spanish were. They wanted to dispossess the British, while greedily gathering up everything for themselves:

> But it Is said that the Spanish usurpations are not merely confined to the dispossession of the British from their own discoveries in those parts; they are not satisfied with the uninterrupted and undisturbed possession of that vast range of American continent, extending nearly from the rising to setting of the sun; they have the arrogance to assume an exclusive right to the gates, locks, and keys of the whole Pacific, to the exclusive monopoly of an ocean, and its numerous islands, which embrace in their extent almost one half of the globe.[12]

The appeals from Meares and Etches—both in person behind the scenes with their powerful business and political connections and in public through the voracious reading appetites of patriotic citizenry—had their desired effect: Prime Minister William Pitt ("The Younger," to distinguish him from his father, also named William Pitt and prime minister in his time) was determined to fight back against Spanish aggression, even to the point of war.

6

THE NOOTKA CRISIS

BEFORE GETTING INTO the diplomatic conflict between Britain and Spain at Nootka from 1789 to 1790, it will be helpful to briefly review Spain's presence in North America at this time and to provide some context for its actions on the Pacific Northwest coast.

We know from our first chapter that Spain, along with France, had been a major naval power in the 1770s, providing critical support to the American revolutionaries in achieving independence from Britain. That pleased the nation well. But Spain had been disappointed when their ally France had lost the Battle of the Saintes and, consequently, failed to deprive Britain of the more financially lucrative sugar-producing colonies in the Caribbean. Spain had been ambitious to acquire new territories for itself and its allies, especially where acquiring them was detrimental to her enemies. That was, in essence, Spain's goal in the Americas.

Despite having a somewhat diminished footprint in the region at the end of the American Revolutionary War, Spain still had plenty of presence in the area. Its possessions in the years shortly after the Revolutionary War included all of present-day Florida, the Colony of Louisiana (which was pretty much everything west of the Mississippi River, bordered to the south and west by New Spain), and New Spain (which was most of the southwestern part of the continent including present-day Mexico, Texas, New Mexico, Arizona, Nevada, Utah, and California). Only the regions currently known as (roughly) Oregon, Washington, and Idaho were unclaimed by any colonial power.

Spain was so well established in the area because its presence in the Americas extended back a couple hundred years. It is well known that Christopher Columbus arrived near the east coast of the American continent in 1492. But it is less well known that Columbus's discovery caused Spanish rulers Ferdinand and Isabella to enlist papal support in 1493 for their claims to the New World. They believed, correctly, that a papal endorsement would restrict the actions of their rival, Portugal, and discourage any other possible competitors. The Spanish-born pope Alexander VI accommodated their request and issued a bull—an official edict—establishing a vertical line of demarcation from pole to pole 100 leagues (about 320 miles) west of the Cape Verde Islands. According to this bull, Spain was given exclusive rights to all the newly discovered and undiscovered lands west of the line. Portugal was entitled to everything east of the line.[1]

While the bull was everything Spain had hoped for, and was respected by its Catholic colleagues, the English Crown did not acknowledge its authority at all. Henry VII, in full defiance of the bull, sent John Cabot sailing across the pope's line to Newfoundland in 1497, though at that time England had little interest in continental North America and was content to look the other way.

Indigenous Peoples on the American continent would not have that luxury. The bull—the *Inter Caetera* of 1493—was issued by a religious leader, with religious considerations hardwired into the document; it was not just flowery language but a very serious and significant part of the law. The bull stated clearly that neither Spain nor Portugal was allowed to occupy any territory already in the hands of a Christian ruler. And not only that, it also required that the Christian powers of Spain and Portugal actively convert any non-Christians they encountered in their new territories:

> Moreover we command you in virtue of holy obedience that, employing all due diligence in the premises, as you also promise—nor do we doubt your compliance therein in accordance with your loyalty and royal greatness of spirit—you should appoint to the aforesaid mainlands and islands worthy, God-fearing, learned, skilled, and experienced men, in order to instruct the aforesaid inhabitants and residents in the Catholic faith and train them in good morals.[2]

The religious aspect of this geographic policy would have a significant impact on Indigenous Peoples, particularly in the first instances of its execution upon the Incas, Tainos, and Aztecs. But it was also a policy the Spanish would take with them to the Pacific Northwest. The ships of Pérez and Martínez always included Catholic priests among their crew. Father Junípero Serra sailed with them on the *Santiago*, as did two Franciscan friars named Juan Crespí and Tomás de la Peña.

Following this bull, Spain claimed not only the land to the west of the demarcation line, but also the coast of the continent and the ocean beyond. The fact that these lands and oceans were unseen, unexplored, and uncharted didn't matter. It belonged to Spain. The pope himself had said so.

Columbus's discovery also captured the imagination of other Spanish adventurers. In 1513, Vasco Núñez de Balboa became the first European to cross the Isthmus of Panama and encounter the Pacific Ocean from the American continent. Later, in 1520, Ferdinand Magellan extended Spain's claim across the Pacific, sailing from Spain to the Philippines (where he was killed). His crew then completed the first known circumnavigation of the world. Spain's constant probing west was an attempt to find a profitable westerly trade route to the markets of Asia at a time when, by virtue of the *Inter Caetera* bull, Portugal had the exclusive right to trade via an easterly direction.

Shortly after Magellan's voyage across the Pacific, the Kingdom of New Spain was established on the American continent, with Mexico City designated as its capital. In 1542, the Viceroy of New Spain, Antonio de Mendoza, ordered Juan Rodríguez Cabrillo to sail north from Barra de Navidad, Mexico, on what was basically a reconnaissance mission. The voyage resulted in claims to San Diego and Santa Monica Bays. Cabrillo made it as far north as Drakes Bay (just north of present-day San Francisco) before dying of an infection. His lieutenant, Bartolomé Ferrer, carried on with the mission, possibly reaching as far as 44 degrees north (the present-day California–Oregon border area).

But while these northerly missions helped fill in the gaps on maps and charts, Spain found little else of interest or value there. It continued to be more attracted to the mineral wealth found to the south and the Asian markets that lay farther west, across the Pacific. For most of the next two centuries, Spain traded Mexican silver for Asian silk and spice. This commerce was briefly, but unambiguously, interrupted by English explorer Francis Drake on the *Golden Hind* in 1579. His interception of the Spanish galleon *Nuestra Señora de la Concepción* off the west coast of present-day Ecuador relieved Spain of a large fortune: eighty pounds of gold, twenty-six tons of silver, and dozens of chests of coins. The memory of that humiliation also made Spanish sailors wary of English and, after England's 1707 union with Scotland, British vessels, and well-motivated to take advantage of any opportunities for revenge.

Yet there were a few other times when Spain tentatively ventured north: In 1595, Francisco de Gali and Sebastián Cermeño made observations along the California coast, documenting Monterey Bay. A few years later, in 1602, Sebastián Vizcaíno toured that coast again and named San Diego, Santa Catalina, Santa Barbara, Monterey, and Carmel. But aside from these few expeditions, points north of present-day California were ignored.

There was just one exception, and it would turn out to be a fairly important one. In 1774, forty-nine-year-old naval officer Juan Josef Pérez Hernández (known simply as Pérez) was instructed by Antonio María Bucareli y Ursúa, Viceroy of New Spain, to sail north from the Spanish base at San Blas, Mexico. He was to observe the coastline north of present-day California and to report back on any signs of Russian activity south of Alaska. His second-in-command was thirty-two-year-old Esteban José Martínez. They made it as far north as the present-day Alaska–Canada border and, on their way back south, dropped anchor at a harbour they called Surgidero de San Lorenzo (Nootka). Without leaving their ship, they conducted some trade with the Indigenous people there. A few days later they passed within sight of a large mountain, which they named Sierra Nevada de Santa Rosalia (Snowy Peak of Saint Rosalia).[3] Today it is known as Mount Olympus.

Other than this one voyage by Pérez, Spain—like everyone else, it must be said—had very little interest in the Pacific Northwest coast until Cook wrote about the potential for acquiring fur there for trade in China.

It is worth noting that, in addition to the authority of the papal bull, Spain based its territorial claims on two additional principles: "immemorial possession" (meaning possession was held so long ago that no living person witnessed its beginning) and that sovereignty was acquired by discovery and by the formal acts of taking possession. From the Spanish point of view, it was enough to visit a place, declare it discovered, and claim it. It was quite unnecessary to disembark from one's ship, negotiate with Indigenous Peoples to buy land, or establish factories, forts, or farms. This was a critical difference between Spain and Britain: the Spanish believed in possession by declaration; the British believed in possession by occupation.

This was the context in which Martínez was sent to Nootka in 1789. Spanish authorities considered his instructions to be entirely reasonable: he was to re-establish relations with the Indigenous people, and if he encountered any Russian or British ships there, he was to "explain with prudent firmness but without being led into harsh expression" the reasons why Spain had claimed this part of the coast.[4]

Despite the very reasonable tone of his instructions, Martínez, as we read in the previous chapter, exercised them with great prejudice and little restraint. Nevertheless, it is clear that when Martínez took formal possession of Nootka in 1789, he thought he was doing so on the solid grounds that Spain's sovereignty had been sanctioned by the papal bull of 1493, and because he and Pérez had dropped anchor in the bay in 1774. He was heavy-handed and punitive, but he believed he was within his rights.

Spanish diplomats in Europe would agree that the fact Juan Pérez Hernández had sailed his ship *Santiago* to Friendly Cove in 1774 was sufficient proof of sovereignty. From the British perspective, the fact that Cook disembarked at Friendly Cove four years later, built temporary structures, and lived among the Indigenous people was a far more significant consideration and one that trumped Spanish claims.

Britain Reacts

Word of the incidents at Nootka arrived in London a few months before John Meares showed up in April of 1790. The British charge d'affaires in Madrid, Anthony Merry, heard about the event through his professional contacts and from undercover intelligence sources, and relayed the early sketches of information back to London in January of 1790. Though early, these reports were thin on details. Officials in London were formally advised of the incident in February when the Spanish ambassador, the Marquis del Campo, delivered an official protest. The Spanish account was, naturally, biased in the interests of Spain and demanded that King George stop his subjects from trading in Spanish territory. In his official note, del Campo requested that His Britannic Majesty restrain his subjects from making expeditions to territory claimed by Spain, and asserted Spain's sovereignty by virtue of its prior exploration and claims.

To this the British foreign minister, the Duke of Leeds, responded (with the approval of Prime Minister Pitt) that no discussion of Spain's claims to the territory could be entertained until the confiscated property had been restored to its British owners and the dignity of the British government fully restored. As the Duke stated, "It might not be unbecoming of the dignity of the government to insist upon satisfaction for that insult before entering upon other subjects." This new policy of "satisfaction before discussion" was difficult for Spain to accept, since it basically required them to apologize before being able to explain why they felt they didn't have anything to apologize for. Nevertheless, that was the British response.

At virtually the same time, Leeds received another communication from Merry advising that Spain was reinforcing its garrisons and preparing a fleet of twelve ships to defend its claims. Furthermore, it was understood from Merry and other sources that Spain was reaching out to other European powers to establish alliances; France, Russia, Austria, and Prussia all received entreaties to stand with Spain on its claims.

When Meares arrived in London in April, he set the cat among the pigeons. Pitt's government was already agitated by Spain's presumptions, but Meares made certain they were livid and outraged. He set about stoking the fires of righteous and patriotic indignation, first in his personal meetings with his and the Etches brothers' connections and then in his *Memorial* document. Appended to his account were letters and statements from witnesses that documented the hostile acts of Martínez and quantified the commercial losses. The statement from the officers and men of the *North West America* serves as one such example. They declared that their ship

> did barter and trade with the Natives of the North West Coast of America, for Two hundred and Fifteen Sea Otter Skins of good and prime Quality; that the said Number of Two hundred and Fifteen Sea Otter Skins, were put on Board of the Sloop *Princess Royal*, of London, belonging to the Associated Merchants, for their Use and Advantages. That the said Robert Funter and his Crew were removed

> Prisoners on Board [i.e., they were removed and made prisoners on board] the said Spanish Ships of War, to their Vexation, Detriment, and Loss; and that the said Schooner *N. W. America* was taken out of his Care, and given up to the Plunder of the Subjects of his Catholic Majesty; that the Colours of Spain were hoisted on Board the said *N. W. America*; that every Formality was used by the Spaniards, by sprinkling Holy Water, &c. on the above Vessel, in order to cover their unjust and cruel Proceedings.[5]

In late April, thirty-year-old Prime Minister Pitt received cabinet approval of his request to mobilize the Royal Navy. On May 5, the same time that Meares's *Memorial* was released to the public, Pitt appealed to the House of Commons for special funding for the navy, and a massive sum of £1 million was approved. In the House, Pitt demanded colourfully that Spain surrender a claim that was "the most absurd and exorbitant that could be imagined, a claim which they had never heard before, which was indefinite in its extent and which originated in no treaty, no formal establishment of a colony, nor rested on any one of those grounds on which claims of sovereignty, navigation and commerce usually rested."[6]

In the House of Commons, as well as the coffee houses of London, political leaders and philosophers argued the merits of who was in the right and who was in the wrong. Spain held to its belief that it had prior claim to Nootka and the entire coast from California to Alaska. The British ridiculed the idea that a pope could confer the monopoly of two continents and an ocean. Britain argued that merely exploring and formally declaring possession of a country did not grant any rights of sovereignty. The fact that Pérez had sailed through Nootka in 1774 was acknowledged, but he had never set foot on the land. They argued that Cook first setting foot at Nootka made all the difference in the world. Pérez had sailed through, but only Cook had landed.

Edmund Burke, member of Parliament and philosopher, took the discussion even further, arguing that sovereignty actually belonged to the Indigenous Peoples. Many today would agree.

In the meantime, the machinery of war continued to move forward. Diplomats scrambled furiously to build military alliances and come to some kind of agreement between the two main powers before blood was spilled. By the end of June, Britain had formed an alliance with Holland and gained the passive support of Prussia. Spain had sought an alliance with their old ally France, but with mixed results. On one hand, the French had indicated they would provide aid, subject to ratification by the new Constituent Assembly; on the other hand, Spain was uneasy about the new republic and feared that too close an association might infect its own political system with anti-monarchical fever.

Diplomacy and De-escalation

In the end, Spain made the calculation that if it fought a war alone against the British, it would lose. By the end of July, Spain agreed to restore the ships and land that had been confiscated by Martínez at Nootka.

Holding that territorial sovereignty must be "founded on actual occupation and established possession, prior to any other European nation," Pitt rejected Spain's claims and considered them invalid "in any part of the continent North of the Spanish settlements in California." But he did not argue that the area should belong exclusively to Britain; he wanted access for everyone. The Pacific Northwest coast, he argued, "should be open to all European nations to make such establishments by virtue of a bona-fide purchase, occupation and possession; though it would not be just that such establishments should exclude other nations from a commerce which they had previously carried on upon such coast."[7]

Though the conflict at Nootka was the inspiration for this policy, the notion that sovereignty had to be based on occupation—not just on the Spanish principle of declaration or discovery—would in time become a key pillar of British foreign policy. The principle continues even to this day with regard to the Falkland Islands. Argentina claims sovereignty by right of discovery, while Britain declares sovereignty by right of occupation.

In any event, by the end of October, Spain was beaten down by a combination of persistent negotiation and sabre-rattling. They agreed to sign the Nootka Convention and its five articles.

The first two articles renounced Spain's claims to exclusive control of the area and confirmed that Spain would make good on the losses to the King George's Sound Company–Associated Merchants. Article III agreed that the British and Spanish ships in the area would not molest each other "in navigating or carrying on their fisheries in the Pacific Ocean or in the South Seas, or in landing on the coasts of those areas in places not already occupied, for the purpose of carrying on their commerce with the natives of the country or of making establishments there."[8] Article IV clarified that British ships should stay at least ten leagues away from any part of the coast already occupied by Spain. Article V established that both British and Spanish ships should have free access at Nootka and along the coast between California and Alaska, and should be free to carry on their commerce without molestation where either party might form a settlement.

With agreements formally established at the highest level of government, the next step was to put those words into action. Spain had to formally return the seized lands at Nootka to Britain. The task of receiving them was assigned to one of Captain Cook's former midshipmen, George Vancouver.

7

GEORGE VANCOUVER, DIPLOMAT

IT IS ONE THING to make an agreement in the parliament of Britain or the court of Spain, but another thing to make those words come to life. An agreement not acted upon is hardly an agreement at all. On Team Britain, the task of putting the Nootka Convention into action fell to British naval officer George Vancouver.

Though only thirty-three years old when he received the assignment, Vancouver had been at sea for sixteen years and had an excellent resume. He was well suited to the task. His first job at sea had been as a teenage midshipman on Cook's second voyage around the world; after three years of daily on-the-job training in navigation, charting, and all aspects of surviving life aboard a vessel thousands of miles away from home or help, he was qualified enough to be made a senior midshipman on Cook's third voyage, in 1778—the one that had taken them to Nootka.

Cook's third voyage had also been his last, and Vancouver had been present when Cook was cut down on that Hawaiian beach in 1779. He was also, therefore, under no misapprehension of the dangers that could befall a ship's captain who mismanaged relations with Indigenous Peoples far away from home.

On his return from the last Cook mission, in 1780, Vancouver was promoted to lieutenant and appointed to the fourteen-gun sloop HMS *Martin,* cruising in the English Channel to protect Britain's commerce and sovereignty. After two years patrolling home waters, HMS *Martin* sailed to the West Indies, where the crew captured a Spanish vessel near Jamaica. Vancouver was then assigned to the seventy-four-gun ship HMS *Fame,* joining the victorious crew a month after their historic service at the Battle of the Saintes, the last significant sea battle of the American Revolutionary War. He spent the next six years sailing between the Caribbean and England, gaining more experience on the fifty-gun HMS *Europa.* When Pitt mobilized the navy in May 1790, Vancouver was briefly assigned to HMS *Courageux* (a French ship captured by Britain thirty years earlier) as part of the Spanish Armament fleet before being tapped to command HMS *Discovery.*

The Vancouver Expedition, as it came to be known, had three mission pillars: botany, geography, and diplomacy. The most important of these for our purposes is the latter. It was up to George Vancouver to personally, on behalf of the Crown, officially accept the return of the properties seized by Spain at Nootka. His instructions from the Admiralty, though written in a style that is less than plain to the contemporary reader, are worth repeating all the same:

> And whereas you will receive herewith a duplicate of a letter from Count Florida Blanca, to the Spanish officer commanding at Nootka (together with a translation thereof), signifying His Catholic Majesty's orders to cause such

> officer as may be appointed on the part of His Britannic Majesty, to be put in possession of the buildings, and districts, or parcels of lands therein described, which were occupied by His Majesty's subjects in the month of April, 1789, agreeable to the first article of the late convention, (a copy of which has been sent to you) and to deliver up any persons in the service of British subjects who may have been detained in those parts; in case, therefore, you shall receive this at Nootka, you are to deliver to the Spanish officer, commanding at that port, the above-mentioned letter from Count Florida Blanca, and to receive from him, comfortably thereto, on the part of His Britannic Majesty, possession of the buildings and districts, and parcels of land, of which His Majesty's subjects were possessed at the above-mentioned period.[1]

In addition to taking back the seized properties at Nootka, he was also instructed to provide safe passage back to China for any of the King George's Sound Company–Associated Merchants workers who had been stranded there, and to treat them equally as everyone else:

> If, during your continuance on the American coast, you should meet with any of the Chinese who were employed by Mr. Meares and his associates, or any of his Majesty's subjects, who may have been in captivity, you are to receive them on board the sloop you command, and to accommodate them in the best manner you may be able, until such time as opportunities may be found of sending them to the different places to which they may be desirous of being conveyed; victualling them during their continuance on board, in the same manner as the other persons on board the said sloop are victualled.

The ship placed under Vancouver's command, HMS *Discovery*, was about 100 feet long and held a crew of as many men. It was armed with ten four-pounder cannons and ten smaller swivel cannons—enough to defend itself, but nothing like the seventy-four guns that had been on the 165-foot *Fame*.[2] Perhaps more importantly, in addition to guns, the new ship carried the latest in high-tech navigational equipment: an Arnold chronometer.[3] The chronometer was critical for measuring longitude, and the ones developed by Arnold were state of the art. The one on the *Discovery*, marked No. 176, was an improvement over Arnold's innovative marine chronometer No. 3, which had accompanied Cook on his second voyage under supervision of two astronomers appointed by the Board of Longitude.[4] This new technology would help Vancouver produce coastal charts that were more precise and more accurate than ever before. If the elusive Northwest Passage was discovered by Vancouver, there would be no doubt about how to find it again.

Among HMS *Discovery*'s crew were some familiar names: Peter Puget was appointed second lieutenant (under First Lieutenant Zachary Mudge); he had served on HMS *Europa* at the same time as Vancouver, as a teenage midshipman. Third Lieutenant Joseph Baker was another former HMS *Europa* shipmate. Joseph Whidbey, who Vancouver had known as the ship's master on HMS *Europa*, was appointed master of HMS *Discovery*. Archibald Menzies, veteran of the Battle of the Saintes and botanist-surgeon aboard KGSC *Prince of Wales*, was assigned to the ship by Sir Joseph Banks.

Following the recent mutiny on HMS *Bounty*, commanded by Cook veteran William Bligh, the Admiralty had decided, in March of 1791, that all principal ships be accompanied by a second ship. HMS *Chatham* was dedicated to this task and put under the command of twenty-nine-year-old William Broughton. Though young by present-day standards, Broughton, like Vancouver, had sixteen years' experience in the navy. Having sailed previously in North America, the East Indies, and the Mediterranean, and having served aboard the massive 104-gun HMS *Victory*, he was well prepared for his first command. The *Chatham* had been built a couple of years earlier than the *Discovery*, in 1788, but was still relatively new when acquired and armed with four three-pounder guns and six swivels. Smaller than the *Discovery*, but with the advantage of a copper-sheathed hull, the *Chatham* carried a crew of fifty-five men.[5]

James Johnstone, former employee of the King George's Sound Company (he had commanded KGSC *Prince of Wales* on its return to England from China, with John Etches and Archibald Menzies) and also a veteran of the Battle of the Saintes, was engaged as HMS *Chatham*'s master.

A third vessel, HMS *Daedalus*, was also assigned to the mission as the supply ship. Its task would be to shuttle supplies, diplomatic and other correspondence, and materials between the two other ships and London. Richard Hergest, who Vancouver knew from Cook's second and third voyages, and who was also deeply affected by Cook's murder, was given command.

With ships fully stocked and prepared, Vancouver left for Nootka in April of 1791 and sailed into Friendly Cove in August the following year. Vancouver did his best to be cheerful upon reaching their destination, but he was slightly dispirited, having just learned from a rendezvous with HMS *Daedalus* that Hergest had been killed, like Cook, on a beach in Hawaii weeks earlier.[6]

The Nootka Summit

When the British ships sailed into Friendly Cove, the Spanish were dutifully waiting. The gruff and aggressive Martínez, who had sparked the crisis, was long gone, replaced by the fashionable, elegant, gregarious, forty-nine-year-old Juan Francisco de la Bodega y Quadra, commander of the Spanish naval forces along the Pacific coast of North America. Quadra had come from his base in San Blas, Mexico, and had been at Nootka since March. Johnstone and Menzies were startled by the changes to the port. In the four years since they had been there with the King George's Sound Company, the Spanish had clearly made themselves comfortable.

On the shore, a large Spanish flag was flying high for all to see, and Quadra had deployed his blacksmiths and carpenters to build and enhance the evolving domestic infrastructure—chicken pens, a fenced-off vegetable garden, houses, barracks—and had constructed a magnificent mansion complete with European-style drawing room, a balcony over the entrance, servants' hall and kitchen, guard room, and a dining hall where Quadra, his officers, and distinguished guests could dine off his silver plates and drink Madeira from his crystal goblets.

The ships in the harbour were as bedazzling as Quadra's dinner table. In addition to Quadra's ship there were several others, including the *Sutil*, under the command of Captain Galiano, and the *Mexicana*, commanded by Captain Valdés, each proudly flying the Spanish colours. HMS *Discovery* saluted them with thirteen guns and the honour was returned.[7] The cove that the King George's Sound Company had been among the first Europeans to visit in 1787 was becoming a popular destination. In addition to the Spanish and British ships, American captain Robert Gray was also present. Menzies wrote in his journal: "There were at this time ten Vessels riding at Anchor in this small Cove, besides two small ones building on shore . . . and this perhaps was the greatest number of Vessels hitherto collected together in this Sound at any one period."[8]

In addition to building his mansion and gardens over the past five months, Quadra had plenty of time to talk with others who had been present during the conflict with Martínez. Among them were Captain Robert Gray and the Mowachaht Chief Maquinna—both of whom poured cold water on Meares's claims, giving Quadra the impression that much had been exaggerated.

Again, we are reminded that timing can sometimes be everything. Had Vancouver arrived at Nootka before Quadra, he would have held the upper hand. Instead, when Vancouver presented his copy of the letter from Count Florida Blanca, Quadra said that he would return only the plot of land on which Meares had built his shelter—a plot, according to his sources, of perhaps just 900 square feet. Vancouver was under the impression the entire harbour should be returned. In principle they were agreed, but in detail they were at loggerheads. Eventually, they agreed to do nothing, but they agreed to do it amicably, and that alone was a sign of progress.

After exchanging their diplomatic notes and discussing relations between Spain and Britain, Vancouver and Quadra decided to update Chief Maquinna on their plans. They left their ships anchored at Friendly Cove and made for the nearby village of Tahsis in small boats (two from HMS *Discovery*, one from HMS *Chatham*, and a large Spanish launch).[9] The Spanish went ahead and the British party, arriving near Tahsis toward the end of the day, decided to camp overnight on shore so they could make a grand entrance the following morning.

Menzies, travelling with Vancouver, wrote that after breakfast the next day:

> We all embarked in the boats and made a kind of martial parade with our little musical band before the Village of Tashees, where we landed amidst the noisy acclamations of the natives. Maquinna together with his brother and attendants received us on the beach, and we were conducted to the Chief's House which was large and spacious and occupied by himself, his brother and other families of distinction. Here we found the women decently seated on mats spread on little risings on each side of the house and benches were placed at one end covered over with rich furs and clean mats for the party to set down on. We first advanced to the Royal Mat to pay our respects to the Chiefs wives and daughter, the latter was a young girl about thirteen years of age named Apinnas, who the Spaniards informed us had been lately recognized and inaugurated in a most pompous and solemn manner by the whole tribe as the successor of her father.

The delegates then witnessed, and were among the first Europeans to describe, a Potlatch ceremony:

> When the natives were assembled on this occasion, a throne was erected on which the young Princess was seated by her father, and from thence copper iron beads etc. and every other article of any value the Chief possessed was thrown down and scattered in the most profuse manner amongst

> the people, who scrambled for it and expressed their approbation by continual plaudits. After this ceremony they continued their rejoicing by feasting singing and dancing for some days, till the Chief with respect to riches was brought almost upon a level with the poorest of his tribe.

With these ceremonies and reunions over, the Spanish turned to the business at hand. Quadra explained to Maquinna that the Spanish would be leaving and the British would be staying.

> As soon as the Party was seated [Señor] Quadra explained to the Chief the purport of our visit and with a disinterested zeal which marked his benign character he said every thing in recommending Captain Vancouver, Mr. Broughton together with their Officers and the English Nation in general to his kind attention and to a friendly intercourse with all his tribe; he assured him of the friendship and good understanding which subsisted between the English and Spaniards, and that the latter were only to quit his territories by a mutual agreement between the two Nations.[10]

In a private moment, the two diplomats agreed that assigning their names to the entire island would be an appropriate gesture to signify and cement the goodwill that existed toward each other and their nations. Of this, Menzies would later write in a letter to his patron Banks: "Our commander has already perpetuated his name on the coast for the great island we circumnavigated last summer, of which Nootka is a part," adding, perhaps somewhat cheekily, that it was "modestly named Quadra and Vancouver's Island."[11]

Spain Departs

While Vancouver and Quadra had not been able to agree on what specific territory was to be surrendered and received—largely because neither of them had been given clear instructions or details on this point—they were able to agree that the Spanish influence in the area would generally ramp down while the British could ramp up unrestricted. To that extent, they were able to fulfill at least the spirit of their orders, and of the Convention's several articles. Concrete steps were taken to decommission the "crisis" that had afflicted their two countries. There would be no war over Nootka or the Pacific Northwest.

Any animosity that had existed between the British and Spanish along the Pacific Northwest coast was now considered to be in the past. Menzies's journal provides a first-hand account of the sentiments of those who were there when the Spanish left for California: "It was but natural to feel some reluctance at parting as during our stay at Nootka the Spanish Officers and we lived on the most amicable footing. Our frequent and social meetings at [Señor] Quadra's hospitable mansion afforded constant opportunity of testifying our mutual regard and friendship for each other, by that harmony and good understanding which always marked our convivial hours. In short... we passed our time together cheerfully and happy."[12]

It was hoped that some additional correspondence from London or Madrid might provide more definitive details regarding the territory to be surrendered and received, and Quadra invited Vancouver to meet him again at his base in San Francisco in October. When Vancouver undertook to do this, he passed the entrance to the Columbia River on his way south.

The sandbar at the mouth of the Columbia was too great an obstacle for HMS *Discovery*, but Broughton was able to navigate two boats from HMS *Chatham* into the river and made it as far as the Columbia River Gorge, just past present-day Portland, Oregon. At that point, he named the north shore Vancouver, after George Vancouver, and named the towering mountain visible to the southeast Mount Hood, after Viscount Samuel Hood, a Royal Navy admiral and veteran of both the Battle of Chesapeake and the Battle of the Saintes. Along the river route, as was the tradition, Broughton named a number of places after members of the crew: Walker Island was named for the surgeon of HMS *Chatham*, William Walker; Menzies Island for the surgeon-botanist on HMS *Discovery*; Johnston Island for Lieutenant James Johnston of HMS *Discovery*; and Point Sherriff after HMS *Chatham*'s mate John Sherriff. He also named places for members of the Admiralty, family friends, and even for incidents and geographic features—like Pillar Rock and Warrior Point.

Only one other non-Indigenous ship had ever entered the vicinity of the Columbia River from the ocean. American captain Robert Gray, commander of *Columbia Rediviva*, had managed to cross the sandbar six months earlier on his way north to the Nootka area.

When Vancouver's two ships made it to San Francisco, the Spanish garrison and the Franciscan fathers at the mission gave their new friends a warm welcome. Both sides followed tradition and fired salutes from their cannons. The Spanish used a brass cannon lashed to a log of wood, firing it from a location at the south end of where the Golden Gate Bridge now spans the narrows. From this meeting came nothing more than further friendly, collegial relations. Neither side had received further instructions on what to do about the specifics of the Convention.

In the end, two more Nootka Conventions were drafted and enacted without the participation of Vancouver.

Resolution and Restoration

Ultimately, a 1794 Convention finally settled the Nootka question. It agreed that Spain would hand over to Britain the lands they had been dispossessed of, and then both powers would withdraw completely. To resolve the issue of the King George's Sound Company–Associated Merchants' land claims that had been advanced so dramatically by John Etches and John Meares, a 1793 Convention simply agreed to provide a generous financial settlement of $210,000. No one doubted that the Spanish had probably overcompensated the aggrieved entrepreneurs, but the matter was now settled for good, so perhaps the Spanish considered it money well spent.

Article I of the February 1793 version of the document resolved financial claims and read as follows:

> His Catholic Majesty, besides having restored the ship *Argonaut*, the restoration of which took place in the port of San Blas in the year 1791 [1790] agrees to pay as indemnity to the parties Interested in it the amount of two hundred and ten thousand hard dollars in speele [specie], it being understood that this sum is to serve as compensation and complete indemnification for all their losses, whatever they may be, without any exception, and without leaving the possibility of a future remonstrance on any pretext or motive.[13]

A third Convention, in January 1794, set out terms for the mutual abandonment of possession of Nootka. It called for official delegates to meet at Nootka and sign documents affirming that the lands had been restored and

> that then the British official shall unfurl the British flag over the land so restored in sign of possession. And that after these formalities the officials of the two Crowns shall withdraw, respectively, their people from the said port of Nootka. Further, their said Majesties have agreed that the subjects of both nations shall have the liberty of frequenting the said port whenever they wish and of constructing there temporary buildings to accommodate them during their residence on such occasions. But neither of the said parties shall form any permanent establishment in the said port or claim any right of sovereignty or territorial dominion there to the exclusion of the other.

This all came to a conclusion and was executed at Nootka in March of 1795. The British commissioner assigned to the role (since Vancouver had left for England) was Sir Thomas Pierce. Remarkably, he travelled from Spain to Mexico to San Blas to Nootka in order to fulfill this task. His Spanish accomplice was Manuel de Álava, the new commandant of the Spanish base at San Blas (replacing Quadra, who had died the previous March). What a disappointment for Vancouver and Quadra that they did not get to place their signatures on the final documents that resolved the issue for good.

The Nootka Conventions did more than right the wrongs of a rash act by a haughty Spanish captain against a modest flotilla of British ships belonging to the King George's Sound Company's newly formed Associated Merchants Company. They effectively put an end to Spain's centuries-old claim of exclusive sovereignty over the west coast of America, and marked the beginning of the end of its empire. Britain had achieved a remarkable thing: it prevented Spain from colonizing the entire coast of the American continent north of California without firing a shot or occupying it themselves.

An Accurate Map of North America c. 1780. In the decades immediately following the American Revolution, the west coast of North America remained mostly unknown, uncharted, and of little interest to the new republic. THOMAS BOWEN, 1780S

The Spanish Empire in North America, 1790. After Pope Alexander VI's papal bull of 1493, and well into the 1700s, the Spanish considered most of North America to be part of their empire—including the entire west coast from California to Alaska. ERIC LEINBERGER

OPPOSITE Spain solidified its claims to the northwest coast of the continent by reading the Requerimiento at landing points all around the region identified as the Territorio de Nutca. ERIC LEINBERGER

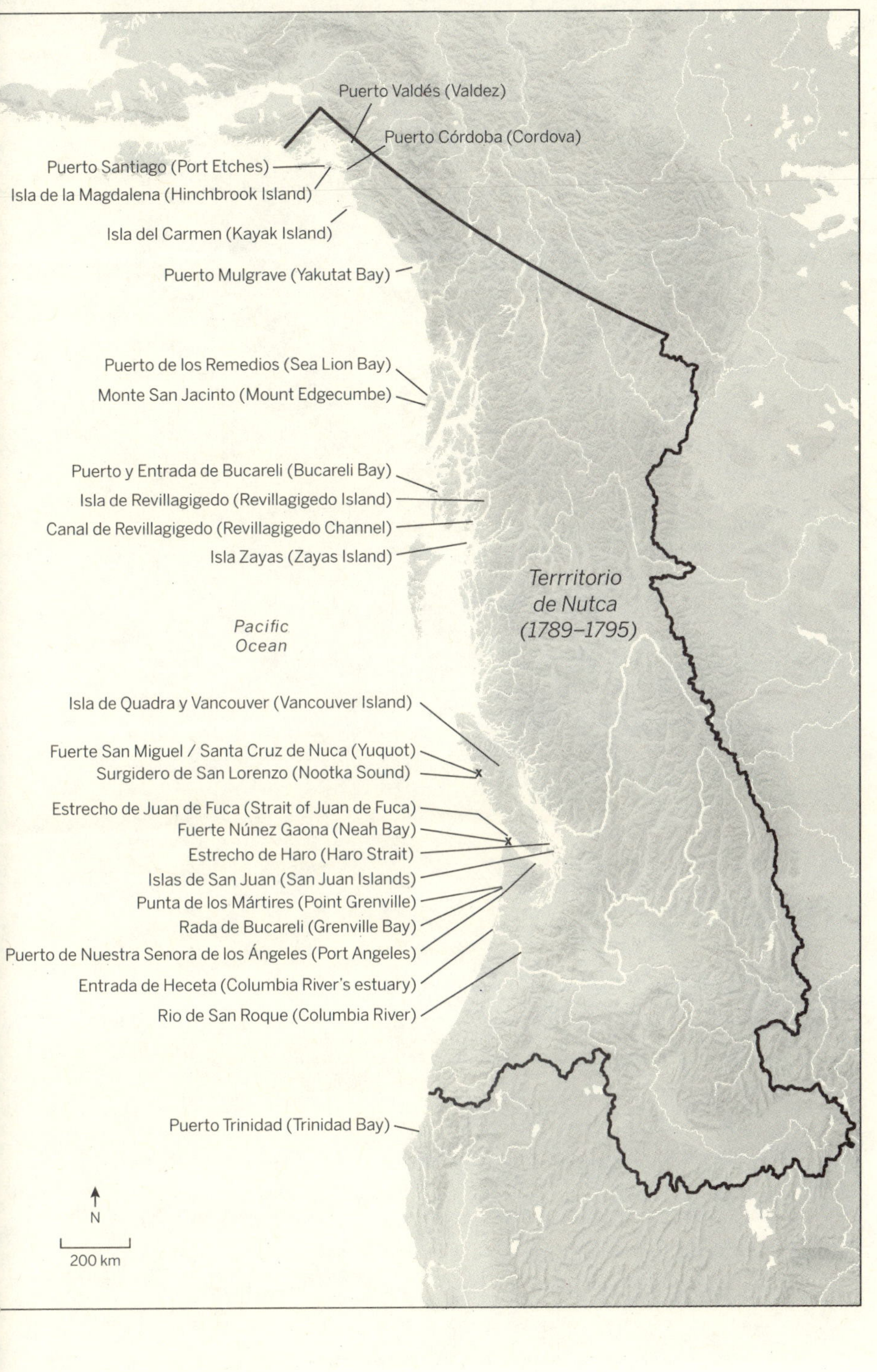

Puerto Valdés (Valdez)
Puerto Córdoba (Cordova)
Puerto Santiago (Port Etches)
Isla de la Magdalena (Hinchbrook Island)
Isla del Carmen (Kayak Island)
Puerto Mulgrave (Yakutat Bay)
Puerto de los Remedios (Sea Lion Bay)
Monte San Jacinto (Mount Edgecumbe)
Puerto y Entrada de Bucareli (Bucareli Bay)
Isla de Revillagigedo (Revillagigedo Island)
Canal de Revillagigedo (Revillagigedo Channel)
Isla Zayas (Zayas Island)
Terrritorio de Nutca (1789–1795)
Pacific Ocean
Isla de Quadra y Vancouver (Vancouver Island)
Fuerte San Miguel / Santa Cruz de Nuca (Yuquot)
Surgidero de San Lorenzo (Nootka Sound)
Estrecho de Juan de Fuca (Strait of Juan de Fuca)
Fuerte Núnez Gaona (Neah Bay)
Estrecho de Haro (Haro Strait)
Islas de San Juan (San Juan Islands)
Punta de los Mártires (Point Grenville)
Rada de Bucareli (Grenville Bay)
Puerto de Nuestra Senora de los Ángeles (Port Angeles)
Entrada de Heceta (Columbia River's estuary)
Rio de San Roque (Columbia River)
Puerto Trinidad (Trinidad Bay)
N
200 km

The Apotheosis of Captain Cook. The influence of Cook's voyages on those who sailed with him, and those who read of his exploits, cannot be overstated. This engraving, created fifteen years after his death, shows Cook ascending to heaven with the help of Britannia and Fame after being slain at Kealakekua Bay in Hawaii. JOHN WEBBER, 1794 / IMAGE © THE TRUSTEES OF THE BRITISH MUSEUM

OPPOSITE, TOP *View of the Spanish Fort and Cove at Nootka Sound.* In 1793, the Spanish fort, complete with ten artillery canons, and the Spanish frigate *Princesa*, with twenty-six canons, dominated Friendly Cove/ Cala de Los Amigos. SIGISMUND BACSTROM, 1793. COURTESY OF BEINECKE RARE BOOK AND MANUSCRIPT LIBRARY, YALE UNIVERSITY

BOTTOM *Contest between England and Spain for the Dominion of the Seas, 1790.* When this British cartoon was published in 1790, the United States had yet to establish its navy, and the French had not recovered from their devastating losses at the Battle of the Saintes. The battle for dominion of the seas was between Britain (George III) and Spain (Charles IV). In the cartoon, George III is backed by Neptune while Charles IV is backed by the Pope. In anticipation of victory, Fame emerges from clouds holding a laurel wreath above George III's head. COURTESY OF BEINECKE RARE BOOK AND MANUSCRIPT LIBRARY, YALE UNIVERSITY

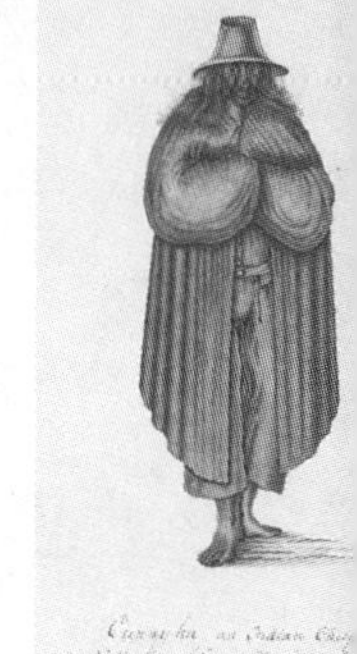

LEFT *A Native of King George's Sound.* The region that Britain and Spain had nearly gone to war over had been occupied by Indigenous Peoples for more than ten thousand years. ETCHING BY WILLIAM ELLIS, 1782. PUBLIC DOMAIN

TOP, RIGHT This Nuu-chah-nulth hat, woven from cedar or spruce, was collected at Nootka Sound during Cook's research voyage and later donated to the British Museum by botanist Joseph Banks in 1780. IMAGE © THE TRUSTEES OF THE BRITISH MUSEUM

BOTTOM, RIGHT *Oachey, a Chief in Norfolk Sound* (left) and *Cunny Ha, an Indian Chief on the North Side of Queen Charlotte's Island* (right). Botanists on the ships that visited the Pacific Northwest enthusiastically recorded the hairstyles, clothing, jewellery, and deportment of the many Indigenous men and women they observed. BY SIGISMUND BACSTROM, 1793 (LEFT). COURTESY OF BEINECKE RARE BOOK AND MANUSCRIPT LIBRARY, YALE UNIVERSITY (RIGHT)

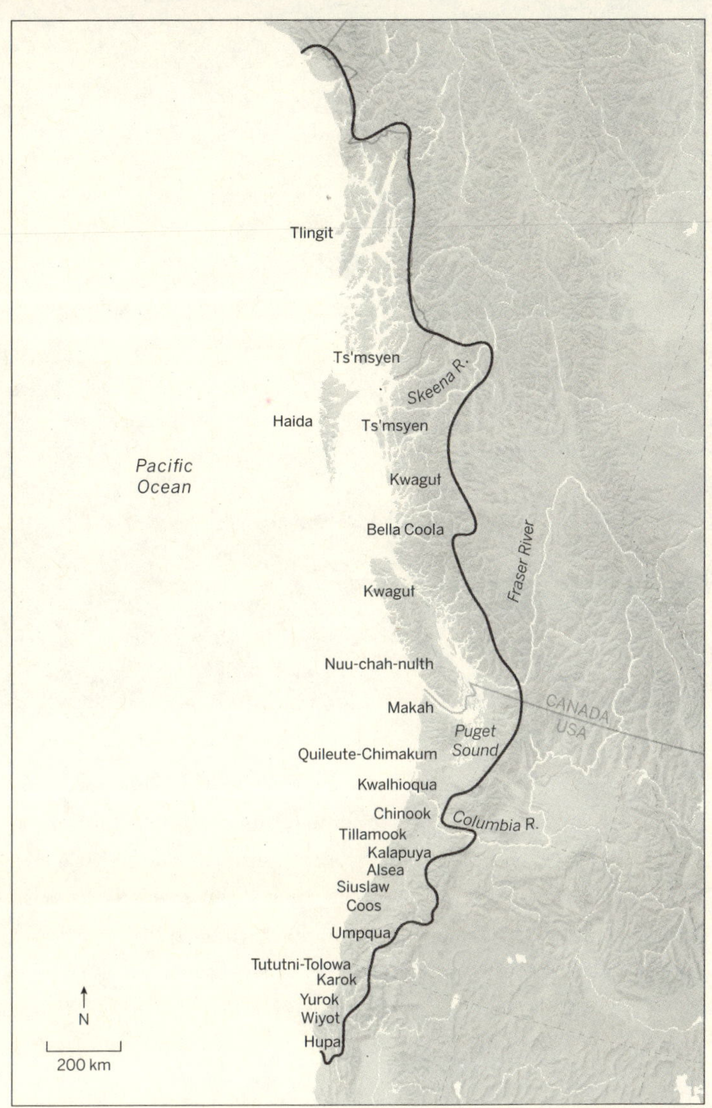

Peoples of the Pacific Northwest. The earliest European visitors to the Pacific Northwest coast had no idea which Indigenous Nations lived in which parts of the coast, or what political, social, or other relationships existed between them. These were revealed through trial and error. This map indicates a present-day understanding of names and locations. ERIC LEINBERGER

We kept the western shore on board. Ships of the King George's Sound Company were among the first to trade for fur along the coast of the Pacific Northwest and, politically, the most consequential. Because they were licensed to trade in the area by the British Crown, the Spanish assault on the KGSC ships, and disruption of their trade, was consequently deemed an assault on Britain. MARK RICHARD MYERS

PART TWO

Coastal Culture and Shock

8

COASTAL CONTACT

THE DISPUTES between Spain and Britain over territory on the Pacific Northwest coast were nothing new. Long before the Europeans arrived on the scene, Indigenous tribes had been competing among themselves for control of and access to marine resources. What the Europeans brought to the scene was a new stream of resources—copper, iron, firearms—and political allegiances that complicated existing lines of tension and created new ones.

The general area that Britain and Spain had argued—and almost gone to war—over had been occupied by coastal Indigenous Peoples for more than ten thousand years. But of course, the Indigenous Peoples who lived there at the time of European contact did not think of themselves in that communal way any more than the Europeans thought of themselves as "Europeans." The Indigenous Peoples considered themselves members of their own individual tribes, at home in their own territories, with their own languages, histories, and beliefs. The geographic area they occupied was vast, with many inlets and coves, and was also an area of great density of different languages. The broader region running south from the Gulf of Alaska to the present-day Oregon–California border and inland to the Coast Mountains of British Columbia and the Cascade Range of Washington and Oregon included as many as forty-five languages in thirteen language families.[1]

The area that is the focus of much of our narrative, Nootka Sound, was part of a cultural region that stretched south about 500 miles, from the northern tip of what is now Vancouver Island to the mouth of the Columbia River farther to the south. At the time Cook visited, in 1778, the Nootka Sound area was thought to have a population of about 2,600 people. When Alejandro Malaspina visited the area in 1791, the estimate was 4,000. The reality was probably somewhere between the two.

The coastal Indigenous Peoples, including those in the Nootka Sound area, lived in orderly societies with their own hierarchies based on extended family groups. Some tribes were on friendly terms with each other, in some cases held together through intermarriage. Others were wary of each other and experienced occasional, sometimes violent, conflict. While kinship networks were important, political power was competitive, and those with the most resources—and the most control over resources—held the greatest power. Those leaders who could provide the most resources for their people held the most influence and authority over others. They could muster warriors from neighbouring villages either for group defence, or for raids on others.

When the first ships from Spain, Britain, Russia, and America visited the northwest coast and met the people there, the Europeans did not know—as we do today—that they were meeting separate tribes like the Heiltsuk, Haida, Nuxalk, Tlingit, Nuu-chah-nulth, Makah, Salish, Kwakwa̱ka̱'wakw,

Ts'msyen, and others. They did not know that the territories around Friendly Cove belonged to the Yuquot-Tahsis Confederacy, Tlupana, Muchalaht, and Hesquiaht. The voyagers were as unfamiliar with the ethnographic situation as they were with the geographic, possibly even more so. But they soon discovered that the Indigenous societies valued commercial trade; and they came to understand that the acquisition and distribution of wealth was a core attribute and status symbol of the powerful. This would prove to be an immediate, if not entirely smooth, area of mutual understanding and collaboration.

For the Indigenous Peoples, the arrival of these first few foreign ships provided a rare opportunity to trade for exotic goods—copper and iron being most attractive—mainly in exchange for fur, but also for food and other items. The leading families were able to maintain and advance their social positions by accumulating and then distributing material wealth obtained through canny trade with the visitors. This was the system that Vancouver and Quadra experienced with Maquinna in the previous chapter. This accumulation and display of wealth at the local level also helped prevent encroachment by neighbouring groups.

Because this hierarchical system already existed at the time of first contact with Europeans, it was natural that established Indigenous leaders would take control of the acquisition, preparation, and trade of fur within a given area. At Nootka Sound, Chief Maquinna dominated the scene. To the south in Clayoquot Sound, Chief Wickaninnish controlled trade. On the Olympic Peninsula, south of the Strait of Juan de Fuca, Chief Tatoosh was in charge. They each exercised control over trading empires in the interior, organized labour, and set the terms for trade at the coast. As their wealth grew, so did their prestige, because they were able to redistribute more and more goods in their communities.

Maquinna, Wickaninnish, and Tatoosh, though separate, considered themselves of equal stature in their communities. As coastal peoples, their territory was not just the land they lived on, but also the seas they sailed and harvested. Whales, salmon, and seals were their property to manage, to own, and to distribute. The foreign ships that arrived in their territories with new goods aboard were also viewed within this context. Each Chief claimed rights to control the distribution of the bounty, treating the visiting ships as they would dead whales that had drifted into their territory.

An extreme but clear example of this occurred in 1788, when John Meares was in Wickaninnish's territory and some men from a neighbouring village attempted to trade with Meares, without the chief's consent. To establish his right to control trade with Meares, Wickaninnish dispatched warriors in many canoes to capture those other men, one of whom was dragged into the woods and executed. Just as they did with other resources in their territory, Chiefs moved quickly and unambiguously to establish and maintain control over sources of wealth.

To the Indigenous Peoples, it was understood that each dominant local Chief controlled the trading relationships. To the visiting Europeans, unfamiliar with the protocols or the leaders' territorial boundary lines, these actions often seemed puzzling and occasionally difficult to navigate. In 1778, ten years before the Meares incident above, Cook had been puzzled by Maquinna's efforts to control access to his ship. Each newcomer would stumble clumsily into unknown (to them) sovereign tribal territories and attempt to establish friendly trade relationships.

But as long as both European and Indigenous cultures shared an interest in trade, respected social hierarchies, valued the accumulation of wealth, and understood that giving it away was something only the powerful could afford to do, they were able to make common ground. The linguistic challenges may have been many, but the language of trade and commerce was easily understood.

Precisely when first contact took place, and between whom, is difficult to pinpoint. Russian traders from the Alaska area had occasionally ventured south. But the first European to visit the area may have been Sir Francis Drake, briefly, in 1579. Juan de Fuca is believed to have been to the area in 1592, also briefly. But we know the first properly documented encounter between northwest coast Indigenous Peoples and Europeans was nearly two hundred years later, when Juan Pérez visited the area in 1774. His accounts are among the earliest records of the people, customs, and culture that existed in this area at that time. They are worth reviewing here so we can better understand the state of the region and the nature of early visitor–Indigenous relations at that time.

Pérez and the *Santiago*, 1774

Pérez arrived in the area from the Spanish naval base in San Blas, Mexico. He had been instructed to sail north as far as 60 degrees north latitude—roughly as far as present-day Skagway, Alaska—to assert Spanish sovereignty over the west coast. His 82-foot frigate *Santiago* accommodated eighty-eight official members and some additional passengers, including two priests. He did not make it as far north as planned, but by August of that year he arrived at about 55 degrees north latitude, where he encountered the Haida People of Haida Gwaii. After spreading feathers on the water near Pérez's boat, the Haida proceeded to trade with his crew, offering sea otter skins and items made from cedar trees—hats, blankets—in exchange for metal goods.

On his first encounter with the Haida people, Pérez wrote in his journal: "The men were of good stature of body, well-formed and smiling expressions, beautiful eyes, and good looking; the hair tied, and compared to fashion of a wig with a tail. Some wore it tied in the back and had beards and moustaches in the fashion of the Chinese people. The first action they did when they approached within a gunshot of the ship was to begin to sing their motet in unison and cast feathers in the water." He added that "their arms were open making a cross, and put their arms on the other's bosom in the same manner, an appropriate sign of their peacefulness."[2]

Confirming the established trading nature of the people, he observed:

> They are very enlivened to trade and to sell according to the acuity of their dealings with us, because before they would give any trifles, they had to hold in their hands the items of their dealings, considering and satisfying their likes with a look, and if pleased, to ask for more, making it understood that if we did not give more, they would not pay. Noticing this, one could believe that they have had frequent commerce amongst them.
>
> All their trade is reduced to giving pelts of animals such as sea wolf, otter, and bears. They also have a special white wool and I don't know the species of animal that produces the wool they extract. They weave beautiful blankets and I collected four. They are not large, but are well woven and wrought.[3]

He noted that the three canoes he saw were swift, very well made, and of one piece of wood, with the largest carrying nine men and the other two each carrying seven. The next day he met more Haida people, including two women and some children. He wrote:

> Among the twenty-one canoes, we saw two full of women with some children on their bosom, and other older children. They were all good looking, white, and blonde, many of them wore bracelets of iron and copper and some headbands of the same. They wear clothes of pelts tailor fit to their body. The lower lip in the middle has a hole, and in it they put a colored shell that strikes on the nose when they speak, but they have regular movement. Those that wore it are apparently married, because some of the young girls were not wearing it. They are of a good build, like the men.[4]

The observation about bracelets of iron and copper suggests that while he was the first to document his observations, he was not the first outsider to trade with the Haida.

Sailing farther south, Pérez repeated his boat-to-boat trade. Eventually he arrived at Nootka... except he decided to call it "Surgidero de San Lorenzo."

Cook, HMS *Resolution*, and HMS *Discovery*, 1778

A more extended intercultural exchange occurred with Cook and his two ships in 1778. As noted earlier, Cook stayed among the Mowachaht at Nootka for most of April and found them friendly and eager to trade. Again, Second Lieutenant

John Rickman's account of their first encounters is a useful source of information. Not fully understanding local customs, he nevertheless documented what were likely Chief Maquinna's successful efforts to exercise his right to control trade with HMS *Resolution* and HMS *Discovery*.

This incident happened just a couple of days after arriving at Friendly Cove. Cook and his crew feared they were about to be attacked by several hundred Mowachaht. Instead the attack was on Indigenous people who had come to trade without permission. Rickman recorded the event:

> On the 3rd [of April], a large body of Indians were seen paddling along the Sound, mostly armed with spears from twenty to thirty feet long, and with bows and arrows very neatly made. On their nearer approach they too were heard to tune up their war-song, and to brandish their weapons, as if in defiance of an enemy. Their number was alarming, there being not less than between three and four hundred of them in their war canoes, who we apprehended were come to attack us; but we afterwards understood they were come to attack a body of their enemies on the opposite shore, whom they afterwards engaged, and returned victorious.[5]

On April 22, a similar event occurred. This time a small party of Indigenous traders were intercepted after they had conducted their business with Cook's ships. The traders had hardly left the ship, wrote Rickman, "when another body of Indians appeared, more than double the number of the former, who hemmed them all into the cove, and stript them of every thing they had about them, and then came and traded with us."[6]

Strange, the *Captain Cook*, and the *Experiment*, 1786

Charles Stuart Strange, the fur trader from Bombay, was motivated by profit; his journals suggest he was not much interested in ethnographic studies or cross-cultural understanding, except where it facilitated trade. If we are generous, we might note that his crew was in rough shape when they arrived in Friendly Cove in June of 1786, and his attitude may not have been the best. Risking one's life in the hope of a big payoff might have that effect. However, while Strange was happy to remain mostly on board the *Captain Cook*, another more curious traveller, thirty-two-year-old Alexander Walker, on Strange's second ship, the *Experiment*, has left us with more helpful first impressions.

Walker reported that he and other crew members walked around Friendly Cove and Yuquot freely and unarmed, "with as much security, as if we had been on the banks of the Thames." He noted again what others have said: the Mowachaht were astute traders, carefully evaluating items offered in trade, focusing on items of metal and copper, and increasing their price as trade continued. With regard to Maquinna, son of the Maquinna who had greeted Cook, Walker observed that despite his unkempt appearance he was "a stout handsome young man, with a fine manly countenance, and being fond of our company, soon became our favourite." He was honest and shrewd and "the most intelligent person we met with."[7]

Walker initially suspected that cannibalism was practised among the Mowachaht. But, after passing more time among them, he began to think the Mowachaht were merely pulling his leg.

Hanna, the *Sea Otter*, 1786

We have already read about the 1785 voyage of the unlicensed *Sea Otter* under command of James Hanna (see page 38). That mission was successful enough to merit a return visit in 1786, when the ship's second mate, a Mr. Elliot, wrote a short sketch of the people he encountered. This account was written in August of 1786, the same time that the KGSC's *Prince of Wales* was slipping out of London, and just a few weeks after Strange had left Nootka. Mr. Elliot gave his first impression of the Mowachaht:

> They are of a middle statu[r]e, stout and muscular built, of a dark copper colour, and very fierce countenance, which they heighten by smearing their whole body with red clay, mixed with fish oil, and streaking their faces with black; they also daub their hair with clay, and powder it with white down of birds. The dress of the men is a skin or matt (which they work of stripes of some tough bark very neat), tied round the neck; and open before, with a hat made of stained twigs, like basket-work, of the form of a sugar-loaf. The women wear a hat also, and the skins tied round their middle, which, with the help of a round matt and a hole in the center, through which they put their heads, and which hangs down to their middle, forming a complete covering... The men, when going to battle or expedition, are always perfectly naked.

He went on to observe: "Fish appear to be their chief provision in summer, and indeed they dry a great quantity for winter; they eat the whale, porpoise, and everything they can catch; I have seen them frequently take a mouthful of a fish even before taking it off the hook; in winter they have sea otters, seals, bears, wolves, and sundry other wild beasts, but no vegetable, nor any substitute for bread." Perhaps falling victim to the same joke played on Walker a few weeks earlier, Elliot wrote that the Mowachaht "eat their captives and enemies killed in battle, and I believe their own dead also; as, on our first arrival, they brought us for sale a great number of skulls, hands, feet, and other human bones."

Mind you, Elliot also reported that the Mowachaht seemed to think the Europeans were cannibals. Apparently they had mistaken his ship's white-painted wooden rigging blocks for human skulls.

Like Pérez before him, Mr. Elliot also wrote about the canoes: "They are cut out of the solid tree. I saw one of them, which was seventy-three feet long, eight feet broad and had seats for thirty men to paddle, besides which she could easily have carried twenty more."[8]

Colnett, KGSC *Prince Of Wales*, and KGSC *Princess Royal*, 1787

Arriving at Friendly Cove the summer after Hanna and Mr. Elliot, James Colnett had many of the same first impressions. His journals note that he was visited upon arrival by two Chiefs, "McCulagh & Clataluka," and presented each of them with a grenadiers cap. This was probably Chief Maquinna and his brother ("catlati" being the Nuu-chah-nulth word for brother). But while Colnett's notes are matter-of-fact, a more detailed and colourful account of the KGSC traders' first encounters can be gleaned from the journals of crewman Andrew Bracey Taylor, another veteran of the British Royal

Navy. The twenty-nine-year-old's writings begin by identifying the name of the village and its leadership:

> The Town which stands very pleasant, the Natives call Nutka. The Village is under the Government of two Chiefs of nearly equal power, they are both keen clever men well acquainted with barter, in all its Stages, as well, with distant tribes for Skins, as with us in the sale of them, and they spare no pains in getting them into their possession. If their is any difference in their authority Maquilla has the preference, he speaks some English.

Taylor also took pains to describe the appearance of the men, women, and children:

> They use a red kind of ore to paint their faces & utensils with & set little Value on it nor our vermillion altho' they prefer'd it would not give the smallest article in exchange they have also black & white which they mark their faces with, the latter gives them a horrid aspect. The Inhabitants are of a middling size neither corpulent nor lean, the Visage mostly round and full, and sometimes broad & high prominent Cheeks their nose flat and wide nostrils the eye small and black rather dull than sparkling the mouth round & lips mostly thick, their teeth good & regular, very few young men wear their beards, & scarce an old man without one, the Hair of their Heads is dark inclining to Black & thick & on many of them a good length hanging down over the Shoulders & forehead in a wild manner but when going on a visit, it's dress'd in different manners ornamented with the white down of Birds. Their complexion when wash'd clear of paint is a Shade whiter than the People of the society

Isles & the Women had appearance of a Colour in their Cheeks. The Children whose skin had not been died with paint were nearly as white as Europeans.

He took notes on the buildings and canoes, and the artwork that adorned them:

The largest Building is generally in the Middle of the Village & Occupied by the Chief[.] On the two beams which form the length of the House are paintings resembling Human figures & the supporters of these beams are large posts of wood those at each end has a human face carv'd on & in the mouth teeth fix'd. The remainder of their House is made up with a small rafters & boards;... The canoes are well calculated[,] the largest carrying twenty or thirty people, the smallest two & three[;] they are form'd out of one tree growing narrower at each end the stern the lowest the Bow having a good rake forward & carried up much higher than the other end some of them have carving & Painting on their Stern and gunnel & the inside cut in Grooves [which] at a distance look like timbers they swim without outriggers & the seats are round sticks.

Taylor's notes also reveal the challenges of verbal communication, and the crew's inability to understand, except through tone and temperament, what was being said. One incident captures the situation particularly well: "We were surrounded by the Natives in their Canoes[.] In one of the larger Canoes were several troublesome elderly Men, one in particular whom we took for a Chief, a sourly fellow stood up and harangued the Natives alongside for near an hour without ceasing[;] we were quite ignorant respecting the purport of the oration, yet we were sure He found himself offended at something, and we knew He must be some person of consequence as his Clamour commanded general attention."

The Europeans struggled to understand the local languages, but tried their best. The natives, wrote Taylor, "generally took great pains to instruct those who were desirous of learning their language, but 'tis extremely difficult to get acquainted with, and I have minded in asking the name of any particular article that in asking six different Men I have received as many different name[s], but 'tis scarcely fair to say each Man had a different name for the articles it might in consequence of some misunderstanding in the question asked."

In addition to trying the learn the local languages, the KGSC crew attempted to understand local religious practices. Taylor explained in his journal that they did not get any fish from the local people for two Sundays in a row, and this led them to wonder if it was a sacred day. To explore the hypothesis, the ship's surgeon, Archibald Menzies, was sent to the village to investigate: "He was received very cordially by the Natives there was about two hundred present[;] they placed him on a clean Mat, by the side of Oughomeize, the Chief of this district. He remained with them an hour without discovering any religious ceremony or anything worthy of notice, unless 'twas one Woman endeavouring to relieve a sick Child of its pain by friction. This She performed with great affection and tenderness, at the same time singing a doleful song."

The KGSC traders continued their cultural exchange with musical performances, but with little success. "On the 17th a small organ of the Captain's was played to the Indians, but the musick to them was not so attractive as the small brass pipes, those they conceived would make pretty ornaments for their Ears and Noses. The Drum and fife was also tried, but they disapproved of the Noise."

A final account from Taylor describes his admiration for the Chief, who explained local hunting methods through a masked performance:

> Oughomeize our Chief paid us frequent visits. He appeared to me to be a man who had raised himself to his Command of the District by his bravery[;] he was a great favourite of mine. This fellow possessed some humour, and could pronounce a number of English words very well. This evening he described to us their method of killing Sea Otters and other animals, by putting on his head a wooden mask resembling feintly the head of some wild animal and covering his body with a Skin, then placing himself on the Deck in the attitude of the Animal he was supposed to pursue. In this manner in the Winter Season they hunt in the Woods, mixing occasionally with various animals, and being prepared with daggers, they watch proper opportunity to stab them[;] sometimes they watch in the Woods with long spears, thus ornamented till the animal comes near enough to strike them. Whether they are expert or industrious at this I cannot say, but should suppose they are, and if this trade is continued, no doubt 'Twill lead them to a close application for the benefit of Barter.[9]

A Gitxaała Account

Indigenous accounts of first contact with European visitors were not written down in journals, as they were by Europeans like Taylor, Elliot, Walker, Rickman, and Pérez. Instead, these stories were passed down through oral tradition. Fortunately, in 1916 Nisga'a hereditary chief and ethnographer William Beynon visited Gitxaała and recorded several stories on wax cylinders. One of them was the story of the origins of the name "Sabaen," ascribed to a Kanhade head chief among the Gitxaała.

The account relayed to Beynon likely related to the visit to the area by King George's Sound Company commander James Colnett, who arrived on KGSC *Prince of Wales* in September 1787. The recorded account was later transcribed as follows:

> The people were all living on the south end of Pitt Island. Here they gathered their winter food of halibut and fur animals, seals and otter... One day, two Gitrhala men set out from their village to fish for halibut and were so absorbed in fishing that they failed to notice a large boat approaching. When one of them looked up, he saw a huge being with many wings approaching towards them. They at once thought it was a monster which lived in the nearby rocks. They were at the time fishing over a spenarnorh ("abode of monster") from which a huge Raven used to emerge (a crest of 'Arhlawaels, Kanhade). They thought that the monster had now taken a new form and was approaching to do them harm. So they drew up their fishing lines, which were made of kelp (mawrh) and paddled in for the shore. There, they thought they would be safe. The man that was sitting in the stern had the rope of the canoe fastened around his waist.
>
> Then they landed, the man in the bow of the canoe ran up into the woods, and the man in the stern got up and tried to follow, but failed to untie the rope from his waist. It tightened and he fell down and was overtaken by these strange beings, who resembled human beings. They came up to where he was lying and untied the rope, and he now set up and looked at them and became frightened.

To protect himself he urinated in his hand, and rubbed the urine all over his body. The Gitrhala used to protect themselves from monsters and supernatural beings and ghosts, by rubbing themselves with their urine, thus breaking off any bad influence of the supernatural beings. If anything appeared to do them harm they would throw their urine at it. The urine was always kept close at hand in their houses and never wasted. These strange men now picked him up and made motions for him to come down to the canoe. They pointed first to the canoe and then to the halibut, and then to their mouths. This they kept on doing while saying "Soap," which they gave him and took a halibut from the canoe. The Gitrhala man thought that they were giving him a name. Then they made signs for him to cut the halibut up for them. So he took his knife of albatross bill and began to cut up the fish. These strangers took the fish from him and cut it up quickly. He was then frightened on seeing their weapons for cutting. These strangers then motioned him to build a fire, and he went down to his canoe and brought out his firing outfit (gyins), and began to build a fire. He worked a long time. Meanwhile, these men had gathered some moss and got their flint-lock revolvers, and set it off. When the Gitrhala man heard the report, he fell right over and "died" (sadaek, suddenly died, meaning fainted away). As he came to, he saw a huge fire burning, and now knew that these men were supernatural. So to give himself double protection, he again urinated in his hand and bathed his body. The men came to him and made motions for him to cook fish. He then went down to his canoe and got his cooking box and set stones in the fire, and filled his box up with water. As soon as the stones were hot, he put the halibut in and then the hot stones in the cooking box and kept on changing the stones. The strangers looked on for a while, and then one of them went down to the boat and got a large pot and put water in it and put the whole halibut in the pot and then boiled it on the fire. The Gitrhala man was now much frightened. When the fish was cooked, the men got out something else out of another pot which the Gitrhala man thought to be maggot (this was rice), and began to eat. They poured upon the rice black stuff which the Gitrhala knew to be the rot of people (this was molasses). They made motions for him to eat, but he was so afraid that he could not move. He now saw that they were eating and that they would not harm him. So he called out to the other man, "Come on down. They are eating. They won't touch anybody." They were eating the rot of people, along with maggots, and they were also eating adaeran (a fungus growth on trees) much like a mushroom, very dry, and large. These were biscuits.

AFTER THESE MEN had finished eating, they made signs to the Gitrhala to show them where they lived. When they understood them, one of them made signs for them to go down to the canoe. The men got into their boat and the Gitrhala in their canoe were towed by these strangers, and they pointed out where was their village. When these strangers let them go they paddled away to their village, and the strangers went away.

WHEN THE GITRHALA arrived at their home they told all the people what they had seen and where they had left the strangers. Then the Gitrhala man said, "They gave me the name Sabaen." This is what it sounded like to him, but the white man was thought to have said Soap, because that is what he gave them. They kept it for some time before they found out what it was used for. He then assumed the name of Sabaen and referred it to Sabaehlnahlkuhlehl-hagwilaw'rh, "The offspring of Hagwilaw'rh runs suddenly."

A FEW DAYS passed by and these strangers landed in the village. Everyone ran away but these two men and the Chief Ahlawaels, a Kanhade, stayed there and entertained them to a hallaeit dance. They first gave them food, but the white men (so they were) would not eat it. Arhlawaels then got his narhorh out, which was Alaerem-mekshilk, "Continually moving white weasel," a headress, and he moved out to the centre of the house and began to dance. The weasel was on his hat and to all accounts was dead. The chief moved faster and faster, then the meksihlk came to life and moved up and around the top of the hat. The dancer now danced very hard[,] the meksihlk moved faster and faster then ran out on the arms of the dancer and around his robe. When the dancer slowed down, the weasel moved slower and, as the dancer stopped, the weasel went up again to its former resting place. (The weasel was dead and not alive, but moved around mechanically by strings being pulled). The chief then took a sea-otter robe and gave it to the elder man, who seemed to be in command, and to all the rest, bear robes, seal robes, and mink robes.

These Gitrhala are not the same people as Hale met and got his name from, but came before them. [10]

These earliest recorded descriptions of connections between Pacific Northwest Indigenous Peoples and the broader trading world show all parties struggling to understand each other's language, status, values, allegiances, and protocols, but generally managing to get by. If the goal was to conduct mutually beneficial trade, that goal was achieved. If the goal was also to establish enduring friendships, alliances, and mutual understanding, much of the appropriate groundwork was laid.

But the earliest days of connection were not without conflict, and sometimes deadly violence. Those stories also need to be told.

9

COASTAL CONFLICT

THE RECORDS of first contact between European visitors and the Indigenous Peoples of the Pacific Northwest reflect mutual curiosity and desire for satisfactory trade relationships. But there are also records of conflict, sometimes deadly. Though regrettable, history is full of examples, some due to disagreement or ignorance, others by design, and still others by accident. Reviewing some of the early cases helps us understand the nature of the emerging relationship between Indigenous Peoples and their visitors at this time.

As noted, conflict between local tribes existed before Europeans arrived. A nineteenth-century oral history relayed to Brigham Young University professor Albert B. Reagan by the Quileute People of the Cape Flattery and Tatoosh Island area (on the southern side of the entrance to the Strait of Juan de Fuca) tells of conflict with the neighbouring Makah. The story relayed that the Quileute warriors had pushed the Makah to the north side of the strait, onto what is now Vancouver Island, and, fearing a counterattack, had subsequently raided the Makah village in a pre-emptive strike. Reagan wrote that "with whale bone and stones and clubs, clam shell knives, and yew wood daggers [the Quileutes] dealt death on every side."[1] This was, unsurprisingly, met with a retaliatory counterattack of equal violence that left a Quileute village a smouldering ruin with many dead.

Oral histories recorded in the early twentieth century tell how Chief Wickaninnish had initially been leader of an inland tribe before expanding to the coast. Having outstripped local food resources, but also having a large number of warriors, he declared war on the coastal Kelsamites and drove them out of their village, Opitsaht, by force. He continued to expand his authority throughout Clayoquot Sound with repeated raids to gain control over the coastal resources of salmon, halibut, and whales. He then secured his power and built his leadership status by redistributing his wealth through lavish Potlatches.

These conflicts in what is now northern Washington State and southwestern Vancouver Island were all about establishing control over lucrative marine resources and the optimal marine harvesting sites. These territories, and the rights to them resulting from various battles and negotiated alliances over many generations, were changed forever after Cook alerted the commercial seafaring community to the possibilities of the area's fur trade.

Soon, ships were visiting the coves, inlets, harbours, and bays, not only from neighbouring tribes but also from places much farther away: Canton, Macao, Bombay, Calcutta, London, San Blas, and Boston. Such was the volume of visits and commerce that by the end of the eighteenth century, British sales in the maritime fur trade had reached nearly 300,000 Spanish dollars; the Spanish, American, and French traders pulled another 150,000 out of the market.

These commercial ships arrived with mixed agendas: some to get rich quick, others to establish permanent factories, like the ones in Bombay and Macao, from which they could run long-term trading operations and build even greater institutional wealth. The British ships sent in the name of King George III were more interested in ruling the seas than the land. The Spanish ships sent in the name of King Charles IV were, at least initially, sent to claim the land and convert the Indigenous Peoples to Christianity. While all sought to achieve their goals without loss of life, and were keen to establish Indigenous partnerships, they all collectively contributed to a disruption in the established political, territorial, and economic norms in the area.

Occasionally in that milieu, violence happened.

Most violent conflict was accidental. Sometimes it was intentional. Always it was tragic. What follows are some of the stories, shared as before so we can better understand the evolving relationship between local peoples and their earliest recorded visitors. We will start with a Spanish visit in 1775 and end with Maquinna in 1803.

Heceta and Quadra, the *Santiago*, and the *Sonora*, 1775

One year after Pérez's first brief visit to Friendly Cove, his colleague Bruno de Heceta was given command of the *Santiago* and sent back to the area to do what Pérez had not been able to do: make land and formally claim it for Spain. He was accompanied by Juan Francisco de la Bodega y Quadra on the schooner *Sonora*. The ships became briefly separated off the coast of present-day Washington State, to the west of Olympic National Park. Both commanders were thirty-two years old.

On July 13, 1775, the *Sonora* was close to land near the mouth of the Quinault River, about 130 kilometres south of the entrance to the Strait of Juan de Fuca. Several Indigenous people approached in a canoe, keen to conduct trade. Quadra invited them on board and presents were exchanged. All ended well. The following morning, on July 14, still waiting for reunion with the *Santiago*, Quadra sent seven crew members ashore to collect fresh water and wood for a topmast. When his crew reached land, they were immediately ambushed by over two hundred warriors. Five sailors were cut down; two escaped into the sea but, unable to swim safely back to land or to the *Sonora*, they drowned.

Quadra did not know that the people who had visited him the previous day were from the Quileute Nation, while the people his crew encountered on shore were Quinault Nation. He also didn't know he had sailed into waters the two tribal nations were competing for. So when the traders from the Quileute came back to visit him again on the fourteenth, after a land attack they knew nothing about, Quadra was on the defensive, thinking he was about to be attacked again by the Quinault. When the Quileute canoe drew within range, he gave the order to fire the ship's swivel gun and killed seven out of nine people in the canoe.

It was only then that the *Santiago* came onto the scene, arriving from a point farther south where that same morning they had made land, dutifully erected a cross, and read the Requerimiento, asserting Spanish rule and encouraging Indigenous Peoples' conversion to Christianity.[2]

Cook, HMS *Resolution*, and HMS *Discovery*, 1778

Cook's visit to Friendly Cove in 1778 lasted several weeks and involved extended onshore visits. This prolonged contact, with multiple daily interactions among many strangers with little to no shared language or understanding, created a high risk for misunderstandings. That the visit ended on good terms between all parties is a credit to the diplomacy of Cook and the authority of Maquinna.

But there was one close call. Blood was nearly spilled over an iron bolt. Lieutenant Rickman recorded the incident thus:

> About the same time another Indian made free with a bolt from the armourer's forge; but was seen in the act, and an endeavour made to wrest it from him but he instantly jumped overboard, and gave it to one of his companions, who was making off with it, till fired at with small shot, which brought him back, and he surrendered it, but with such a fierceness expressed in his countenance as sufficiently indicated his intent. In a moment every Indian in the cove disappeared, and in less than three hours, more than 900 of them assembled in the sound, and being uncloathed (which is their custom when they mean to engage) began their war-song, and approached the ships. We were in readiness to give them a warm reception; but seeing our preparations, and perhaps not liking our countenance, they all laid down their arms, and putting on their cloaths, came peaceably round the ship without offering the least incivility.[3]

Cook and his crew, on their scientific expedition, were motivated to exercise diplomacy while charting the coast, making astronomical observations, collecting plants, and trading for artefacts. But many of the commercial traders who followed in his wake, after his revelations about the fur opportunities there, were much less cautious.

Hanna and the *Sea Otter*, 1785

James Hanna arrived at Nootka in August of 1785. He traded successfully enough, but his visit was nowhere near as peaceful as Cook's. One incident was likely the result of misunderstanding, another the result of ignorance.

The incident caused by misunderstanding was much the same as the one avoided by Cook. The details are lost to time, but the core elements of the story are this: A Mowachaht visitor to the *Sea Otter* had taken a chisel. Hanna believed the chisel to have been stolen and fired on a canoe containing the perceived thief. The Mowachaht then counterattacked. Hanna fired some more. Twenty Indigenous people—including women and children—lost their lives.

In another version of this story, the person who took the chisel thought it had been given to him in exchange for furs. It is also possible that, the ship being within the realm of the tribe's other marine resources, the person removing the chisel from the ship merely considered it his rightful bounty to harvest. But regardless of whether it was a trade gone wrong, a theft, or an appropriation, it is clear that neither party understood the territorial or property rights of the other, and lives were tragically lost as a result. Fear may also have been a factor; Hanna's ship was small and he could easily have been ransacked, or worse. Did he feel a need to show force?

The second incident, the one caused by ignorance, was recorded by Martínez when he was visiting the area four years later. According to his notes,

> One day, when Macuina, the principal chief of the village of this port where we are lying, went on board [Hanna's] ship to visit him, and when they had seated him near the binnacle, they sprinkled a little powder under his chair,

> giving him to understand that this was an honour which they showed to chiefs. He supposed that the powder was dark coloured sand, but he soon felt its effect, when one of the Englishmen set off the charge. Poor Macuina was raised from the deck by the explosion and had his buttocks scorched; he showed me the scars.[4]

It is unclear whether this incident happened before or after the other one. Some accounts suggest the former. If so, then perhaps it was this humiliating incident—not the chisel—that triggered the attack on Hanna's ship. It may be that it was actually Hanna's juvenile assault on Maquinna's dignity that caused the attack on his ship, and the subsequent loss of twenty lives.

That Hanna and Maquinna subsequently achieved some form of détente and were able to continue to trade with each other seems remarkable.

Strange, the *Captain Cook*, and the *Experiment*, 1786

A similar event took place the following year, when James Strange arrived on the scene in the *Captain Cook*, accompanied by the *Experiment*. After some days of trading and generally good relations between Strange's men and the Nuu-chah-nulth, an unfortunate incident broke the peace. An Indigenous person was accused of stealing a copper kettle and two seamen's jackets from one of the *Captain Cook* crew. Complaints were made and the items eventually returned, but Strange demanded the thief be surrendered to his custody, taken on board his ship, and flogged. The event was alarming, confusing, and frightening.

Alexander Walker, reflecting on the event in his journal, lamented that "our conduct on this occasion had neither justice, nor policy, to recommend it. The restitution of the articles and the placing of the person of the offender in our hands, ought to have satisfied all the claims of justice. By preferring a different conduct, we lost a fine opportunity of establishing a character for moderation and humanity. The affair was... ill managed. It was calculated to produce irritation and suspicion, instead of those calmer and more dignified impressions, which ought to attend the prosecution of Justice."[5]

Colnett, KGSC *Prince of Wales*, and KGSC *Princess Royal*, 1787

Nobody died while Colnett's two ships were at Nootka. But, as with Strange, tempers were raised, muskets fired, and blows exchanged, all because of perceived acts of theft.

The most egregious act was when KGSC *Princess Royal*'s chief mate punched Mowachaht chief Oughomeize in the head. Andrew Taylor's journal relates the story, beginning with an incident of theft on July 19:

> The Carpenters were at work on shore upon the *Princess Royals* Mast, when one of the Natives took an opportunity of stealing a Drawing knife... The thief was known and pursued. Captain Duncan was landing at the time & made the alarm to the Ship, a boat was sent, but ere she arrived at the Spot the Carpenter recovered his knife. the Canoes round the Ship were brought too with Pistols, and detained along side, several Musquets fired to bring the Man too, 'twas quite a sham fight for some Musquets went off, but most of them missed fire. no damage was done, but

the natives were all much frighten'd and became shy of the Ship for a while.

On the following day, a similar incident occurred, except this time the Chief was on board the *Princess Royal* and became caught up in the chaos and conflict. Taylor explains:

> Some of the Indians were detected in prising off the guard plate of the *Princess Royals* Main chains. when discovered they made for the Shore a Boat was Man'd and armed expeditiously and Captain Duncan pursued them up the Northwest Arm but could not come near them before they took to the Bush. He seized one of the Canoes and brought on board and She was destroyed immediately. two three Pounders were fired off without doing any damage. Poor Oughomeize the Chief came worst off in this fray. He was on board sometime ere this happened, and when the small arms was fired the Chief became noisy and harangued the Natives in their Canoes along side, but to what purpose none could tell, probably through fear finding himself detained, or whether he was advising those along side to act offensively I could not tell. He was repeatedly desired to hold his Tongue, which he refused, probably from being ignorant of our desires… [T]he Chief mate gave him a violent blow on the side of his head. His behaviour on the occasion was truly characteristic of the Indian, receiving the blow with a smile of Contempt, then looking on the Chief Mate with a sullen countenance, and expressed his disatisfaction by a Shrug of his Shoulder, as much as to say Ah! is it so! but I'll be revenged.

As with Walker, Taylor was aware their actions with regard to the Chief had taken their relationships backward, possibly establishing a score to be settled later. Thinking about the destroyed canoe, he reflected on his colleagues' actions with regret:

> Our Conduct respecting the Canoe was in my opinion highly blameable, for twas uncertain whether the Canoe belonged to the person, or persons concerned, or to an innocent Family. though I conceived punishment to be necessary in some degree to deter others from thievery, still the punishment inflicted on those occasions should never exceed the bounds of reason but one should rather be guided by the nature of the Crime taking care to make examples of the guilty only. in this Case the punishment far exceeded the Crime.[6]

Martínez, the *Princesa*, and the *San Carlos*, 1789

Esteban José Martínez, the Spanish commander who confiscated the ships of the King George's Sound Company and nearly triggered a war between two great powers, behaved even more harshly toward the Indigenous Peoples at Nootka than toward the British. His own ship's naturalist, José Mariano Moziño, described him as a "ferocious pirate who[se] avarice did not respect a single thing."[7]

One day, after the Spanish had confiscated the KGSC ships, local Chief Callicum, second in rank only to Maquinna, approached Martínez on his ship, *Princesa*, and complained that Martínez had been treating the British poorly. He called Martínez a wicked man and gave him a dressing down for seizing the ships of the Mowachahts' British friends. This greatly offended Martínez and, as Callicum was leaving the ship, he raised his weapon and attempted to shoot him. His weapon misfired, but another member of his crew took the shot and Callicum fell into the water, dead.

Murdering a Chief was not the worst of Martínez's legacies at Nootka. Oral histories say the blacksmith shop he established doubled as a rapists' den and torture chamber where the ship's crew forced themselves on the local women on threat of pain from a hot poker. The violence and intimidation that were the hallmarks of Martínez's leadership were repeated by his crew.

Perhaps Martínez was attempting to establish Spanish sovereignty over the local people just as he wished to establish it over the sea and the land. He had planted a cross, conducted a mass, and read the Requerimiento, but maybe he thought more needed to be done. In any event, his actions cast a chill over relations for a long time. Immediately after Callicum's murder, Maquinna left for safety among the Tla-o-qui-aht with Chief Wickaninnish, and word spread throughout the region that the Spanish should be approached with extreme caution. When the Spanish attempted to establish a base at Cape Flattery, some 200 kilometres southeast of Nootka, near the entrance to the Strait of Juan de Fuca, they were violently repelled by the Makah. When they attempted to establish a fort at nearby Neah Bay in 1792, they were persistently resisted by the Makah. One Spaniard, accused of rape, was taken away and killed in the woods. In rage, or revenge, the Spanish commander fired on canoes from his ship (again the *Princesa*), killing all except a boy and a girl.

Gray and the *Columbia Rediviva*, 1792

American commercial trader Robert Gray seems to have had, at least on one documented occasion, a temper—or a strategy—every bit as extreme as Martínez's. Gray had set sail from the east coast of America on the *Columbia Rediviva*, a 250-ton ship, crewed by fifty men and armed with twelve carriage guns, in 1790. Loaded with a cargo of blue cloth, copper, and iron, the ship's four-year mission was to acquire fur in the Pacific Northwest and sell it for profit in China. The ship had no licence, no scientific mission, and no government backing. The enterprise was purely commercial, owned by three Boston investors.

Gray spent many months sailing along and about the Pacific Northwest, by and large trading successfully and amicably with the different peoples and tribes. But there was one glaring exception, in March of 1792. Gray had spent the winter in the Clayoquot Sound area, near the village of Opitsaht, building a small ten-man sloop, the *Adventure*, to be used to gather fur in the Queen Charlotte Isles the following summer. But after many months of friendly relations between the Americans and the Tla-o-qui-aht people of the Nuu-chah-nulth Nation, things began to get tense. The story, recorded in the journal of eighteen-year-old crewman John Boit, tells of suspicious interactions between the local Chiefs and a Hawaiian lad who was one of the *Columbia*'s crew:

> This day severall chiefs came on board, one of which we found was busily employ'd talking with our Sandwich Island lad. Their conversation was soon put a stop to, and the Lad examin'd, but he denyd that the Chief ask'd him any improper questions. These Natives, always behaving so friendly, occasion'd us to place too much confidence in them, and what a pity it is, that we cou'd not leave this port, with that opinion of them which we had heretofore held; But alas! We find them to be still a savage tribe, and only

> waiting an opportunity for to Massacre the whole of us, in cold blood.

This account seems a paranoid reaction, but it was followed shortly with a confession that seemed to confirm their fears:

> But fortunately, in the evening, the Sandwich Island lad made a confession to his Master, (as follows): He said Tatoochkasettle, (the Chief) told him, that Wickananish was about to take the Ship and Massacre all the Crew, and said he shou'd be a great man if he wou'd wet our Musketts, and steal for him some Bulletts.

Boit then explained that "the Chiefs had been telling us for some time that they was going to war with a distant tribe and wish'd for us to lend them Musketts and Ammunition, which some of these fellows used as well as ourselves. We had observed of late that they did not seem so cheerful as common, but seem'd to be deeply wrapt in thought."

What precisely went through the Americans' minds is impossible to know. Rightly or wrongly, they feared attack. Their commander, Gray, decided they should stay in the area only as long as it took to finish building the *Adventure*, then leave. But for reasons unknown, he then made a dreadful decision. Boit gives his first-hand account:

> I am sorry to be under the necessity of remarking that this day I was sent, with three boats all well man'd and arm'd, to destroy the village of Opitsatah. It was a Command I was no ways tenacious of, and am grieved to think Capt. Gray shou'd let his passions go so far. This village was about half a mile in diameter, and contained upwards of 200 Houses,

> generally well built for Indians; every door that you enter'd was in resemblance to an human and Beasts head, the passage being through the mouth, besides which there was much more rude carved work about the dwellings some of which was by no means inelegant. This fine village, the work of Ages, was in a short time totally destroy'd.[8]

Perhaps, like Martínez, Gray was trying to establish his dominance. Outnumbered, but with superior firepower, maybe he was trying to send a warning message: "Do not plot against me." Or maybe he overreacted in a fit of pique. We shall likely never know.[9]

Vancouver, HMS *Discovery*, and HMS *Chatham*, 1793

Even though George Vancouver was on an official diplomatic mission in the Pacific Northwest, determined to avoid conflict, he was not able to complete his mission without encountering violence.

The most extreme instance he experienced occurred in August of 1793 on the shores of what today is southern Alaska, about 180 kilometres north of Prince Rupert. Vancouver was leading a routine survey of the coast, with two small boats from HMS *Discovery* assigned to the task. This expedition was just another of the hundreds his crew had performed along the coast over the past two summers. Some local Tlingit people arrived on the scene by canoe and the small boats began their customary trade and gift exchange. But within minutes, blood was spilled in canoe and boat alike.

Vancouver's surgeon-botanist Archibald Menzies was in one of the small boats and later recorded the event in his journal. Four canoes containing about thirty-six people approached his boat "caroling and holding up Sea Otter Skins with all the alluring signs of friendship; as soon as they joined us they threw two of these skins into the boat and took the first things that were offered in return with apparent satisfaction without driving a bargain for them as the Natives we had hitherto met with generally did."[10] Vancouver was nearby in the other small boat conducting his survey.

Then more canoes arrived on the scene, and the two small boats were nearly surrounded.

Trading continued but anxieties were raised when one of the Tlingit men reached for one of the muskets in Vancouver's boat. Menzies had observed earlier that there were more firearms in the area than when he had visited with Colnett on KGSC *Prince of Wales* six years earlier. He noted that several were inferior to those of English manufacture, "as their Barrels were secured to the Stocks by means of Iron hoops" rather than brass. He suspected, as did Vancouver, that commercial traders in the area had been responsible for the escalation in arms trade and had been driving hard bargains in exchange for low-quality weapons.

Now, they received confirmation. "This Indian," wrote Vancouver later, "by means of signs and words too expressive to be mistaken, gave us clearly to understand, that they had reason to complain of one or more muskets that they had purchased, which burst into pieces on being fired: a fraud which I know has been practiced too frequently, not only on this coast, but at the Sandwich [Hawaiian], and other islands in the Pacific Ocean. These defects have not arisen from ignorance or mismanagement on the part of the Indians, but from the baseness of the metal and imperfect workmanship of the firearms." He added, "We had reason to suspect that they had been ill-treated in their traffic with white men."[11]

Although Vancouver understood that the Tlingit men had been cheated, he had always been reticent to trade in weapons, and resisted the plea to do so now. However, seeing that there were quality British muskets in the boats, the Tlingit men continued to press Vancouver to trade for them. When he again refused, they decided to help themselves. This is when things truly spiralled out of control. The Tlingit grabbed for the better weapons and whatever else they could take from the boats. If they were not to be given justice, they would take it.

Vancouver then decided it was time to make a hasty departure and ordered both boats to retreat. But, wrote Menzies, "a young man . . . who appeared to be a chief with his war dress on and a mask resembling a fox's head jump'd into the boat."[12] He directed his group to grab the boats' oars to prevent them from leaving. Now immobilized and surrounded by fifty angry men with spears, daggers, and some unreliable muskets, the Europeans responded by raising their weapons too.

Now everyone was pointing a weapon at everyone else.

Vancouver's diplomacy had achieved some brief success in defusing the situation. But before temperatures could properly cool, his efforts were confounded by vociferous entreaties of a female member of the tribe (in Vancouver's words, "their female conductress") who "seemed to put forth all the powers of her turbulent tongue to excite, or rather to compel the men, to act with hostility towards us."[13] Responding to her plea, one of the warriors raised his musket, aimed it at Vancouver, and pulled the trigger . . . to no effect. Whether it was a lucky misfire, or the man was making a point about the poor quality of the arms he had previously purchased, Vancouver would never know. Others then let loose with their spears. When one flew directly toward Seaman Robert Betton's chest, quick reactions allowed him, at the last minute, to deflect the blow and save his own life, but a second spear hit him in the thigh and he went down. Within seconds Seaman George Bridgeman also caught a spear in his thigh, delivered with such force that the tip passed clean through. Vancouver, perhaps fearing he was seconds away from Cook's fate, gave the order to fire: "Seeing no alternative left for our preservation against numbers so superior, but by making use of the coercive means we had in our power, I gave directions to fire; this instantly taking effect from both boats, was, to my great astonishment, attended with the desired effect, and we had the happiness of finding ourselves immediately relieved from a situation of the most imminent danger."[14]

Now able to grasp their oars, the men rowed the small boats away from shore as fast as possible, desperate to get beyond the range of the spears and arrows. About a quarter mile from shore, they rested so that the surgeon could safely attend to the wounded. "I had the satisfaction," Vancouver wrote later, "to learn from Mr. Menzies, after he had dressed the wounds, that he considered neither of them likely to be attended with any present danger."[15]

Vancouver reflected on the incident afterwards and worried that commercial traders were acting unethically and unwisely. In his journal, he wrote that many of the traders

> have not only pursued a line of conduct, diametrically opposite to the true principles of justice in their commercial dealings, but have fomented discords, and stirred up contentions, between the different tribes... [i]n order to increase the demand for these destructive engines [the muskets]. They have been likewise eager to instruct the natives in the use of European arms of all descriptions; and have shewn by their own example, that they consider gain as the only object of pursuit; and whither this be acquired by fair and honorable means, or otherwise, so long as the

> advantage is secured, the manner how it is obtained seems to have been, with too many of them, but a very secondary consideration.[16]

The increase in trade of weapons—muskets and swords—was a problem Vancouver was wise to worry about. Trading in cheap and low-quality weapons for quick gain was also a problem. The unlicensed, independent, get-rich-quick traders had no motive to build good relations with or among the Indigenous Peoples they encountered along the coast. As the number of predatory traders increased in the years following the Nootka Crisis and Vancouver's mission, the frustrations of the local people increased.

What once was a connection point between the Pacific Northwest and Asia for European powers and government-sanctioned organizations like the East India Company was becoming a connection for American traders sailing out of Boston. Americans were not just trading with Europe; they were increasingly trading with Asia too. One consequence of this was that Friendly Cove became a trading hub under Mowachaht control, with Maquinna controlling access to European and American traders and becoming increasingly powerful and important. The other consequence, however, was that both the traditional economic activity of whaling and fishing and the established political hierarchies were disrupted.

These issues and circumstances collided dramatically in 1803.

Maquinna and the *Boston*, 1803

In March of 1803 John Salter, captain of the commercial trader *Boston*, sailed into Nootka Sound to refresh his supplies and conduct repairs before heading farther north to trade for furs. Like Gray and other enterprising Americans, Salter had sailed from the east coast port of Boston. His ship was owned by private investors.

The business plan was simple: to trade its cargo of English cloths, Dutch blankets, looking glasses, beads, knives, razors, sugar and molasses, rum, ammunition, cutlasses, pistols, and three thousand muskets and fowling pieces for furs that could be sold for great profit in China.

The *Boston* never made it to China, and neither did its crew.

The ship arrived at Friendly Cove in March of 1803 and anchored about four miles farther north. The reception was by now typical and routine. Maquinna visited the ship, gifts were exchanged, meals were shared. But one of the gifts presented to Maquinna, a double-barrelled fowling gun, turned out to be faulty. After two shots, the lock broke. When Maquinna complained, Salter became indignant and offensive.

Maquinna by this point had had enough of being abused and threatened by some of the Cove's visitors. Martínez's murder of Callicum fourteen years earlier had not been forgotten, Gray's actions at Clayoquot Sound were still reverberating in the area, and numerous other disputes and grievances were piling on top of each other. Maquinna decided enough was enough.

Shortly after the rude exchange with Salter, Maquinna returned to the vessel accompanied by some warriors. First, they convinced some of the crew to leave the ship and go fishing for salmon some distance away. Then they boarded the ship and killed all but two of the crew. Each body was beheaded and the quarterdeck of the *Boston* was decorated with the sailors' heads. Those who had left to go fishing were found and killed too. The ship was stripped of all its cargo, its cannon, and anything useful, and then burned to ashes.

Only two men were spared: John Jewitt and John Thompson kept their lives but served as Maquinna's slaves until their release was negotiated by another American ship, the *Lydia*, in 1805.

Jewitt, the ship's twenty-year-old blacksmith and armourer, later wrote a popular book about his years in captivity. Though written a few years after his rescue, undoubtedly with a view toward pleasing an appreciative audience, his account of the inciting event is worth repeating. Jewitt reported that the day after receiving the gun from Salter,

> Maquina came on board with nine pair of wild ducks, as a present; at the same time he brought with him the gun, one of the locks of which he had broken, telling the captain that it was peshak, that is, bad. Captain Salter was very much offended at this observation, and, considering it as a mark of contempt for his present, he called the king a liar, adding other opprobrious terms, and, taking the gun from him, tossed it indignantly into the cabin, and, calling me to him, said, "John, this fellow has broken this beautiful fowling-piece, see if you can mend it." On examining it, I told him that it could be done. As I have already observed, Maquina knew a number of English words, and unfortunately understood but too well the meaning of the reproachful terms that the captain addressed to him. He said not a word in reply, but his countenance successfully expressed the rage he felt, though he exerted himself to suppress it, and I observed him, while the captain was speaking, repeatedly put his hand to his throat, and rub it on his bosom, which he afterward told me was to keep down his heart, which was rising into his throat and choking him.[17]

A slightly different version of this incident was included in a written statement made by Jewitt's rescuer, Captain Samuel Hill of the *Lydia*. According to Hill, who would have received his information directly from Jewitt and likely also from Maquinna when conducting negotiations, Maquinna was not just assaulted verbally but also physically: "Maquinnah borrowed a double barrelled musket of Captain Salter for the purpose of shooting fowls; he re-turned on the 19th [the next day], bringing several pair of ducks of which he made a present to Capt. Salter; at the same time presented him with the musket and informed him he had broken one of the locks.— Capt. Salter used some very harsh threats on this occasion and taking the musket by the barrel he struck Maquinnah on the head with the breach of the musket."

Three days after being insulted and assaulted, Hill continued, "Maquinnah went on board the *Boston*, attended by a number of his chiefs and warriors; Maquinnah was painted and had a mask in imitation of a bear's head: When they came alongside of the ship they all shouted several times and Maquinnah performed a kind of mystical ceremony." Then,

> Capt. Salter invited Maquinnah to dine with him, which he accordingly did: While they were at table Maquinnah observed to Capt. Salter that there was great plenty of salmon in Friendly Cove and expressed his surprise that Capt. Salter did not send his officers and people to take salmon, which he said other captains had often done; Capt. Salter immediately turned to Mr. Delouisa, his first officer, and expressed a wish for some salmon.—Mr. Delouisa set out immediately with nine men, in the pinnace [small boat], accompanied with the drum and fife, in order to take salmon in Friendly Cove.

Once the crew aboard the pinnace was out of sight, the massacre began. "Maquinnah, who at the same instant seized Capt. Salter, and threw him overboard, where the old women in the canoes along side, killed him with their paddles, and he expired, crying out 'Wha-cosh, Maquinnah,'[18] while Maquinnah looking over the ship's side, laughed at the farce of the old women beating Salter's brains out with their paddles!"[19] In short order the entire crew were killed.

This grim incident suggests Maquinna, and no doubt other Indigenous people in the region, were becoming fed up with the rudeness—and perhaps also the greed (trading with low-quality materials)—of the traders flooding the region at the tail end of the eighteenth century.

Unfortunately, the nineteenth century would see more of the same.

By 1830, the United States had expanded considerably westward, thanks in no small part to the Louisiana Purchase in 1803. However, access to the west coast was blocked by Mexico to the south and Britain in the north. The disputed British Columbia District/Oregon Territory was the only thing stopping the country from extending "from sea to shining sea."
ERIC LEINBERGER

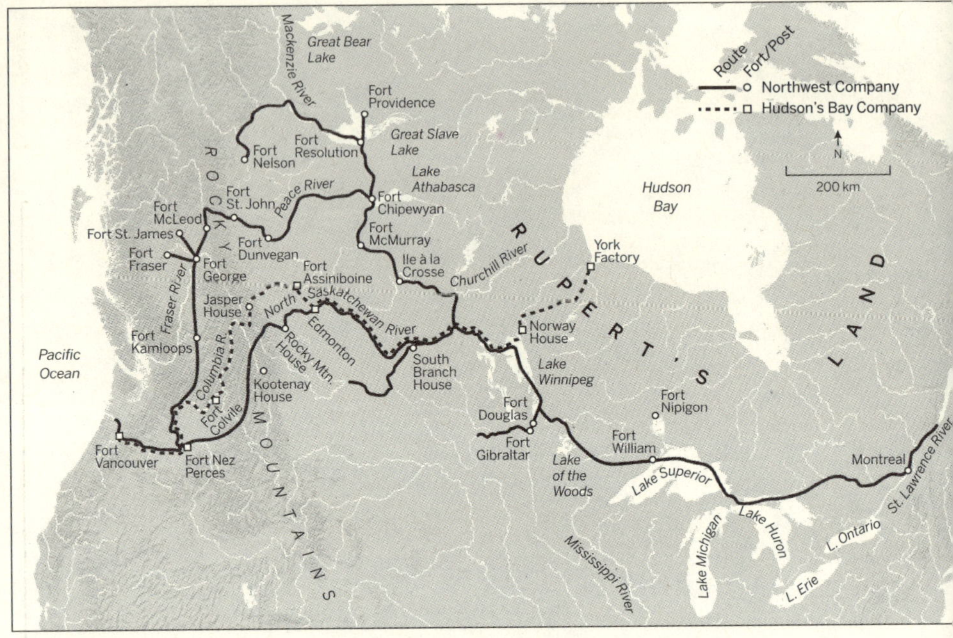

TOP The Columbia River was strategically important to both the North West Company and the Hudson's Bay Company, enabling each to expand trade from British North America to markets in Asia. ERIC LEINBERGER

OPPOSITE, TOP LEFT The Pacific Fur Company established Fort Astoria near the mouth of the Columbia River in 1811 but the business was soon taken over by the North West Company. After a visit by the twenty-six-gun British ship HMS *Racoon*, during the War of 1812, the fort was renamed Fort George. WATERCOLOUR BY GENERAL SIR HENRY JAMES, 1845. PUBLIC DOMAIN

OPPOSITE, TOP RIGHT The Hudson's Bay Company's Fort Vancouver, located farther upriver at the place William Broughton named for George Vancouver in 1792, was established in 1824 and became a vibrant trade and social hub linking the Pacific to the interior at York Factory on Hudson Bay. LITHOGRAPH, SARONY, MAJOR & KNAPP, 1855. LIBRARY OF CONGRESS PRINTS AND PHOTOGRAPHS DIVISION, WASHINGTON, DC

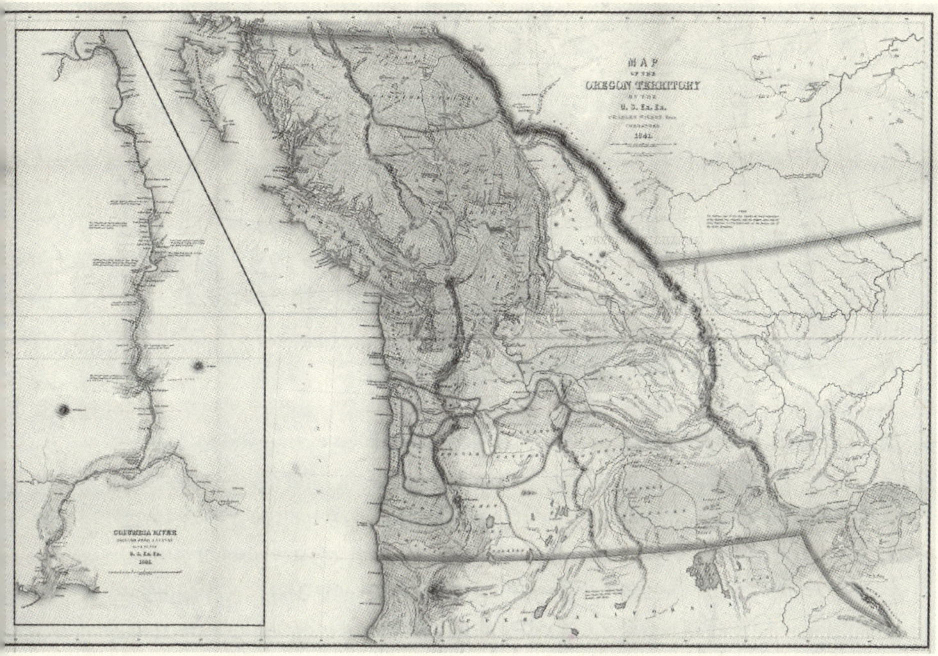

BOTTOM Less than a century after the thirteen colonies on the east coast declared their independence, American maps, such as this one from 1841, reflected the prevailing view that the US territory extended all the way to the west coast, from California to Alaska. LIBRARY OF CONGRESS GEOGRAPHY AND MAP DIVISION, WASHINGTON, DC

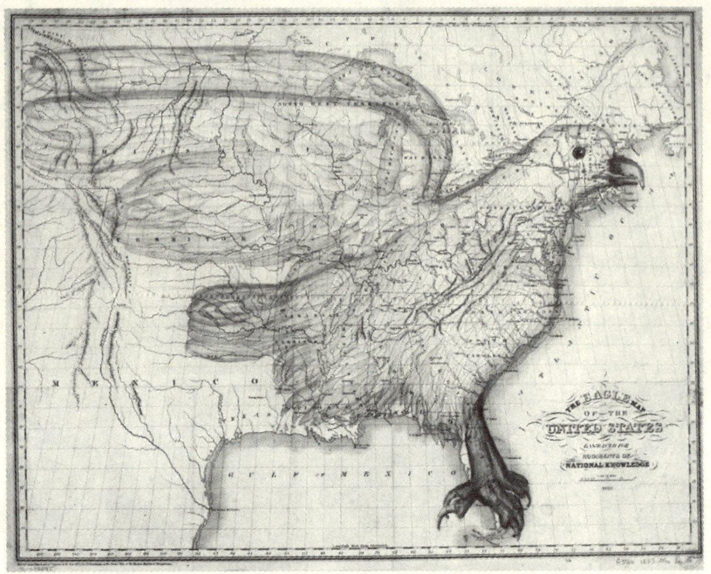

The Eagle Map was designed to serve as a memory device for young American students learning their country's geography. The top of the eagle's wings run along the forty-ninth parallel to the Rocky Mountains, as agreed with Britain in the 1814 Treaty of Ghent, but the unresolved question of the west coast is not included. EAGLE MAP OF THE UNITED STATES, 1833. LIBRARY OF CONGRESS GEOGRAPHY AND MAP DIVISION, WASHINGTON, DC

OPPOSITE, TOP *American Progress*, 1872. The ideal of American Manifest Destiny was captured in this 1872 painting by John Gast. The work shows a bible-holding fair-haired Liberty moving westward, with Indigenous Peoples being replaced by settlers, land converted to agricultural use, and trails replaced by steam engines as cities rise in the east. LIBRARY OF CONGRESS GEOGRAPHY AND MAP DIVISION, WASHINGTON, DC

BOTTOM *Ultimatum on the Oregon question.* In this 1846 political cartoon, Queen Victoria states: "I've opened my ports for the admission of your corn, and I offer to settle the Oregon business by arbitration! What more can you expect! Beware how you rouse the British Lion!" President Polk replies: "You opened your ports to keep you from starvation! I offered to settle the Oregon question at 49 degrees and you refused—I won't arbitrate—I go the whole figure to 54'42 which if you'll agree to, I will negotiate!" EDWARD WILLIAMS CLAY. US LIBRARY OF CONGRESS

Members of the first Legislative Council at the Birdcages, 1870. Sandwiched between Oregon and Alaska, and geographically locked between the ocean and the Rocky Mountains, the colony of British Columbia in the 1860s was alone and vulnerable. Ultimately, and with a railway connection to eastern markets as part of the bargain, the colony's political leaders voted to join Canada. FREDERICK DALLY. IMAGE C-06178 COURTESY OF THE ROYAL BC MUSEUM AND ARCHIVES

PART THREE

The 1800s

10

THE BRITISH EAST GOES WEST

WHILE EUROPEAN traders had been visiting the Pacific Northwest over the thirty-year period following the American Revolutionary War, and sorting out their boundaries and territories there between each other and the Indigenous Peoples, the authorities on the Atlantic side of the continent had been doing much the same.

Immediately after the Revolutionary War, as mentioned in our first chapter, thousands of people loyal to the British Crown had fled north from the new republic—as many as thirty-five thousand people from the State of New York alone.[1] These refugees included white loyalists, freed or escaped slaves, and Indigenous Peoples who had aligned themselves with the British forces and were no longer welcome in the United States. Most arrived without homes, jobs, or land to call their own. The administrative challenges of resettling these masses were enormous; so great, in fact, that the British colony of Nova Scotia was almost immediately restructured into three individual colonies to manage the burden: Cape

Breton, New Brunswick, and Nova Scotia. The British Parliament in Westminster also passed the Constitution Act in 1791,[2] which created the two main colonies of Upper Canada and Lower Canada, and gave each their own legislative council and assemblies such that they could better govern their own domestic affairs.[3]

Over the next few decades, the authorities in these British-controlled parts of North America negotiated a dozen or more land surrender treaties with the various Anishinaabe Peoples living along the shores of the St. Lawrence River and the lower Great Lakes area to establish an agricultural region that provided land for farmers and helped to compensate Indigenous allies for losses incurred during the war with the Americans.

The result of this diplomatic work was that, by the end of the 1700s, the east coast, and the eastern side of the North American continent, was—in stark contrast to the west coast—well known, well charted, well mapped, and well secured. The British had stitched the northeastern part of the continent together with dozens of treaties, acts, and other legal documents accumulated over a century or more. Relations with the United States to the south were also relatively stabilized.

This regional stability presented an opening, and an opportunity, for the commercial fur traders based out of Montreal to expand their enterprise farther west overland. What follows is a brief summary of this expansion by British North Americans.

To the West Coast by Land

The first mover in this enterprise was the Hudson's Bay Company, officially founded in 1670. Like the East India Company established seventy years earlier, it was a legal entity licensed by the Crown in London to conduct trade in a faraway place. Charles II had granted the charter to "The Governor and Company of Adventurers of England, trading into Hudson Bay" and gave them an exclusive trading monopoly over the entire Hudson Bay drainage basin—an ill-defined and little-known area of some 1.5 million square miles.

The Hudson's Bay Company had done very well at the task of exporting fur from British North America to European markets, but it had no access to the Pacific or the Asian markets. Trade was strictly from west to east, from Hudson Bay to the Atlantic. If Cook had discovered a Northwest Passage, things would have changed quickly and dramatically; the Hudson's Bay Company would have been able to control a trade route from China to London. But the leadership of the Hudson's Bay Company, like that of the East India Company, was comfortable with the near monopoly it already enjoyed and was not hugely motivated to explore further.

The risk of developing new trade routes to and markets on the west coast fell to lesser, more hungry competitors—in this case, to the North West Company.

Established in Montreal in 1779, the North West Company was not much different from the King George's Sound Company created by Richard Etches six years later. The general idea was the same: A small group of investors pooled their money and raised capital to form a company that would compete for the lucrative fur trade. The main difference was that the fur trade was to be conducted overland, not by sea; and the movement of fur would flow easterly toward the Atlantic markets, not west toward the Pacific markets. Competition against the behemoth Hudson's Bay Company was challenging and expensive principally because the North West Company was not licensed to use Hudson Bay to transport its goods to the Atlantic; instead, it had to haul its goods by canoe over multiple river routes to Montreal, where buyers could ship product south to American markets or east to Europe via the St. Lawrence River. This was more labour-intensive and thus more costly, and also took more time.

But the North West Company's competitive disadvantage against the Hudson's Bay Company motivated it to explore farther west and seek a potentially game-changing west coast port for trade.

Mackenzie

With much effort and persistence, the North West Company did eventually complete, and chart for the first time, a land route to the Pacific coast. The distinction of achieving this feat fell to Alexander Mackenzie, a partner who had been with the company since he was a fifteen-year-old clerk. Like many others living in Montreal at the time, his family had moved there from New York during the American Revolutionary War, arriving in 1778. He had proven his abilities quickly; by the time he was twenty he was managing a trading post in what is now northern Saskatchewan, about 900 kilometres southwest of Hudson Bay.

Five years later, motivated to find cheaper supply routes for his fur company and tantalized by the prospect of finding a route to the west coast, Mackenzie made two attempts at the task. The first, undertaken over three months in the summer of 1789, took him to the Arctic. It was a fascinating round trip of nearly 5,000 kilometres, but the route he thought would connect Fort Chipewyan to the Pacific was a dud. He advanced knowledge of the country and its terrain, but gained no commercial advantage for the North West

Company. His second voyage, mainly conducted over the summer of the following year, would be a bit more successful.

For this second voyage, Mackenzie set out from Fort Fork, a trading post on the Peace River, located about 100 kilometres northeast of present-day Grande Prairie, Alberta. Heading west on the Peace River and over the Rocky Mountains, he eventually connected with what he thought was the northernmost point of the Columbia River—the same Columbia River Cook had sailed past in 1778, and which Gray and Vancouver had both explored in 1792. He followed it south for about 300 kilometres before finding the route unnavigable due to waterfalls and rapids. On advice from Indigenous guides, he then took a route west on a river he named West Road, for a final push toward the coast.

By the end of Thursday, July 4, 1793, he was able to record in his journal hopeful notes that his final destination was within striking distance:

> At sunset, an elderly man and three other natives joined us from the westward. The former bore a lance, which very much resembled a Serjeant's halberd. He had lately received it, by way of barter, from the natives of the Sea-Coast, who procured it from the white men. We should meet, he said, with many of his countrymen, who had just returned from thence. According to his report, it did not require more than six days' journey, for people who are not heavily laden, to reach the country of those with whom they bartered their skins for iron, etc, and from thence it was not quite two days' march to the sea.

Continuing to follow the advice of Indigenous guides encountered along the way, Mackenzie and his party of nine men moved indomitably westward through rain, flies, hail, and snow. After a few more days, Mackenzie reported contact with a family familiar with the coast. The man of the family, he wrote, "willingly conversed with my interpreter, to whom he made himself more intelligible, than our guides had been able to do." When the man was apprised of Mackenzie's mission, he introduced his wife and Mackenzie observed a form of dress that would have been familiar to the seagoing adventurers of our earlier chapters. The woman, wrote Mackenzie,

> was decorated with ornaments of various kinds, such as large blue beads, either pendant from her ears, encircling her neck, or braided in her hair: she also wore bracelets of brass, copper, and horn. Her garments consisted of a kind of tunic, which was covered with a robe of matted bark, fringed round the bottom with skin of the sea otter. None of the women whom I had seen since we crossed the mountain wore this kind of tunic; their blankets being merely girt round the waist. She had learned the language of her husband's tribe, and confirmed his account, that we were at no great distance from the sea.

Two weeks later, on July 19, Mackenzie was close enough to the coast to be eating salmon and recording objects obtained in trade with the Spanish—perhaps even traded by Martínez or Quadra. His journal records: "I paid a visit to the chief, who presented me with a roasted salmon; he then opened one of his chests, and took out of it a garment of blue cloth, decorated with brass buttons; and another of flowered cotton, which I supposed were Spanish."

Within a couple of days he would be able to leave a more permanent testament to his achievement. Near present-day Bella Coola, Mackenzie "mixed up some vermillion in melted grease, and inscribed, in large characters, on the south-east face of the rock on which we had slept last night, this brief memorial—'Alexander Mackenzie, from Canada, by land, the twenty-second of July, one thousand seven hundred and ninety-three.'" Even today it is a much sought landmark and perhaps the most famous bit of graffiti in the country.

Mackenzie was the first to reach this destination by land from the east, but he learned he was not the first European to reach Bella Coola. In addition to seeing things like the halberd, the copper items, and the blue cloth, he was told by the local Indigenous People, the Nuxalk, that two other Europeans, "Macubah" and "Bensins," had recently visited them by boat: "These men also told me that Macubah had been there, and left his ship behind a point of land in the channel, south-west from us; from whence he had come to their village in boats, which these people represented by imitating our manner of rowing. When I offered them what they did not choose to accept for the otter-skin, they shook their heads, and very distinctly answered, 'No, no.' And to mark their refusal of anything we asked from them, they emphatically employed the same British monosyllable."[4]

It would not be until he returned to Montreal or London and read the accounts and journals of Vancouver's Voyage of Discovery (first published in 1798) that the penny would drop: Macubah was Vancouver and Bensins was his surgeon-botanist, Menzies.[5] He had missed them by mere days.

But, again, while Mackenzie had made an adventurous and historic round-trip voyage of nearly 4,000 kilometres, and this time had located prime access to the Pacific, he had not found a route that would achieve his commercial aims. This route through swamps, over rocky trails and mountains, and through rapids was not viable for trade purposes. The North West Company had still not found a better way to compete against the Hudson's Bay Company.

A few years later, the North West Company gave the challenge another attempt. This time a new partner, Simon Fraser, took up the cause.

Fraser

Like Mackenzie, Fraser had ended up in Montreal following his family's flight from New York. His father had fought and died for the British in the Revolutionary War, and after the war it was clear his family were no longer welcome there. Also like Mackenzie, he had been a keen and talented clerk in the North West Company who quickly made partner. After a dozen years managing trading posts in the Athabasca area of what is now Alberta, and then establishing the first trading posts west of the Rockies, Fraser was tasked to trace the Columbia River—noted by Mackenzie in his reports—to its mouth on the Pacific.

In May of 1808, the thirty-two-year-old began his assignment. Leaving Fort George (present-day Prince George), he led a large party of some twenty-four persons on their 800-kilometre expedition south. Having accumulated more experience in the area in the years since Mackenzie had attempted the voyage, with a better-supplied party and more established relations with local Indigenous guides, Fraser made swift progress. By early July he was in the region of the present-day city of New Westminster, just 20 kilometres from the salt waters of the Strait of Georgia. It was at about this point in his journey that Fraser's challenge changed from physical to human. Barriers such as rapids and currents were supplemented now by personal and cultural barriers. He was advised by the Indigenous People near New Westminster—

where he had, like Mackenzie, seen the red and blue cloth traded by British and Spanish visitors—not to venture any farther west.

On July 2, he wrote in his journal: "The Indians advised us not to advance any further, as the natives of the coast or Islanders were at war with them, being very malicious, and will destroy us. Upon seeing us slight their advice and going to embark, they gathered round our canoe and hauled it out of the water." But he continued anyway, taking the north arm of the river toward the sea. Before too long he made it to the coast, and a Musqueam village. "At last we came in sight of a gulph or bay of the sea [the Strait of Georgia]; this the Indians called Pas-hil-roe. It runs in a S.W. & N.E. direction. In this bay are several high and rocky Islands whose summits are covered with snow. On the right shore we noticed a village called by the Natives Misquiame."

Unfortunately, Fraser's encounters with the Musqueam were such that he felt it best to retreat back up the river. Arguments over canoes, skirmishes over equipment, and the dire warnings he had received earlier in the day left him feeling threatened and vulnerable. After many weeks of intrepid travel to his destination, he was only able to stay there a few hours at most.

To make matters worse, he also realized that the latitude of the river's mouth did not match the latitude of the Columbia as recorded by Vancouver, Broughton, and Gray. "This River, therefore, is not the Columbia," he wrote.[6] His delight at having navigated to the mouth of the Columbia was instantly deflated. He was actually about 300 kilometres north and slightly east of his intended destination. It turns out he had navigated down what we now call the Fraser River, which empties into the Pacific Ocean just south of present-day Vancouver. The hills and rocky islands he saw at the Strait of Georgia were likely part of what was then called Quadra and Vancouver Island.

But still the North West Company persisted in its search for a viable trade route to the Pacific.

The next adventurers to take up the challenge were David Thompson and John Stuart.

Thompson and Stuart

It was the experienced and talented forty-one-year-old Thompson who succeeded, in 1811, in finding a connection to the real Columbia River and to its mouth on the coast. His work was refined a couple of years later by thirty-three-year-old Stuart, who had been second in command during Fraser's voyage five years earlier. He worked out a viable trading route to the coast via the Columbia.

Thanks to their efforts, by 1814 it was possible at last for the North West Company's trading posts on the western side of the North American continent to be resupplied by ships arriving from the Pacific. For commercial and practical purposes, the mouth of the Columbia River was now established as the southernmost point of British North America.

Yet while the commercial opportunities of the west coast had captured the attention of fur traders, the political leadership in the cities of York (now Toronto), Montreal, and London was more concerned with the hostile attitude that was re-emerging from the American Republic to their south.

The peace and security achieved after the Revolutionary War were beginning to slip.

11

WAR, TREATY, AND CONVENTION

WEAK AND diminished as the new United States was in the years immediately following the Revolutionary War, the country had made great advances over the following decades. Its economy was improving, and the nation was proud and confident, revelling in its liberty from European monarchs and empires. The animosity toward Britain and things British that had existed during the war continued.

This ongoing hostile attitude toward Britain was aggravated by events in Europe. While Fraser, Stuart, Thompson, and others had been plotting their voyages west from Montreal to chart rivers on the North American continent, Napoleon Bonaparte had been charging east from Paris to conquer Europe for France. The French Crown had fallen shortly after Vancouver returned from Nootka,[1] and Napoleon had become the First Consul seven years later. By 1800, France was the dominant power on the continent of Europe. In 1804, the year after Maquinna destroyed the *Boston*, Napoleon became emperor.

These events on the other side of the Atlantic inevitably affected politics and the economy on the east coast of North America. In addition to traditional forms of warfare, the French and the British also resolved to attack each other through trade embargoes and naval blockades. As a consequence, the United States was often piggy-in-the-middle: The French would not let the Americans ship goods to British ports. The British would not let Americans ship goods to ports on continental Europe. Occasionally, skirmishes between American and British ships occurred on the Atlantic, and the Americans became increasingly frustrated with the situation.

The Americans would have liked to engage the British at sea. The US Navy, though only formally established in 1798, was a not-inconsiderable force: with about as many ships in the area as the Royal Navy had near Halifax, it could argue for being evenly matched. The US had seven frigates, while the British had one ship-of-the-line and seven frigates. But that was only the number of ships in the local region. Worldwide, Britain had 130 ships-of-the-line and 600 frigates, many of which could be redirected into the area if needed.[2] A naval war between the US and Britain was out of the question.

But a land war seemed viable.

The War of 1812

The United States' fourth president, sixty-one-year-old James Madison, was keen on the idea. His predecessor in office, Thomas Jefferson, had signed legislation establishing the United States Military Academy, West Point, ten years earlier, and its leaders were eager to demonstrate their prowess. Madison's military advisor, General Henry Dearborn, also in his early sixties, worked hard to convince him that British North America was vulnerable to attack by land. Having already taken thirteen colonies away from the Crown, American leaders imagined they could do it again—this time permanently removing Britain from the continent.

With many citizens still glowing with anti-monarchist revolutionary zeal, harbouring anti-British spirit, and eager to expand their new republic north and west, Madison saw war as a way to not only find relief from the blockades but also achieve nationalistic objectives.

So in June of 1812, President Madison signed a declaration of war against Great Britain.

It did not go well.

A key error in their plan was a miscalculation of British troop strength. The Americans had underestimated the effectiveness of the work the British had done to form alliances with Indigenous Nations hostile to American expansion. The greatest of these was their alliance with Shawnee Chief Tecumseh, who created and led a united force of skilled and highly motivated Indigenous warriors, including those from the Potawatomi, Ojibwe, Shawnee, Odawa, Kickapoo and other Nations who had for years been resisting American expansion into their traditional territories. In August, just two months after Madison had declared war, the American forces suffered their first casualties when Indigenous forces under Tecumseh and British forces under General Isaac Brock orchestrated a coordinated and humiliating defeat at Fort Detroit.

The Americans would get their own back eight months later by setting York ablaze, and by achieving some naval victories in the Great Lakes, but these victories were mostly small and brief.

Madison's miscalculation about the land war was compounded by his underestimation of the potential role of the British naval forces. He had counted the British ships in Halifax but had overlooked the forces stationed in Bermuda. Despite the lessons of the Battle of the Saintes—or perhaps having not learned them because that battle was fought on their behalf by France—the Americans soon discovered what a great mistake this oversight was.

Vice Admiral Alexander Cochrane, responsible for the British fleet based in the Caribbean, sent forces north to engage in the war. In a move similar to that of former Virginia governor Lord Dunmore in the previous war, Cochrane offered transportation to anyone wanting to leave the United States. Though not explicitly or exclusively directed toward the slave population, Cochrane's declaration, signed in Bermuda in April 1814, stated: "That all those who may be disposed to emigrate from the United States will, with their Families, be received on board of His majesty's Ships or Vessels of War, or at the Military Posts that may be established, upon or near the Coast of the United States when they will have their choice of either entering into His Majesty's Sea or Land Forces, or of being sent as FREE Settlers to the British Possessions in North America or the West Indies, where they will meet with all due encouragement."

The offer, circulated everywhere, but particularly among the Black population in the US south, encouraged thousands of current and former slaves to desert to the British side. Cochrane's manoeuvre reduced the Americans' labour force, fomented internal political discord, and further disrupted its economy. The population of Nova Scotia surged again, as it had during and after the Revolutionary War thirty years before.

An interesting side note to this naval action concerns Robert Barrie. Years before, Barrie had been a young midshipman on George Vancouver's HMS *Discovery* and was now the commander of one of the British ships in the War of 1812, the seventy-four-gun HMS *Dragon*. Barrie successfully liberated ten slaves from Virginia tobacco farmer Thomas Whittington when he anchored his ship close enough to shore that the British flag could be seen from land. Seeing it, and knowing of Cochrane's offer, the resourceful slaves had rowed to his ship and thus to freedom.

As a follow-up to his disruptive declaration, Cochrane also contributed a thousand marines to the sacking of the US capital, causing Madison to flee the White House.

By the end of 1814, the United States was keen to put an end to hostilities. No territory had been gained by the effort and its economy was in distress. The value of imports had fallen 25 percent from before the war, and exports had fallen from $108 million to less than $7 million.[3] By the end of the year, American and British diplomats would sign the Treaty of Ghent, in Ghent, Belgium, to formally end the war.[4]

And this is where our story about the west coast becomes more interesting, for it was during these treaty negotiations that the fate of the west was discussed and shaped—both by design and by ambivalence.

The Treaty of Ghent in 1814

The British, indebted to Tecumseh and other Indigenous allies, had opened the Ghent discussions with a demand for creation of an Indian Territory that would designate a large area of the interior, west of the Appalachian Mountains (the western border of the US at that time), to Indigenous Peoples. The Mississippi and Ohio Rivers would be the Indian Territory's eastern border, and it would extend as far south as the Gulf of Mexico and as far north as Lake Erie. It would potentially encompass much of what today are the states of Alabama, Louisiana, Mississippi, Arkansas, Kentucky, Missouri, Tennessee, and West Virginia.

This demand was also an attempt by the British to live up to the direction given by George III in his Proclamation of 1763. But it was a touchy subject for the Americans. Much ado had been raised about tea tax and the merits of self-government prior to the revolution, but one of the disgruntled colonists' greatest frustrations had been this Proclamation, which came at the end of the Seven Years' War with France. The intent of the Proclamation was to lay out a new administrative structure for British North America and establish procedures and protocols for Britain's relations with North America's Indigenous Peoples. It was also intended, in no small measure, to apply the brakes to the pre-revolutionary colonial governors and settlers who were itching to expand farther west.

The Proclamation's bottom line was that no land negotiations were to be held with Indigenous Peoples unless authorized by the Crown. It read, in part: "We do hereby strictly forbid, on Pain of Our Displeasure, all Our loving Subjects from making any Purchases or Settlements whatever, or taking Possession of any of the Lands above reserved, without Our especial Leave and Licence for that Purpose first obtained."

The reason for this was not because George III was, as his detractors would say, a tyrannical megalomaniac. The reason was that he knew that unregulated and irregular land purchases were counterproductive to peaceful relations with Indigenous Peoples. His Proclamation was clear on this point:

> And whereas great Frauds and Abuses have been committed in the purchasing Lands of the Indians, to the great Prejudice of Our Interests, and to the great Dissatisfaction of the said Indians; in order therefore to prevent such Irregularities for the future, and to the End that the Indians may be convinced of Our Justice, and determined Resolution to remove all reasonable Cause of Discontent, We do, with the Advice of Our Privy Council, strictly enjoin and require, that no private Person do presume to make any Purchase from the said Indians of any Lands reserved to the said Indians, within those Parts of Our Colonies where We have thought proper to allow Settlement.[5]

A third reason the British pushed for the Indian Territory was that it would create a strategic buffer between themselves and the Americans. It would also preserve the existing and emerging fur-trading relationships that were active in and around the Great Lakes and points farther west.

But the American delegates, who would not recognize any Indigenous representatives at the discussions (aside from Britain acting as their proxy), refused to bend. So adamant were they on this point that one of Britain's three negotiators, Henry Goulburn, would later remark: "Till I came here, I had no idea of the fixed determination which there is in the heart of every American to extirpate the Indians and appropriate their territory."[6]

Ultimately, both sides agreed to a *status quo ante bellum* agreement: The belligerents basically agreed to set borders and relationships back to the way they had been before the war.[7] The Treaty allowed the Americans to save face and permitted the British to focus on other parts of their global empire. Neither side could claim to have "won" the war.

As had happened immediately after the 1783 Treaty of Paris, the months and years following the 1814 Treaty of Ghent brought not just peace but also social, administrative, and economic aftershock. Borders had to be redrawn, people had to be moved, commerce had to be re-established. Between 1815 and 1860, the British administrators in North America negotiated a number of additional treaties with Indigenous Peoples covering all the remaining lands of Upper Canada, from the productive agricultural lands south of Lake Huron to the resource-rich lands around Lake Superior and Georgian Bay. They also worked with the Americans to resolve outstanding issues regarding the borders, demilitarize the vessels on the Great Lakes, and address other matters.

But the fate of the west, so far as the officials were concerned, was still very much a large question mark. The North West Company had made the connection from the Rocky Mountains to the Pacific Ocean via the Columbia River, but that was private business—the British government was not claiming that as its own territory. It still maintained the position it had taken with Spain in the Nootka Conventions: Let everyone trade freely there.

The Convention of 1818

It was not until 1818 that the British and American governments were compelled to put their positions about the west down on paper, and even then the terms were temporary and broad. This was done through the Convention of 1818, a document designed to tidy up unresolved and emerging issues between the two countries. The document had six articles. The first was all about fishing rights on the east coast, near Newfoundland. The fourth reaffirmed a previous (1815) convention regulating trade between the two countries. The fifth established that the United States was "entitled to the Restitution of, or full Compensation for all or any Slaves" that had fled to British North America during the recent war. The sixth merely noted the date that the convention would come into effect.

The second and third articles are particularly germane to our story.

Article II established for the first time that the international boundary between British North America and the United States would run along the forty-ninth parallel from Lake of the Woods (the most southeasterly corner of present-day Manitoba) to the Rocky Mountains, just over 1,000 kilometres to the west. But the straight horizontal border line to the Rocky Mountains was as far as the negotiators were able to go, and as much as they were able to agree with. What happened to the border after that was left an open question.

Article III attempted to address this unresolved aspect of the second article. But it was precise only to the degree that it accurately identified the ambiguity of the situation. The third article said simply that the area west of the Rocky Mountains should remain free and open to both countries for another ten years: "Any Country that may be claimed by either Party on the North West Coast of America, Westward of the Stony [Rocky] Mountains, shall, together with its Harbours, Bays, and Creeks, and the Navigation of all Rivers within the same be free and open, for the term of ten Years from the date of the Signature of the present Convention, to the Vessels, Citizens, and Subjects of the Two Powers."

Both sides had interests in this western area, and both agreed that the other should not possess it. This "Columbia District," as the British called it, was named for the Columbia River (explored and mapped by the North West Company's Stuart and Thompson) that formed the natural north–south border from the Rocky Mountains to the Pacific Ocean. The Americans preferred to designate the area as the "Oregon Territory," since American explorer Jonathan Carver had written of a mythical Oregon River ("River of the West") in a 1778 book. The area comprised everything west of the Rocky Mountains, including 1,000 kilometres of coastline from the mouth of the Columbia River to the border of Alaska.

The Americans were confident they had a strong card to play with regard to any future claim to the area: They got there first. The American Robert Gray had been the first to enter the Columbia, crossing the sand barrier between the Pacific and its mouth a few months before British naval officer William Broughton.[8] They could also argue that they had been the first to establish a trade factory at the mouth of the Columbia, but this was a weak technical point: The fort established there in 1811 by the American-owned Pacific Fur Company lasted barely more than a couple of years before being taken over by the British-owned North West Company.[9]

The British were also confident with regard to any claim they might have for the Columbia District in the years ahead. They would note that Broughton and boats from HMS *Chatham* had crossed the sandbar at the mouth of the Columbia and had explored and charted its route for over 150 kilometres inland. They would also note that Thompson of the North West Company had navigated to its mouth from the interior in 1811 and, thanks to Stuart, the North West Company had been actively using the river to transport goods from British North America to the Pacific since the end of 1813.

Shortly after the North West Company took over the Pacific Fur Company fort (Fort Astoria), it was visited by the British twenty-six-gun HMS *Racoon,* which, in the fervour of the war going on at that time, promptly rechristened it Fort George.

The event was documented by a witness: "The captain took a British Union Jack, which he had brought on shore for the occasion, and caused it to be run up to the top of the staff; then, taking a bottle of Madeira wine, he broke it on the flag-staff, declaring in a loud voice, that he took possession of the establishment and of the country in the name of His Britannic Majesty; and changed the name of Astoria to Fort George."[10]

In the next few years, the British position became stronger still. The North West Company was taken over by the mighty Hudson's Bay Company, and the Columbia River route joined the many other rivers and tributaries that crisscrossed the northern part of the continent and formed a vital part of the York Factory Express route that connected to the Company's York Factory on the southeastern shore of Hudson Bay.

By 1825, the Hudson's Bay Company had established Fort Vancouver on the Columbia River, about 150 kilometres from the ocean, to serve as the headquarters of the company's interior fur trade. It was no modest affair: From here the entire western operations of the company, covering some 1.8 million square miles of territory—from Russian Alaska to Spanish California, and from the Rocky Mountains to the Pacific—would be managed and administered.

Within a decade, the Hudson's Bay Company would have the Pacific west coast region serviced by SS *Beaver*, its first steam-powered ship.

By 1840, the Columbia District seemed very much under British control.

Yet at this time, the Americans were already making other plans for the Oregon Territory.

12

THE AMERICANS GO WEST

EXPANSION FROM east to west happened on both sides of the newly established border between the United States and British North America, but the approach of each country toward expansion was markedly different. One key difference was based on legal principle: The British still maintained, as they had during the Nootka Crisis, that sovereignty over any land was based on occupation and development; the Americans, however, subscribed more closely to the Spanish principles of declaration and discovery.

But perhaps the greater difference between the two was the scope of ambition. The British in the late 1700s had interests all over the world. They were already a "superpower" and their concern was managing what they had. The Americans had only their thirteen colonies . . . and they wanted more.

What exactly drove American expansion westward is hard to say. One reason may be that their attempt to expand northward had failed badly. But whatever the motivation, it is indisputable that by 1814, less than forty years after gaining independence, the United States was poised to create for itself a massive continental empire. From the American point of view, George III's 1763 Proclamation protecting Indigenous property rights in North America was rendered null and void in all of the American continent immediately after independence. Members of Indigenous Nations were left out of the Treaty of Paris discussions in 1783, just as they were left out of the Treaty of Ghent in 1814. Everything to the west, it seemed, was up for grabs.

Much of the American expansion was achieved through a strategy that combined diplomacy with either penalties or rewards. Their first major expansion westward was by purchase, when the Louisiana Territory was acquired from France in 1803. Then under control of Napoleon, who was at war with Britain and spreading his forces across Europe, France had little interest in Louisiana, which nobody had yet fully charted or explored. Indeed, the French had only just acquired it two years earlier from Spain, as part of a land-swap deal called the Treaty of Aranjuez. But in 1803, France didn't need vast amounts of unknown land on a continent far away; what it needed was cash. Wars are expensive, after all. So in exchange for $15 million, France sold Louisiana to the US.[1] What the Americans received in return was another two million square kilometres of territory. They also took a significant step toward removing the old European monarchies from the continent.

Lewis and Clark

As had happened north of the border, small but important steps toward westward expansion were also achieved by overland exploration. Here, again, the American approach with regard to reaching the Pacific coast overland from the east was substantially different from that taken by the British. For one thing, the most celebrated expedition was government-sponsored. Meriwether Lewis and William Clark are generally portrayed as merry plant-collecting adventurers, and perhaps they were; but they were also officers in the US Army. The mission they famously led was a forty-five-man army unit known as the Corps of Discovery, created by President Jefferson specifically for the purpose of claiming and discovering the territory he had purchased from France, and for extending the US claims all the way to the west coast.

Commerce was also a part of the mission but, unlike the British at Nootka, Jefferson was not interested in opening up trade for all countries. He wanted to secure the trade exclusively for the United States. He had been mulling the idea for some time, and while negotiating the Louisiana Purchase with France, he had discussed it with French naturalist and politician Bernard Germain Etienne de La Ville-sur-Illon, Comte de Lacépède. Evidence of this is recorded in their written correspondence.

In a letter to Jefferson around this time, Lacépède specifically mentioned the search for the Columbia River and provided directions on how to find it:

> The river you seek might well be the Columbia that your compatriot Mr. Gray discovered in 1788 or 1789. Mr. Broughton, one of Captain Vancouver's companions, navigated it northward for a hundred miles in December 1792. He stopped at a place he called Vancouver, located at latitude 45° 27′ N and longitude 237° 50′ E, starting from the London meridian. In this place, the Columbia river is still a quarter of a mile wide. Its depth varies from 12 to 36 English feet. Vancouver Point is thus still far from its

> source, and yet, from this place one can see Mount Hood, at a distance of about twenty leagues.

Lacépède also encouraged Jefferson's nation-building ambitions, suggesting that a transcontinental trade route from one coast to the other would open the United States up to Asian as well as European markets. He added:

> If your country can establish easy communication between New York, for example, and a city founded on the mouth of the Columbia, using rivers, canals, and short portages, imagine what a route this would be for European, Asian, and American commerce. Products from the north would reach it from the Great Lakes and upper Mississippi while goods from the south of the new continent would arrive from the lower Mississippi and from the river in northern New Mexico whose source is close to the 40th parallel. What a great boon for civilization these new routes would be![2]

When Jefferson sent Lewis and Clark on their mission to the coast, he made sure they had Broughton's detailed charts of the Columbia, published in 1798; had read Mackenzie's journal *Voyages from Montreal to the Frozen and Pacific Oceans*, published in 1801; and understood the goal of nation-building through declaration, discovery, and trade.

Jefferson also made sure Lewis and Clark understood his view that the Indigenous Peoples they encountered along the way were living in United States territory. In a confidential letter to Congress, requesting funding for the mission, he wrote that "the Indian tribes residing within the limits of the United States, have, for a considerable time, been growing more and more uneasy at the constant diminution of the territory they occupy."

His assertion that the tribes were "residing within the limits of the United States" would be a surprise to many Indigenous Peoples of the American west whose territories, unbeknownst to them, had been claimed and passed on over three centuries from the pope to the king of Spain, to the emperor of France, and now to the president of the United States. But the Americans retained the notion that they, as the Spaniards before them, had a sacred right to the land and a duty to convert the non-European residents to the ways of the modern world.

To address the concerns of the uneasy tribes, and to open up more land for American expansion, Jefferson had a simple plan: He would introduce the Indigenous Peoples to the benefits of modern agriculture. His plan, outlined to Congress, held two key measures:

> In order peaceably to counteract this [unease], and to provide an extension of territory which the rapid increase of our numbers will call for, two measures are deemed expedient. First: to encourage them to abandon hunting, to apply to the raising stock, to agriculture and domestic manufacture, and thereby prove to themselves that less land and labor will maintain them in this, better than in their former mode of living. The extensive forests necessary in the hunting life, will then become useless, and they will see advantage in exchanging them for the means of improving their farms, and of increasing their domestic comforts. Secondly: to multiply trading houses among them, and place within their reach those things which will contribute more to their domestic comfort, than the possession of extensive, but uncultivated wilds. Experience and reflection will develop to them the wisdom of exchanging what they can spare and we want, for what we can spare and they

> want. In leading them to agriculture, to manufactures, and civilization; in bringing together their and our settlements, and in preparing them ultimately to participate in the benefits of our governments, I trust and believe we are acting for their greatest good.[3]

With these instructions, and armed with intelligence from previous explorers, Lewis and Clark set out from a post on the Missouri River in May of 1804. Heading west with them was a team of forty-three others, mostly, but not exclusively, drawn from the US Army. Clark also brought his slave, York, whom he had inherited from his father four years earlier.[4] And they would rely on Indigenous guides along the way, notably the teenaged woman Sacagawea.

The corps reached the Pacific coast in November of 1805 and made camp. Their camp, which they called Fort Clatsop, was named after the Clatsop People in the area who had met Captain Gray and Lieutenant Broughton ten years earlier. Some of the record of their interaction with the local people can be found in Clark's journal. On December 9, he wrote:

> Proceeded on to the mouth of the Creek which makes a great bend above the mouth of this Creek or to the S. is 3 houses and about 12 families of the Clat Sop Nation, we cross to those houses, which were built on the S. exposur of the hill, Sunk into the ground about 4 feet the walls roof & gable ends are of Split pine boards, the dores Small with a ladder to decend to the iner part of the house, the fires are 2 in the middle of the house their beads ar all around raised about 2½ feet from the bottom flore all covered with mats and under those beads was Stored their bags baskets and useless mats, those people treated me with extrodeanary

> friendship, one man attached himself to me as Soon as I entered the hut, Spred down new mats for me to Set on, gave me fish berries rutes &c. on Small neet platteers of rushes to eate which was repeated, all the Men of the other houses Came and Smoked with me.[5]

After spending the winter months on the coast, the corps began the return journey in March of 1806. As they made their way back to the east coast, the Americans made a new map of the Columbia River, replacing Broughton's names with new ones that reflected American sensibilities. Of all the place names recorded on Broughton's charts, only a handful survived the purge. Thus Baker's Island, named for Lieutenant William Baker of HMS *Discovery,* was renamed Fanny's Island after Clark's younger sister, Menzies Island was renamed Canoe Island, and so on.[6]

The greater effect of the Lewis and Clark expedition was not unlike those of Cook or Vancouver: The corps's journals and reports, amplified by visionary thought-leaders in their capital cities far away, stimulated the adventurous and tantalized the ambitious. Within a few years, many more would follow in their footsteps.

Astor

Among the first Americans, and certainly the most serious, to follow up on the commercial opportunities identified by the Lewis and Clark expedition was a fellow called John Jacob Astor. Like Richard Etches of the King George's Sound Company, who had started his business career as a spirits trader and switched to fur when alerted to the opportunity, Astor was willing and able to make agile and far-sighted business decisions. He had emigrated to the United States from Germany, via London, immediately after the 1783 Treaty of Paris as a twenty-year-old musical instruments salesman. But he soon branched out into the fur business, travelling from his home in New York to Montreal to buy fur at auction from independent traders and from the North West Company. He then sold the furs on to buyers in the United States and Europe.

By 1800, Astor was a major player in the fur business and was also sending fur to China and importing tea and silk and other goods from Asia, routinely doubling his money. By 1807, the forty-four-year-old Astor was a millionaire and one of the wealthiest men in the United States. But he knew he could maximize the return on his investments further if, instead of paying numerous commissions to others for insurance and cartage, he controlled the entire chain of production, from acquiring fur in the hinterlands to shipping and distribution to major ports around the world. Though already wildly more successful than Richard Etches, Astor landed on essentially the same idea as the King George's Sound Company: He would create his own fur company, and with the involvement of likeminded investors and the explicit approval of government allies, he would buy ships and send them to the west coast to trade between there and China.

The only difference between Astor's plan and Etches's was that he would set up a base at Fort Clatsop instead of at Nootka.

Astor wrote to Jefferson explaining his intentions, and in April 1808 Jefferson replied with his full support, saying that "all beyond the Missipi is ours exclusively, and it will be in our power to give our own traders great advantages over their foreign competitors on this side the Missipi. You may be assured that in order to get the whole of this business passed into the hands of our own citizens & to oust foreign traders who so much abuse their privilege by endeavoring to excite the Indians to war on us, every reasonable patronage & facility in the power of the Executive will be afforded."[7]

Astor spent much of the next two years developing his ideas, first creating the American Fur Company and then, with an eye toward the west coast specifically, the Pacific Fur Company. All the while, he was travelling back and forth to Montreal holding various conversations and reviewing various schemes to move his ideas forward.

By March of 1810, things were falling into place. Astor had persuaded former North West Company men to go in on the project with him: Duncan McDougall, Alexander McKay, and Donald McKenzie were experienced traders; McKay had accompanied Alexander Mackenzie on his trips to the Pacific coast in the 1790s. The Pacific Fur Company became a reality on June 23, 1810. If all went as planned, Astor would later merge the new venture into the American Fur Company that he had previously established on the east coast, creating a continental fur empire. It would be, potentially, as big as the Hudson's Bay Company or maybe even the East India Company. Astor's plans were as big as the continent itself.

But the bigger the dream, the mightier the fall—or so it sometimes seems. It was reasonable to expect that the Pacific Fur Company's factory at the mouth of the Columbia River would be a far safer base for the Americans than Nootka, which the British had threatened war over before, but the venture would end tragically nonetheless. As the crew of the *Boston* had discovered to their horror a few years earlier, the Indigenous Peoples of the Pacific Northwest were becoming impatient and intolerant of abusive traders. Having dealt with the Spanish and British traders along the coast for twenty or thirty years or more, the coastal peoples were sophisticated and savvy customers, increasingly wise to dishonest schemers. They would not be the naive pushovers some east coast businessmen and politicians might expect.

Ignorant of cultural and political issues on the northwest coast, and obsessed with his charts, maps, and contracts, Astor forged ahead with his plans.

The Pacific Fur Company commissioned a ship—the *Tonquin*—to voyage from its headquarters in New York City to the mouth of the Columbia River. There the men would set up a trading factory, or fort. From this base, the *Tonquin* would sail up the coast toward Alaska and gather furs before returning to the Columbia and sailing to markets in Asia or back to the east coast. It was essentially the same business plan as that of the King George's Sound Company, but twenty years later and based 400 kilometres farther south.

Despite all his careful and methodical planning, Astor made one fatal mistake. He hired the wrong man to captain the *Tonquin*. On paper, thirty-one-year-old Jonathan Thorn looked good. He was a loyal sixth-generation American and an experienced US Navy veteran who had seen action in the Mediterranean in combat against the Barbary pirates around present-day Libya, Tunisia, and Algeria. And, in the tradition of Royal Navy veterans like James Colnett, he was prepared to take a leave from military service to make his name in a bold commercial venture.

But Thorn had two dangerous flaws. The first was practical: He had no experience of the Pacific Northwest nor with the region's Indigenous culture. The second was personal: He was pathologically lacking in diplomacy. According to the journal of one of the ship's crew, he was a "strict disciplinarian, of a quick and passionate temper, accustomed to exact obedience," with haughty manners and an overbearing disposition.[8]

The first six months of Thorn's command took the *Tonquin* from New York to Hawaii and thence, by March 1811, to the mouth of the Columbia. But here he met the same difficulty as others before him: that almost-impenetrable sandbar. Impetuously, Thorn sent five men in a boat to take soundings of the channel. In the words of one of the *Tonquin*'s crew, "The boat's crew pulled away from the ship; alas! we were never to see her again."[9] The weather was too rough and the way too difficult. A second boat, and three more lives, would be lost under Thorn's command before they eventually found their way past the sandbar and into the estuary of the Columbia.

Within a few days the members of the Pacific Fur Company selected a place on the south side of the river, about 12 miles from the river's mouth, to build their factory. A blacksmith, silversmith, cooper, and several carpenters had travelled from New York to build their 62-by-20-foot warehouse and make preparations to receive the goods collected by the *Tonquin* after the ship completed the voyage north.

By June, they were well enough established that Thorn was able to take the *Tonquin* north toward Nootka, leaving some men behind to mind the warehouse full of trade goods and carry on with the establishment of Fort Astoria. Little did those left behind know that they would be the lucky ones.

After a couple days of successful trading at a village in Clayoquot Sound in Tla-o-qui-aht territory, Thorn insulted one of the principal Nuu-chah-nulth Chiefs, Nookmis. According to legend, Thorn either rubbed Nookmis's face in the skins he had brought for trade or slapped him across the face with a pelt. Either way, this arrogant act had very much the same effect as when Salter of the *Boston* struck Maquinna eight years earlier. The next day the *Tonquin* was visited by a trading party of twenty warriors. Shortly after they had boarded, another twenty arrived. Using weapons hidden among the furs they brought with them, the Tla-o-qui-aht quickly took over the ship. Caught by surprise, and by his own hubris, Thorn attempted to defend himself with a pocket knife. He was soon cut down, along with the rest of the crew. By nightfall all were dead except two people: one was Thorn's Indigenous interpreter, Joseachal, who managed to get safely to shore; the other was an unknown wounded crewman who stayed on board with a plan for revenge.

The day after the massacre, the Tla-o-qui-aht paddled back to the ship to take stock of their prize. The wounded crewman, certain he would not survive but determined to take as many people with him as possible, waited until all the canoes were empty of warriors and then, as they roamed the upper decks of the ship, he lit a fuse to the estimated four-and-a-half tons of gunpowder stored in the hold. The entire ship exploded into smithereens, sending limbs and other body parts high into the air. That unknown crewman became the west coast's first suicide bomber.

The Pacific Fur Company men at Fort Astoria would not find out what had happened until much later, but the effect would be as fatal to their enterprise as it had been to the lives of the *Tonquin*'s crew. Their principal ship, upon which so much of their business plan was based, was nothing but toothpicks. Many of the company's employees, including at least one partner, were dead. And the Indigenous Peoples who lived along the coast were—at best—cautious to trade with the Americans again.

Perhaps it was a good thing, therefore, that members of the North West Company showed up at Fort Astoria in July of 1811 with outdated information about the discussions Astor had held in Montreal a year or so earlier. According to the new arrivals on the scene, Astor had offered the North West

Company members a one-third partnership in the Pacific Fur Company. This was not true, but it did seem plausible. So everyone went along with it until further confirmation could be received.

The next step toward the end of Astor's dreams for the Pacific Fur Company came with the outbreak of the War of 1812. Ships from the Royal Navy were sent to the Columbia River with orders to "protect and render every assistance in your power to the British traders from Canada [meaning the North West Company], and to destroy, and, if possible, totally annihilate any settlements which the Americans [meaning the Pacific Fur Company] may have formed either on the Columbia River or on the neighboring coasts."[10] A ship from the North West Company, the *Isaac Todd*, sailed to the Columbia under protection of the navy's formidable armed escort.

By October 1813, still not having received any further clarification or confirmation of affairs from New York, the Pacific Fur Company's partner at the Fort, Duncan McDougall, officially gave up hope in the venture and sold all the furs, provisions, and manufactured items of the Pacific Fur Company to the North West Company.

The next month, as mentioned in Chapter 11, the British sloop HMS *Racoon* arrived at the Columbia River, captained by William Black and accompanied by North West Company partner John McDonald. Black formally renamed Fort Astoria to Fort George. "The American colors were hauled down from the factory, and the British run up, to the no small chagrin and mortification of those who were American citizens."[11] With this final act accomplished, Astor, having cleared a measly $44,000 for all his efforts, abandoned the project. A note in the *New-York Gazette and General Advertiser* advised that the Pacific Fur Company had been dissolved.[12]

The failure of the Pacific Fur Company, and the loss of Fort Astoria, was not unlike the failure of the King George's Sound Company and the loss of Nootka to the Spanish. Political leaders would continue to squabble, barter, and negotiate over the territory from their capitals far away. And in the meantime, other entrepreneurs, fortune seekers, and adventurers would continue to flock to the west coast across the mountains and down the tributaries that led to the mighty Columbia.

The British North Americans seemed to have the momentum. By 1821, the Hudson's Bay Company bought out the North West Company and assumed ownership of Fort George. A few years later, in 1825, they built another more substantial fort farther upriver at the place Broughton had named after George Vancouver. Over the next twenty years, Fort Vancouver would become the principal trading centre in the region, finally giving the Hudson's Bay Company a transcontinental trade route from the Pacific to Hudson Bay, from China to Montreal to London.

Yet, despite these wins for the Hudson's Bay Company, individual Americans—not just visionary tycoons like Astor—were also eager to push their boundaries to the west, motivated by an unstoppable mix of patriotic zeal, commercial drive, and a sense of what later would be called "manifest destiny."[13] The Americans believed, in the euphoric and patriotic years following the War of Independence, and again after the War of 1812, that they had a duty to grow, dominate, cultivate, and convert the untamed Louisiana and Oregon Territories. They would improve upon the route of Lewis and Clark, eventually finding a more southern pass over the mountains, creating what history would record as the Oregon Trail.

Madison and Monroe

As American adventurers followed in the footsteps of Lewis and Clark, consecutive American presidents followed the legislative nation-building efforts of Jefferson. After the Louisiana Purchase of 1803, President Madison established the northern border with the British in 1814 with the Treaty of Ghent and then negotiated the Adams–Onís Treaty with Spain in 1819. The Adams–Onís Treaty gave Florida to the United States and established its southern border in a zig-zag pattern creeping north and west from the Gulf of Mexico to the forty-second parallel, just south of the Columbia River. A key part of that agreement was Spain's consent to cede its claims to the Pacific Northwest to the United States, further strengthening that country's legal position in future negotiations with the British.[14]

President Monroe took the reins from Madison and followed up on the provisions in the Treaty of Ghent to resolve the matter of the Oregon Territory with Britain, proposing border solutions in 1818 and 1824. His lengthy report to Congress in December 1823 outlined the status of relations with a number of countries and various issues; it specifically mentioned efforts to establish a Pacific west coast boundary between the United States and British North America "by amicable negotiation" and not by war. But he also updated Congress on relations with Russia, saying he was undertaking discussions to sort out "the respective rights and interests of the two nations on the northwest coast of this continent." Who is to say if his words were chosen to send a signal to the British or not, but some eyebrows may have been raised by this apparent suggestion that there were only two nations on the northwest coast: the US and Russia. (No eyebrows were raised about the status, standing, and rights of any Indigenous Nations of the northwest coast being overlooked entirely.)

Monroe also outlined in his report to Congress the general position of the United States with regard to European powers. Basically, his policy (later known as "the Monroe Doctrine") was that the European powers should exit from North America. He declared: "The American continents, by free and independent condition which they have assumed and maintain, are henceforth not to be considered as subjects for future colonization by any European Power." Despite these strong words, Monroe's negotiations with Britain came to nothing during his tenure, and the status of the Oregon Territory remained open ended for another twenty years.

But notice had been served. The American continent was for the Americans, and the European powers should get out.

13

THE OREGON TERRITORY

AS SOMETIMES happens in politics, nothing much changes until people demand action. This is what began to happen in the Oregon Territory in the 1840s.

A key event took place in a small town on the south side—the American side—of the Columbia River at a place with the unusual name of Champoeg, about 45 kilometres southwest of Fort Vancouver. A group of just over one hundred American settlers got together and decided to create a provisional government. Their May 1843 vote barely passed by 52 to 50. But another truism in politics is that a victory is a victory, no matter how small the margin. Having secured approval to proceed with their initiative, the group elected representatives to pressure the American government in Washington, DC, for further action. In particular, they wanted their land claims in the Oregon Territory to be validated and backed up by the full power and authority of the United States.

By this point, the United States had proposed to the British several times that the boundary that ran across the continent along the forty-ninth parallel from the Great Lakes to the

Rocky Mountains should simply be extended all the way to the Pacific Ocean. The British had constantly countered that the border should run westward along the forty-ninth parallel to the Columbia River and then follow the river southwestward down to the Pacific, ending at about the forty-second parallel. Everything north of there, up to the Russian border at the fifty-fourth parallel, would remain in British North America, as the British Columbia District. Everything south of the Columbia River, and east of the Rockies, could be American territory.

Negotiations became more complex when some ambitious Americans—as hinted by Monroe in his earlier remarks about the negotiations with Russia—disagreed with the reasonable proposal for keeping the border at the forty-ninth parallel and pushed for it to go all the way to the fifty-fourth. In the opinion of those Americans, British North America should end at the Rocky Mountains, and America should have the entire west coast, from California to Alaska.

It is no surprise that these extreme views were popular with the many Americans who had already moved west along the Oregon Trail, like those who had settled around Champoeg. These Americans bristled at the idea that British North America extended as far south as the Columbia River, and they were unhappy that the border question was unresolved. They wanted certainty. They wanted action. They wanted America's rights to the territory they occupied to be recognized and made official. These demands and aspirations were eventually heard and took political expression at an "Oregon Convention" held in Cincinnati in July 1843. There, 113 delegates from six states passed resolutions asserting that the right of the United States "to the Oregon Territory from 42 to 54 degrees 40 minutes north latitude is unquestionable."

The Convention, and its support for American expansion all the way north to Alaska, was given legitimacy by the participation of a significant member of the republic's political establishment. Its host was no less than Richard Mentor Johnson, former vice-president of the United States. The sixty-three-year-old Kentuckian had served under President Martin Van Buren from 1837 to 1841 and was adamantly pro-America. He had fought the British and their Indigenous allies in the War of 1812 and even claimed to have killed the renowned warrior Tecumseh. Of course, many other American veterans of that war made the same claim, but Johnson was the only one who campaigned on it in his bid to become a senator. His boisterous supporters chanted his slogan "Rumpsey Dumpsey, Rumpsey Dumpsey, Colonel Johnson killed Tecumseh."

Johnson also had a complicated family background that no doubt shaped his views on expansion and the rights of others. Raised on a plantation he, like explorer William Clark and many others with similar backgrounds, had inherited slaves from his father. One of them was a young woman named Julia Chinn, who was one-eighth Black. He could not, by law, marry her because interracial marriages were not allowed, but he began a relationship with her and they raised two children together. Some held that he was a progressive voice because he acknowledged the relationship openly, treated her publicly as his wife in all regards, and gave her significant authority over management of their business affairs. But others would have been happier if he had kept his personal affairs to himself.

With Johnson's support, the US Congress considered the issue of the Oregon Territory when it met in December 1843, five months after the Convention he had just hosted. Reporting on the discussion, and the political and public attitude at the time, the editor of the *Washington Globe* wrote that the occupation of the Oregon Territory was inevitable. The

American people will conquer it, he said, "not by arms, but by that inflexible law of nature which enables a growing blade of grass to raise a stone—the law of expansion."[1]

It was clear by now that the topic of the Oregon Territory was not just a foreign policy matter between the US and Britain, but would be a domestic political feature of the upcoming presidential election. At the Democratic National Convention in Baltimore, May 1844, delegate James K. Polk made it clear he was on the side of the expansionists. "Let Texas be reannexed, and the authority and laws of the United States be established and maintained within her limits, as also in the Oregon Territory, and let the fixed policy of our government be, not to permit Great Britain or any other foreign power to plant a colony or hold dominion over any portion of the people or territory of either."[2]

Polk went on to win the election, and in his inaugural address to Congress in March 1845, the fifty-year-old president reaffirmed the position of the Baltimore Convention, declaring that it was his duty to "assert and maintain by all constitutional means the right of the United States to that portion of our territory which lies beyond the Rocky Mountains." He also reaffirmed that "our title to the country of the Oregon is 'clear and unquestionable,'" adding that "already are our people preparing to perfect that title by occupying it with their wives and children."

He also laid out his case for American expansion, citing population growth as a key factor. He declared: "Since the Union was formed the number of the States has increased from thirteen to twenty-eight... Our population has increased from three to twenty millions. New communities and States are seeking protection under its aegis, and multitudes from the Old World are flocking to our shores to participate in its blessings." He also attempted to calm the fears of foreign governments concerned by the US's ongoing territorial gains: "Foreign powers do not seem to appreciate the true character of our Government. Our Union is a confederation of independent States, whose policy is peace with each other and all the world. To enlarge its limits is to extend the dominions of peace over additional territories and increasing millions. The world has nothing to fear from military ambition in our Government."

These assertions by Polk made it clear to the British North Americans that the US's claim to all of Oregon was no longer a mere electoral pledge; it was the official policy of his administration. True to his word, Polk moved quickly to resolve the Oregon Territory question with the British negotiators. But having been on the record for previously saying he thought extending the border along the forty-ninth parallel to the coast would satisfy American ambitions, he angered some of his colleagues and many ambitious Americans by not pressing for more.

Initially, the British negotiators were prepared to give Polk's proposal as much attention as they had the ones before, which is to say they were in no rush to accept it. But it soon became apparent that this time would not be like the ones before. This time there was hot and growing domestic political pressure from within the United States, pushing for action. The British could see as well as anyone else that people like former Vice-President Jackson were steamed up and threatening to take matters into their own hands. Slogans like "All of Oregon or none" and "Fifty-four Forty or Fight" became rallying cries. A loud and growing number of people wanted America's west coast to include everything west of the Rockies right up to the fifty-fourth parallel.

By the time Polk triggered discussion to terminate the joint occupation agreement in February 1846, the British understood that if they did not agree with Polk's plan, the matter would not go away quietly. American citizens seemed primed to revolt again. Having already fought two wars with the Americans—first over the thirteen colonies on the east coast, then over the remaining loyal colonies on the north and east coast of British North America—Britain was in no mood to go to war with them a third time. Opting for a diplomatic solution, the negotiators agreed that the US would have the Oregon Territory north of the Columbia River, but only up to the forty-ninth parallel. From the continental coast, the Strait of Juan de Fuca would form another, natural, borderline westward, with Quadra and Vancouver Island remaining under British oversight and the land and islands to the south under the Americans.

Some Americans were upset that the US did not push the British presence off the coast completely, but others, like New York governor William H. Seward, believed the British territory would become American in due course anyway. In a March 1846 speech, he reflected the view of many American political leaders when he remarked, "Let the Oregon question be settled when it may, it will, nevertheless, come back again. Our population is destined to roll its restless waves to the icy barriers of the north, and to encounter oriental civilization on the shores of the Pacific."[3]

Before his term was over, Polk also saw the annexation of Texas in 1845 and—following the Mexican-American War of 1846–1848—the absorption of 55 percent of Mexico by the United States. Under terms of the Treaty of Guadalupe Hidalgo, the ceded territory included what is today the states of California, Nevada, Utah, most of Colorado, New Mexico, and part of Wyoming. The southern US border, under Polk, was established at the Rio Grande. For its part, the US agreed to pay Mexico $15 million "in consideration of the extension acquired by the boundaries of the United States."

Oregon Occupation

With massive new territories acquired through a combination of negotiation, war, and treaty, the Americans then began to aggressively occupy them. In the Oregon Territory, one new resident who had moved there over the Oregon Trail in 1847 was thirty-one-year-old lawyer Samuel Thurston. He had settled in a place that is now Hillsboro, Oregon, located about 20 kilometres southwest of Fort Vancouver. In 1848, he was elected to the Provisional Legislature, and in 1849, he was selected to represent the Oregon Territory in the US Congress. Once there, Thurston advocated on behalf of the territory's new residents to pass the Donation Land Claim Act in 1850. The Act rewarded existing Oregon Territory settlers for their patriotism, granting 320 acres (1.3 square kilometres) of land to every single man, and double that amount to every married couple. In addition to rewarding the early settlers for their patriotism and courage, the Act also motivated others to move west and join them. The Act promised that all those who moved to the territory before 1855 would receive half as much as those already there—still a huge amount of land—as long as they lived on the land and cultivated it for a minimum of four years.

As American newcomers brought their families overland from the east, they also brought eastern American attitudes, not unlike those of the *Tonquin*'s Captain Thorn. This included attitudes toward race. Britain may have outlawed slavery in 1834, but in 1847, President Polk was still buying slaves for his Tennessee plantation, and when the Donation Land Claim Act came into effect, fifteen of the US's thirty-one states were slave states. So it should not come as a surprise that Thurston was concerned about Black Americans moving west. Fully aware that the British had in the past formed alliances with Indigenous warriors like Tecumseh and encouraged Black slaves like Harry Washington to take up arms against America, Thurston was worried that free Black Americans would threaten the way of life of white American settlers. He explained the problem as follows:

> The negroes associate with the Indians and intermarry, and, if their free ingress is encouraged or allowed, there would a relationship spring up between them and the different tribes, and a mixed race would ensue inimical to the whites; and the Indians being led on by the negro who is better acquainted with the customs, language, and manners of the whites, than the Indian, these savages would become much more formidable than they otherwise would, and long bloody wars would be the fruits of the comingling of the races. It is the principle of self-preservation that justifies the actions of the Oregon legislature.[4]

This attitude was held by many of the newcomers who came west to the Oregon Territory in the following decades. When the State of Oregon was eventually created in 1859, it was established as a "free state"; this meant that while slavery was illegal, there was an "exclusionary clause" on the state's legislative books that excluded Black people from living there. So while there was no slavery, no Black people were allowed. The State of Washington, carved out of the northern half of the Oregon Territory up to its northern border with British

Columbia, was also a free state, but by the time it was given statehood in 1889, it had become a mostly white culture.

Britain had a strong claim to the Pacific coast from the mouth of the Columbia River to Alaska, based on the experiences of Lieutenant Broughton in 1792, Thompson in 1811, the occupation of Fort George in 1813, and the establishment of Fort Vancouver in 1825. Nevertheless, the American Republic was, by the end of the 1800s, a continental country. Spain and France were completely out of the picture. Of the major European powers so dominant in the previous century, only Britain retained any possessions on the continent. And by the end of the century, the poem "America" could proudly proclaim United States dominion from sea to sea:

O beautiful for patriot dream
That sees beyond the years
Thine alabaster cities gleam
Undimmed by human tears.
America! America!
God shed His grace on thee,
And crown thy good with brotherhood
From sea to shining sea!

14

THE COLUMBIA DISTRICT

THE COLUMBIA DISTRICT, which once extended from the Columbia River all the way to Alaska, was, at the conclusion of the Oregon Treaty in 1846, reduced to a smaller geographic footprint than it had been before. Yet it was still substantial. The area included 500 kilometres of coastline between the United States and Alaska, the Island of Vancouver (formerly Quadra and Vancouver Island), and the mainland as far east as the Rocky Mountains.

America's claims to the entire west coast had secured the Oregon Territory based on Gray's trip over the sandbar at the mouth of the Columbia, the arrival and claims of the Lewis and Clark expedition, the president's purchase of rights from Spain, Astor's establishment of Fort Astoria, and America's unique sense of destiny. Its claims for the district north of the new border, however, were much weaker. Above the forty-ninth parallel, it was accepted that Cook (or possibly even Drake) had been the first newcomer to actually set foot on Vancouver Island. It was also accepted that Spain had abandoned its claims to that region following the conflict with the British-owned King George's Sound Company and the resulting Nootka Conventions.

In addition to those events, British commercial enterprises had continued to be a stronger force in the region than those of America or anyone else. Maritime trade had continued to visit the area regularly and was increasingly joined by overland British traders such as Mackenzie, Fraser, and Thompson. While it was true the Americans had also been in the area, they had not stuck around. Most of the American activity north of the forty-ninth parallel had been short-term traders looking for quick profit, and some of those ventures, like the *Boston* and *Tonquin*, had been outright disasters.

Unlike the short-lived American Fur Company, the Hudson's Bay Company had a long history and continued to play a dominant role in the western part of British North America. In 1827, two years after establishing Fort Vancouver on the Columbia River, it established Fort Langley on the Fraser River. By the time the new border was agreed, the company's state-of-the-art coastal trade vessel, the steam-powered SS *Beaver*, was routinely running between the Columbia and the Fraser (via Vancouver Island). And in 1843, having seen the political writing on the wall, the HBC had prudently established Fort Victoria—named for Britain's young new monarch—on Vancouver Island.

The Hudson's Bay Company also requested, and received in 1849, a Royal Grant to trade on Vancouver Island. Having just seen the Americans swallow up Fort Vancouver and the bottom third of British Columbia, the British government gave the grant to the Hudson's Bay Company with some additional strings attached: the company had to agree to sell land to settlers at a reasonable price and actively support the development of a colony that would, in time, compete with and undermine the company's trade monopoly. But it was either that or face the fact that the "54-40 or Fight" crowd would take Fort Victoria for itself. It was, after all, located just 30 kilometres north of the new state of Washington—within easy striking distance.

The Hudson's Bay Company agreed to those terms.

It was at this point that Vancouver Island officially became a British colony. The rest of the Columbia District retained its status as an unadministered region, safe for the time being from American aspirations.

The man the Hudson's Bay Company chose to lead their new base at Fort Victoria was an excellent fit for the role, as he was an exemplar of the company and a firm believer in British methods and values.

James Douglas

James Douglas was born in South America (Guyana) to a Scottish father and a Black mother. At the age of nine he was sent to Britain—some say to Scotland, others to England—where he attended school and, among other studies, became fluent in French. At age sixteen he followed in the footsteps of other rambling fur traders like Alexander Mackenzie and became a clerk with the North West Company in Montreal. As that company merged with the Hudson's Bay Company in 1821, Douglas's career continued its upward trajectory. By the time he was twenty-four, in 1827, he was assigned to the trade station at Fort St. James, on the southeastern shore of Stuart Lake, about 100 kilometres northwest of the present-day city of Prince George, British Columbia. From there he helped transport furs down the Fraser River to Fort Vancouver.

It was also at Stuart Lake that Douglas met and married, in 1828, a sixteen-year-old Métis girl, Amelia Connolly, daughter of the fort's manager and his Cree wife. The marriage ceremony, as was the custom among the fur trader community at that time, was performed *à la façon du pays* (in the style of the country)—a ritual service that was a mix of predominantly Indigenous customs and European.

From Fort St. James, Douglas was transferred south to Fort Vancouver, arriving in 1830. Over the next several years the fort prospered and Douglas's career within the Hudson's Bay Company advanced as well. By 1838, he held the position of Chief Trader and was responsible not just for the business affairs of the fort, but was also the de facto political authority in the area. He made sure that the books were in order and that British law was enforced, including efforts to enforce the law against slavery, enacted in Westminster just a few years earlier in 1834. Reporting to his company leaders in London in October 1838, he outlined the actions he had taken to ensure compliance of both Indigenous Peoples and others.

Working with the local Indigenous Peoples, he said he would use persuasion over force, writing that "I am most anxious to second your views, for suppressing the traffic of slaves... With the Natives, I have hitherto endeavoured to discourage this practise by the exertion of moral influence alone." With others he was more forceful: "Against our own people, I took a more active part, and denounced slavery as a state contrary to law; tendering to all unfortunate persons held as slaves, by British subjects, the fullest protection in the enjoyment of their natural rights."[1]

Island Colony

Douglas's commitment to abolition continued as he moved from Fort Vancouver to Fort Victoria in 1849, after the

Oregon Treaty ceded the southern part of the Columbia District to the Americans. Vancouver Island was by then, as previously noted, both a vast Hudson's Bay trading territory and a designated Crown colony. By 1851, Douglas was both the Chief Factor of the Hudson's Bay Company's fort and the British governor of the colony.[2] Some might say this unique role was a massive conflict of interest, but in fact the business and the government were dependent on each other for success. It was not a conflict of interest but a confluence of interest: The Hudson's Bay Company alone was no match for invading Americans, and British North America could not justifiably or effectively defend its territory without having a sufficient number of loyal subjects living within it. Both the business and the community had to thrive together or both would be lost.

One strategy Douglas used to advance both interests was to entice disaffected Black Americans to move from California to the colony of Vancouver Island. Douglas knew that Black Americans—even those who were free—were still being denied full rights in the new republic. News of the US Supreme Court's 1857 legal decision, known as the Dred Scott Decision,[3] had made its way north. Douglas knew it had barred Black Americans from claiming citizenship in the United States and affirmed that Congress had no authority to ban slavery from a federal territory. And Douglas also knew, through Jeremiah Nagle, captain of the trade ship *Commodore*, that an organized, frustrated, and ambitious Black community in San Francisco was looking for freedom and opportunity.

So Douglas sent an open letter to members of the Black community in San Francisco, inviting them to settle in Victoria.

The letter, delivered via Nagle in 1858, received a warm welcome when it arrived. Thirty-five people sailed immediately from San Francisco to Victoria aboard the *Commodore* and, true to his word, Douglas met with their leaders and welcomed them to the colony. He explained that, after nine months of residence, any of the new landowners would have the right to vote and serve on juries; full citizenship in the global British Empire would be theirs after seven years' residency. In the following years over six hundred Black Americans—mostly from California—would make their way north to the relative freedom of the British territory. One of those who arrived in 1858, Lorne Lewis, would even be appointed (by Douglas) as one of the colony's first police constables.

Douglas was not alone in his abolitionist views. In 1860, as many as seven hundred of Victoria's citizens—"philanthropic free blacks and English humanitarians,"[4] according to subsequent American newspaper reports—gathered on the docks to demand the release of a Black American stowaway detained on an American trade ship. The steam-powered sidewheeler SS *Eliza Anderson* had just arrived from Olympia, in the new state of Washington, and word got around that a fourteen-year-old boy, Charles Mitchell, was being held on board against his will. The news wasn't spread by accident: The ship's cook, James Allen, was a Black resident of Victoria determined to help the boy gain his freedom.

Mitchell had been born in Maryland, the son of a white man and an enslaved Black woman. He had made his way to the Pacific west coast having been acquired by James Tilton, the territorial surveyor for the state of Washington. His presence on the *Eliza Anderson*, and his plans for escape, had been discovered while the ship was en route to Victoria and, under direction of the Washington State governor who happened to be on board, Mitchell had been confined to quarters.

Victoria lawyer Henry Crease, a thirty-seven-year-old recent arrival from England via Upper Canada, took up

Mitchell's cause and managed to have a writ of *habeas corpus* issued, demanding Mitchell be personally presented to court. The ship's captain, John Flemming, initially refused to accept the writ, arguing it had no authority on an American vessel. But when Sheriff William Naylor, backed by the angry crowd, threatened to take Mitchell by force, the governor intervened and allowed Flemming to release Mitchell to the sheriff's custody.

The next day, after spending the night in the local jail, Mitchell was presented before the colony's chief justice, David Cameron. The fifty-six-year-old Scotland-born judge knew that Britain had outlawed slavery in its colonies and around the world in 1834, and was undoubtedly also aware of the landmark 1771 Joseph Knight case in Scotland, which found that a person could not be a slave in a country where slavery did not exist. It is no surprise, therefore, that he was able to immediately declare Mitchell a free man. Saying that "no man could be held as a slave on British soil," he ruled that "there being no charge, warrant or commitment against him, I order that the said sheriff do discharge the said Charles from his said custody forthwith."[5]

In addition to welcoming Americans and imposing British law on the colony's growing European population, Douglas had instructions from his Hudson's Bay Company superiors in London regarding the land and other rights of Indigenous Peoples. "With respect to the rights of the natives, you will have to confer with the chiefs of the tribes on that subject, and in your negotiations with them you are to consider the natives as the rightful possessors of such lands," they wrote. But they also clarified that rightful possession was to be granted only as those lands were "occupied by cultivation, or had houses built on, at the time the Island came under the undivided sovereignty of Great Britain in 1846."

This approach was shaped by practices in eastern British North America, which had by this time mostly been surveyed, mapped, labelled, and registered by a variety of treaties and negotiations. It was also shaped by the prevailing view among European settlers that organized agricultural production was a far more efficient and effective way to use land than the activities carried out by Indigenous Peoples up to this point. Douglas's bosses further directed: "The natives will be confirmed in the possession of their lands as long as they occupy and cultivate them themselves, but will not be allowed to sell or dispose of them to any private person, the right to the entire soil having been granted to the Company by the Crown.

"The right to fishing and hunting will be continued to them, and when their lands are registered, and they conform to the same conditions with which other settlers are required to comply, they will enjoy the same rights and privileges" as British subjects.[6]

Following that direction, Douglas negotiated fourteen treaties with as many Indigenous leaders on Vancouver Island over four short years, encompassing nearly 1,000 square kilometres of land in the traditional territories of the people living at Fort Victoria, Fort Rupert, and Nanaimo, covering only the land that Douglas anticipated would be needed for settlement and trade. Despite Douglas's efficiency executing the treaties, they would face some stress tests in future years as their true meaning came into question. While the European leaders considered the treaties to be a bill of sale, some Indigenous leaders considered them to be an annual rental agreement, paid in the form of cash, goods, and gifts. In hindsight, the diversity of languages and cultural traditions involved in this process was bound to inevitably confront, and eventually confound, the nuances of these legal documents.

While all this activity was unfolding on Vancouver Island, the mainland portion of the Columbia District was also experiencing great changes and threats. The political, social, and economic pressures from the United States, which had proved itself reluctant to put any limits on its citizens' ambition for territorial expansion, were very real. There were still plenty of "54-40 or Fight" Americans living in the Oregon Territory who believed the entire west coast should be theirs and cared very little for the border at the forty-ninth parallel.

This pressure gained even greater momentum when gold was discovered on the Fraser River in 1858.

Douglas's days negotiating treaties on Vancouver Island and making plans to build schools, roads, and hospitals and grow the economy through agricultural and lumber development quickly took a back seat to managing events unfolding on the mainland—although the two were intimately interconnected. Some Americans came north by land via Washington State, but many others came by sea from California. Some 300,000 people had rushed to California for its gold rush just ten years earlier, so there were plenty of prospectors with gold fever looking for the next big thing. With Fort Victoria being the mid-point between San Francisco and the mainland gold fields, it experienced a sudden rush of prospectors stopping there on their way to—and from—the Fraser River. Douglas's letters to the colonial secretary in London reveal the change of pace. In May of 1858 he reported on the scene along the Fraser River: "Boats, canoes, and every species of small craft are continually employed in pouring their cargoes into Fraser's River, and it is supposed not less than one thousand whites are already at work, and on the way to the gold districts."[7]

In July of the following year, he reported on the effect in Victoria: "The excitement on the subject of the Fraser's River

Gold Mines has been more than ever exhibited in the rush of the people from all parts of the coast to this Colony. The Custom-House books of this place show a return of 19 steam ships, 9 sailing ships, 14 decked boats, which have entered at the port of Victoria since the 19th of May last, having 6,133 passengers on board, all either bound directly for Fraser's River, or proposing to settle at this place." He added that "we are, therefore, led to the inference that this country and Fraser's River have gained an increase of 10,000 inhabitants with the last six weeks, and the tide of immigration continues to roll onward without any prospect of abatement."[8]

Douglas—the one-time boss of Fort Vancouver—now began to consider the very real possibility that what had happened to Fort Vancouver on the Columbia could happen to Fort Victoria on Vancouver Island and to Fort Langley and any other British establishment on the mainland. The Americans, left unchecked, could simply swarm the place, declare a provisional government, and petition expansionists in Washington, DC, to recognize their authority over the whole of the territory.

Mainland Colony

The authorities in Westminster shared Douglas's concern and acted to protect the territory from American expansion. The first step was to formally declare the mainland portion of the Columbia District a colony. This was done in August 1858, followed immediately by the direction to build a new city—not a Hudson's Bay trading fort this time, but an entirely civilian enterprise—as the capital of British Columbia. The city was to be called New Westminster. It seemed that, for the first time, British colonial officials were fully engaged and interested in the Pacific west coast. Whether it was the discovery of mainland gold, the stubborn desire to thwart the Americans' seemingly unquenchable thirst for expansion, or both is hard to say. But the casual hands-off free-trade attitude Britain had followed since the conflict with Spain at Nootka Sound was now replaced with a more active and presumptive approach.

Out of urgency and Douglas's proven competency, he was appointed governor of this second colony as well as the colony of Vancouver Island—but only on condition that he resign from the Hudson's Bay Company, which he did. The hope was that formally granting colony status to the mainland of the Columbia District would send a strong signal to fortune seekers in nearby Washington State as well as to political leaders in faraway Washington, DC, that any transgression north of the forty-ninth parallel would be resisted with the full force of the British armed forces and would risk a third war between the two nations.

One hundred and fifty Royal Engineers were dispatched to build New Westminster. The colonial secretary assured Douglas that the men were not only trained professional soldiers; being engineers, they were also capable of building roads and bridges and setting out the foundations of the new city and its docks and other facilities for attracting and managing those arriving and trading by water. Critically, the secretary assured Douglas that the soldiers would not abandon their post: "The superior discipline and intelligence of this force... afford ground for expecting that they will be far less likely than ordinary soldiers of the line to yield to the temptation to desertion offered by the gold fields."[9]

As governor of both colonies, Douglas oversaw a pace of change few could have imagined, not just in volume of people, but also in variety. In addition to the white and Black populations moving north from California, many Chinese came too. The first, in 1858, were wealthy merchants who bought properties on Cormorant Street, where they prepared to supply gold seekers and labourers with equipment and supplies for panning gold in the Fraser River.[10] Over the next couple of years some 2,000 Chinese relocated from San Francisco to Victoria as a result of the gold rush.[11]

Another major gold strike on the mainland, in 1860, this time in the region of the Cariboo Mountains, some 400 kilometres north of New Westminster, ensured that the flow of people into British Columbia continued at a stunningly quick pace. But because the Cariboo area was farther north, and closer to the Rocky Mountains in the east, the number of Americans rushing to the area was somewhat watered down by the "overlanders" making their way there from eastern parts of British North America.

Another factor that somewhat tempered American pressures on the colony was the Civil War, which broke out in April 1861. Although the battlefields of the conflict were almost exclusively on the east coast, between North and South, the war had its effects on the west coast, temporarily slowing and detracting from advances there.

Douglas saw an opportunity in the American Civil War to counter the expansionist pressures he had faced for the past twenty years. His plan was to go on the offensive: He thought Britain should take back the Oregon Territory. To Douglas's way of thinking, the fact that the United States military was divided and focused primarily on battlefields on the east coast presented the British with a unique opportunity to attack. Writing to London at the end of December 1861, he argued that with just a handful of ships, Puget Sound could be overtaken, and the Americans could be strategically isolated and cut off from foreign trade. "There is little real difficulty in that operation, as the coast is entirely unprovided with defensive works, and the Fleet may occupy Puget Sound without molestation." From there, one or two regiments of troops could march south toward the Columbia River, taking possession of Washington and Oregon States as they advanced. Simultaneously, another small naval force could be sent south along the coast to the mouth of the Columbia River, and then up the river to occupy it. "With Puget Sound and the line of the Columbia in our hands, we should hold the only navigable outlets of the country, command its trade, and soon compel it to submit to Her Majesty's rule."[12]

But, once again, the British leaders in Westminster preferred not to enter into a third war with the United States. Douglas's invasion plan was allowed to gather dust, and he returned to the business of managing his two colonies.[13]

A New Era

The mid- to late 1860s brought a number of administrative changes to the area. Douglas, a dominant personality in its commercial and political development, retired at age sixty-six. In 1864, Arthur Kennedy took over as governor of the island colony and Frederick Seymour as governor of the mainland colony. In 1866, the two colonies were united as one, with Seymour in charge until he was replaced by Anthony Musgrave in 1869.

These were more than administrative changes. They were also cultural changes. Douglas had spent nearly fifty years in the fur trade before taking a job with the Crown. He'd lived in tents and cabins and wooden forts; he'd paddled canoes, hiked mountains, and ridden horses. He'd broken bread with Indigenous North Americans from the plains to the coast. He understood the land and the people in a way his successors never would.

The new governors were of a different breed. Kennedy had never been to Vancouver Island until arriving there as governor, Seymour had never been to British Columbia, and Musgrave had never stepped foot in either place until arriving as governor of the merged colonies. All three had been colonial administrators in other places—Sierra Leone, Western Australia, Tasmania, Antigua, Honduras, and the West Indies, to name a few. While all were professionals, sincerely committed to building effective and robust institutions of governance, none had the ties to the land that its Indigenous Peoples did, nor had they invested as much time in developing relationships or understanding cultural ways as the early traders did. They were travelling bureaucrats accountable to London, and when their jobs were done, they would move on.

The non-Indigenous newcomers who moved to the area at this time were also, increasingly, of a different kind than those who had come before. The early traders of the late 1700s, arriving by ship and then leaving, were curious about the Indigenous Peoples encountered on the coast, describing them in their journals as "intelligent," "handsome," and "honest." Those arriving in the mid- to late 1800s, planning to stay and build farms and homes, were more likely to take a different attitude. The generation who had risked their lives to get to the west coast, and celebrated their arrival by dining on rats, were soon replaced by a new generation who risked much less to get there and expected much more once they arrived.

Under this new leadership, and with this new community, Douglas's policy of extending rights to Indigenous Peoples as equal subjects of the Crown began to be rolled back. His policy of allowing individual Indigenous people to acquire Crown land just like any European was reversed.

This change in management was a quiet and subtle revolution, but it was a revolution nonetheless, and there would be no going back.

The last governor, Musgrave, faced a different challenge than Douglas had undertaken almost twenty years earlier. Douglas had started with a blank slate. There was no colony, and no government, when Douglas built a fort in Victoria. But now Musgrave was to manage a new colony with a debt of $1.3 million. Incurred mostly by ambitious road-building projects undertaken on the mainland during the gold rush days, this debt was coupled with a post-gold-rush population decline. Not only had the fortune seekers left; many in the Black population also returned to the United States, since President Lincoln's 1863 Emancipation Proclamation gave hope that liberty and prosperity could be enjoyed there at last.

The situation was grave enough to merit comment in the local newspaper. In 1866, the *British Colonist* reported that "the San Francisco steamer takes away to-day fourteen or fifteen families. We say nothing of the able-bodied single men who are leaving us—although every industrious man is worth several hundred dollars to the country—but the loss of a family in our present infant condition can scarcely be computed. Nothing can be a surer index of mismanagement—of gross mismanagement—than such an exodus. It is an indelible disgrace to the colony and its rulers."[14]

Adding to Musgrave's economic challenge were political and social issues: The mainlanders were upset that Victoria, already a well-established commercial capital, had been selected over New Westminster as the capital for the new colony; the islanders were upset that they had to assume one million dollars of mainland debt. There was also political discord. The islanders leaned toward responsible government,[15] but the merger brought them a legislative assembly with fourteen of the council's twenty-three members appointees of the governor.

Musgrave knew the only way to solve the debt problem was to increase revenue from taxes, and the only way to increase taxes was to grow the economy. In these labour-intensive days when agriculture, mining, and forestry were the main industries, the only way to grow the economy was to increase the population and provide increased access to markets through shipping and overland rail transportation.

The fastest, most expedient way to achieve these goals was with yet another merger. But this time it would be with either the Americans to the south or the Canadians to the east.

15

TWO SUITORS

THE COLONY of British Columbia had two suitors eager for a union: Canada and the United States. Both countries were keen to expand their dominion to the west coast of the continent. Both needed a partner to fulfill their nationalist dreams of the future, but each had a different approach. Canada had a firm plan, motivated in part by a desire for self-preservation from the ever-expanding United States. The US had a loose plan based on self-confidence and faith in the inevitability of achieving its manifest destiny.

The Canadian plan to acquire British Columbia was part of a bigger nation-building strategy. For just as the colony of British Columbia had spent recent years adjusting, responding, and adapting to issues on the west coast, the British colonies in the east had been doing exactly the same thing; in their case, the result was a coming together as a new entity called the Dominion of Canada.

The eastern colonies had been working toward this over a period of three years, with discussions and negotiations held first in Quebec, then in Prince Edward Island, and finally ironed out at a conference in London. The outcome of their work came into effect on July 1, 1867, with the passing in the British Parliament of the British North America Act, which formally united three of the five colonies: Canada, Nova Scotia, and New Brunswick. It then divided the province of Canada into two: Quebec and Ontario. The British colonies of Newfoundland and Prince Edward Island had participated in discussions, but for the time being remained independent.

The Act explained that the Dominion of Canada would have its own House of Commons and that the parliament would consist of 181 members "of whom Eighty-two shall be elected for Ontario, Sixty-five for Quebec, Nineteen for Nova Scotia, and Fifteen for New Brunswick." It also explained that a senate would be established with a total of seventy-two senators (twenty-four each for Ontario and Quebec, and twelve each for Nova Scotia and New Brunswick). The senators would be appointed for life. John Macdonald, age fifty-two, was appointed the country's first prime minister.

Like the newly formed United States of 1783, Canada in 1867 was small and militarily weak, entirely dependent on Britain for its national defence.[1] But, also like its southern neighbour, it had ambitions to grow. In fact, territorial expansion was built in to the Canadian constitution. The British North America Act anticipated, and pre-approved, the entrance of other North American colonies into the union: "It shall be lawful for the Queen, by and with the Advice of Her Majesty's Most Honourable Privy Council, on Addresses from the Houses of the Parliament of Canada, and from the Houses of the respective Legislatures of the Colonies or Provinces of Newfoundland, Prince Edward Island, and British Columbia, to admit those Colonies or Provinces, or any of them, into the Union."[2] This provision was rooted in an earlier proposal from the Quebec conference of 1864, unanimously adopted, that called for mechanisms to provide "for the admission into the Union on equitable terms of the North West Territory, British Columbia and Vancouver [Island]."

Immediately after the Dominion was formed, therefore, the new government began a two-pronged expansion strategy: One goal was to purchase the territory under management of the Hudson's Bay Company—Rupert's Land—which spanned from Newfoundland to the Rockies; the other was to convince the independent colony of British Columbia to join Canada. Both actions were undertaken simultaneously.

The second goal depended on achieving the first, as it was unlikely in the extreme that British Columbia would join a country with which it did not share a border.

As Thomas Jefferson had negotiated with Spain and France for their claims on the continent, John A. Macdonald and his colleagues now negotiated with Britain for its claims. Two ministers from Macdonald's cabinet, George-Étienne Cartier and William McDougall, were sent to London to strike a deal with the Hudson's Bay Company. But they were not the only ones interested in Rupert's Land or in British Columbia. American ambitions were well established and, in the aftermath of its bloody but nation-forging Civil War, were gaining fresh momentum.

The aggressive American attitude, and its goal of assimilating British Columbia into its fold, is evident in the plainspoken, unabashed comments of California senator William Gwin when he argued that the US should purchase Alaska. He said it should be done to "displease to the last degree Great Britain and to weaken that power upon the Pacific... Thereby, British Oregon [the British Columbia District] would be isolated by the American barriers both on the northern and southern sides."[3]

Similarly haughty, provocative, and confident comments were made by William Seward when campaigning for Abraham

Lincoln in September 1860.[4] Seward, the former governor of New York who had predicted in 1846 that the Oregon question would eventually come back into play, told an appreciative audience in Saint Paul, Minnesota, that one day the territory to their north would join them in America: "I look off on Prince Rupert's land and Canada, and see there an ingenious, enterprising and ambitious people, occupied with bridging rivers and constructing canals, railroads and telegraphs, to organize and preserve great British provinces north of the great lakes, the St. Lawrence, and around the shores of Hudson bay, and I am able to say, 'It is very well, you are building excellent states to be hereafter admitted into the American Union.'"[5]

The idea of British Columbia joining the United States was not just floating among the parlours, lobbies, and meeting halls frequented by American politicians. There were some regular British Columbians who were sympathetic to the idea as well. In 1866, the same year those families sailed for San Francisco, the American consul in Victoria, Allen Francis, reported to Washington that "the people of Vancouver Island, and British Columbia, are almost unanimous in their desire for annexation to the United States."[6]

Americans continued to press for expansion to the Pacific Northwest coast, proposing concrete actions that would entice British Columbians and frustrate Canadians. In December 1866, Alexander Ramsey, an American senator from Minnesota, presented a memorial to the Senate calling for the construction of a northern transcontinental railroad to the Pacific. His document emphasized "the influence which the construction of this [rail]road will have upon our northern neighbors." Shortly thereafter, the Northern Pacific Railroad Company issued a promotional pamphlet warning of the risk that a Canadian company might build a railroad to British Columbia before the US did: "The construction of such a [rail] road would preclude the idea of political relations between that people and our own."[7]

The next year, Seward, now the powerful US secretary of state, began urging American capitalists to subvert the rights of the Hudson's Bay Company, taking the Company's land as their own.

Macdonald's new government was keenly aware of these US ambitions and was determined to foil them. British North America had been a refuge to loyalists fleeing north after the Revolutionary War, and had survived the aggressive attack of the War of 1812. They were not about to let the Americans slip north of the forty-ninth parallel easily. To make their intentions known to the British Columbians, but also as a warning shot to the United States, the Canadian government officially informed British Columbia, on March 25, 1868, that it desired union with the colony and had approached Great Britain on the subject. It also floated plans to build a transcontinental railroad to link the region with markets in the east.

Undaunted, American politicians continued to advocate annexation of British Columbia. In early summer 1868, during the debate in Congress on the appropriation for the Alaska purchase, congressmen openly expressed their desire to acquire the British colony. Minnesota representative Ignatius Donnelly, no doubt fighting for his railway-building supporters and business-minded constituents, said he viewed the Alaska purchase as a foot in the door of further expansion; it was, he said, "the way to the acquisition by the United States of that great and valuable region, Western British America." Illinois congressman and Civil War veteran Green B. Raum agreed and predicted that in due course British Columbia would "drop into our hands like a ripe pear."[8]

Raum may have overstated and oversimplified the case, but there were some British Columbians who agreed with him.

As consul Francis had noted in 1866, and as Seward had constantly hoped, by the end of the 1860s some British Columbians were beginning to look toward the US for their future. In the fall of 1869, about a hundred business leaders in Victoria drafted an Annexation Petition and sent it to President Grant.[9] They outlined their thoughts, saying they liked being a part of Great Britain but were not at all keen on the idea of being part of Canada: "We are instigated by every sentiment of loyalty to Her Majesty, by our attachment to the laws and institutions of Great Britain and our deep interest in the prosperity of our adopted country, to express our opposition to a severance from England and a confederation with Canada. We admit the Dominion may be aggrandized by confederation, but we can see no benefit either present or future, which can accrue to us therefrom."

In other words, if they could not be a colony of Britain, they would just as soon join the US as Canada.

The sober and practical-minded business leaders, still sensitive to the depression and infrastructure debts that had followed the heady days of the gold rush, went on to say that confederation with Canada would make things easier for Britain, but would do little to improve their lot. The petition continued:

> That confederating this Colony with Canada, may relieve the mother country from the trouble and expense of fostering and protecting this isolated distant Colony, but it cannot free us from our long enduring depression, owing to the lack of population as aforesaid and the continued want

> of home markets for our produce. The only remedy for the evils which beset us, we believe to be in a close union with the adjoining States and Territories, we are already bound to them by a unity of object and interest; nearly all our commercial relations are with them.

The only way forward, said the signatories, was for the US to acquire British Columbia. "We earnestly desire the ACQUISITION of this Colony by the United States. It would result at once in opening to us an unrestricted market for our produce, bring an influx of population and with it induce the investment of capital in our Coal and Quartz Mines and in our forests."[10]

In 1869, the same year Musgrave was installed as governor, William Seward, who had secured the sale of Alaska in 1867, visited Victoria to soften the ground for further expansion. He met with business leaders and floated the idea of an economic alliance between Alaska, BC, Washington, Oregon, and California. He also boasted of never hearing "any person, on either side of the United States border, assert that British Columbia is not part of the American continent."[11] And, as we know from Monroe, the American continent was for Americans.

These machinations were watched closely by the remaining British colonies in the east, and by the newspapers in London. Observing from afar, the *London Daily News* clearly identified the threat of American expansion north of the forty-ninth parallel, but predicted the Americans were not likely to move by force. The republic, the newspaper said, will "probably do nothing precipitately, especially if it perceives that it may equally gain its object without war."[12]

In Ottawa, Alexander Galt was equally alert to the threat. A savvy politician and successful land developer, he knew the best way to stop America from taking Rupert's Land was to prevent them from taking British Columbia. "If the United States desires to outflank us on the west, we must... lay our hands on British Columbia and the Pacific Ocean," he said, adding that "the country cannot be surrounded by the United States."[13]

Thankfully for Galt and the Canadians, after six months of negotiations, the Hudson's Bay Company agreed to transfer Rupert's Land to the Dominion of Canada for just $1.5 million. The company could have gotten much more for it from the United States, which had just recently paid Russia $7.2 million for Alaska.[14] But the Colonial Office knew that allowing Rupert's Land to fall into American hands would put an end to any chance British Columbia would join the Canadians, and they strongly encouraged the Hudson's Bay Company to play ball. Britain calculated it would be far wiser to have the region secured by its Dominion ally at a low price than fall to its trading rival at a higher one.

The transfer of Rupert's Land was instantly one of the largest real estate transactions ever conducted and, like the Louisiana Purchase, helped turn a modest country in the northeast of the continent into an expansive one that reached across North America. The area gained—five times larger than France—was eventually divided among Quebec and Ontario, and later used to form the provinces and territories of present-day Manitoba, Saskatchewan, Alberta, the Northwest Territories, and Nunavut.

The purchase of Rupert's Land, along with the promise of a railroad, offered British Columbia the concrete possibility of a secure overland connection to markets in eastern Canada—infrastructure that could remedy its economic and security woes.

By the end of 1869 the future of the colony of British Columbia was still an open question. Its economy was in the post-gold-rush dumps. It had borrowed and spent a lot of money to build infrastructure and generally administer the territory while thousands flocked there. Now it was left holding a fairly hefty bill after many of the get-rich-quick crowd had pulled up stakes and moved on to greener—or more golden—pastures elsewhere. But it also had a firm offer to join a new country that it shared a border with, which promised a railway link to markets in the east. It was not obliged to accept the offer, of course, but it seemed equally clear that rejecting the offer would lead inevitably to union with the United States either by intention or default.

The matter came to a head when the members of the British Columbia legislature met in March 1870 to debate the issue. They had a decision to make: Which suitor would they fall for, Canada or America?

16

FALLING FOR CANADA

WHETHER OR NOT to join the other former colonies in the Dominion of Canada was less a "debate" than a discussion about what the terms of joining would be. The truth of the matter was that the deck was already stacked in favour of union with Canada, so the outcome was virtually inevitable. If anyone was placing bets, the smart money was on a solid win for Canada.

For one thing, the proposed union was already pre-approved by Canada and supported by the Colonial Office in London—so long as that's what the people in British Columbia wanted. For another, the pro-union governor of British Columbia, forty-one-year-old Anthony Musgrave, had been hand-picked specifically to lead British Columbia in that direction. Canadian prime minister Macdonald had already been lobbying the Colonial Office to have Musgrave's predecessor, Frederick Seymour, replaced with someone more helpful to his cause; so when Seymour died unexpectedly in June 1869, the Colonial Office wasted no time in slipping Musgrave into the role. Macdonald knew Musgrave from his role as governor of Newfoundland, and although Newfoundland had not joined Canada, Macdonald knew he was a proponent of the Canada project. Simply put, Musgrave was Macdonald's choice for governor of British Columbia.

When Musgrave accepted the role, he did so with the desire to be British Columbia's last governor. He arrived with the goal of eliminating his job, then moving on to some other assignment at some other colony in the British Empire. Shortly after arriving, in a private conversation with Speaker of the legislature John Helmcken, he spoke plainly of his aims and told Helmcken the Canadian government wanted British Columbia to join because it was "afraid that B.C. may, if left alone, choose to join the U.S. and the annexation cry makes them anxious."[1]

Musgrave had two influential newspaper editors on his side. Amor De Cosmos, also a member of the legislature, had been a founder and editor of the *British Colonist* in Victoria; and John Robson was editor of *The British Columbian* in New Westminster. Both had been proponents of union for some time, and proved to be powerful allies for the cause. And, as noted earlier, the majority of members on the Legislative Council—fourteen out of twenty-three—were appointees accountable only to the government that he was responsible for managing.

The decision point arrived in March 1870, just seven months after Musgrave took up his post, when the members of the legislature met to debate the issue. The gathering in Victoria—the designated capital of the three-year-old united colony—was held in the bizarre red-painted brick and wooden structure that had been commissioned by Douglas in 1859. Described at various times as something between a Dutch toy and a Chinese pagoda, a pigeon roost and a Chinese washhouse, it was intended to be a mix of a Swiss cottage and

Italian villa. In time, people referred to it as "the birdcages." Given the diversity of characters in the debate, perhaps the venue and its description were apt.

The resolution for the debate was framed as follows:

> *Resolved*, that this Council is of opinion that at this juncture of affairs in British North America, east of the Rocky Mountains, it is very desirable that His Excellency be respectfully requested to take such steps, without delay, as may be deemed by him best adapted to insure the admission of British Columbia into the Confederation on fair and equitable terms, this Council being confident that in advising this step they are expressing the views of the Colonists generally.[2]

Henry Crease, who twenty years earlier had taken up the case of escaped slave Charles Mitchell, was now the colony's attorney general. He succinctly summarized the situation as many saw it, and explained why forming a union with Canada was the best choice: "We are sandwiched between the United States territory to the north and south—indeed on all sides but one, and that one opening toward Canada." He added that "our only option is between remaining a petty, isolated community, fifteen thousand miles from home, eking out a miserable existence on the crumbs of prosperity our powerful and active Republican neighbours choose to allow us, or, by taking our place among the comity of a young and vigorous people, the eastern boundary of whose possession is washed by the Atlantic."[3]

Many shared Crease's view, but the adoption of the resolution was not to pass uncontested. The loudest and most persistent voice against the proposal was that of John Helmcken. The influential forty-five-year-old was a former

Hudson's Bay Company doctor, Douglas's son-in-law, and Speaker of the legislature. He was of the old-school mentality, committed to his patients and his community, not an imported bureaucrat or professional colonial administrator. He represented the view of many who were by and large satisfied with the status quo and skeptical of the rising authorities in the east. He spoke for many when he said, "We are a Colony of England; and I don't know that many people object to being a Colony of England; but I say that very many would object to becoming a Colony of Canada."[4]

The people of British Columbia, he said, had no love for Canada. They cared "little or nothing about the creation of another Empire, Kingdom, or Republic; they have but little sentimentality, and care little about the distinction between the form of Government of Canada and the United States."[5]

Helmcken elaborated on his case further, explaining that Canada was an unknown and faraway place: "It is absurd to attempt to ally ourselves with a people three thousand miles away, without any settlement of the intervening country, with no communication except through the United States and with no telegraphic communication." He added that "Canada is for all practical purposes further removed from us today than England; we know less about her."[6]

Helmcken had harsh words for Britain too. He was certain the empire was conspiring with Canada to unburden itself of its responsibilities. Without revealing the private conversation he had earlier with Musgrave, he told members of the legislature that he felt certain "Her Majesty's Government had no wish to be put to the expense of defending the country; no wish to be involved in quarrels with the United States," and "no wish to keep Canada depending on her support, but rather a wish to force her into independence—to get rid of her altogether."[7]

He was not wrong. Two years earlier, the *London Daily News,* commenting on the threat of American expansion on the North American continent, had observed, "It is equally well understood that it is only while the Canadians desire to remain a part of our Empire that our obligation will exist."[8]

Finally, perhaps out of desperation or frustration, Helmcken opined that the whole issue was likely a waste of time and a distraction from the very real probability the colony and Canada—together or independently—would eventually be taken over by the United States. "It cannot be regarded as improbable that ultimately, not only this Colony but the whole Dominion of Canada will be absorbed by the United States."[9]

At least one member of the legislature expressed a sense of having been hoodwinked by the idea of confederation. Barrister Thomas Lett ("T.L.") Wood said he had initially interpreted it as meaning "a union of free and self-governing states, united by a federal compact for the purposes of maintaining and preserving uniformity in laws and institutions which affect the social and commercial relation of life." But as the debate continued, and the reality of what they were discussing came increasingly into focus, he concluded that what Confederation actually amounted to was "union, incorporation, absorption and annihilation."[10] He had thought Canadian Confederation might be an alternative version of the United States—a union of former colonies—but became increasingly concerned it was merely trading Westminster for Ottawa.

Countering naysayers like Helmcken and Wood was Amor De Cosmos, the forty-five-year-old former *Colonist* newspaper editor. Responding to Helmcken's remarks about the United States, De Cosmos argued that an alliance with Ottawa would be better: "The Honourable Member for Victoria City has said a great deal about centralization. But I say, Sir, that there must be a centre somewhere. We cannot have it in British Columbia, and a centre would be no worse in Ottawa than in Washington. The Pacific Coast, so far as the United States are concerned, is represented at Washington, which is not so large a city as New York."

He continued with a dazzling math-fuelled argument designed to illustrate that British Columbia would have more representation at the seat of power in Ottawa than it would at Washington, DC. "Now, Sir," he said, "the whole of the Pacific States of the United States have only twelve Representatives in Congress—six in the Senate and six in the House of Representatives. California has two Senators and three Representatives; Oregon, two Senators and one Representative; Washington Territory, one Delegate; and Nevada, two Senators and one Representative. Now, it is proposed in the Resolutions to grant to British Columbia twelve Members—four in the Senate and eight in the Commons—a number equal to the whole representation of the Pacific States, with 1,000,000 people, in the United States Congress."

He elaborated his mathematical analysis:

> Again, there are only five States that have more than twelve Members in Congress. They are New York, Pennsylvania, Illinois, Indiana, and Ohio. Take another glance at the representation of the States most remote from Washington. Texas has five Members; Florida, three; Maine, seven; and California, five. Remoteness and small numbers have never caused any of those States to be treated unfairly. Under the popular system of government there, the small States do not go to the wall. Has little Delaware gone to the wall? Has Rhode Island gone to the wall? No; neither would British

> Columbia go to the wall in the Parliament of Canada. The Government of Canada is based on the popular will; and that is the highest of guarantee that we shall be treated fairly by the Dominion.[11]

Joseph Trutch, a forty-four-year-old surveyor and engineer, also came out fully in favour of union. Trutch had come to the coast inspired by the gold rush, first in California, and then in the Oregon Territory, before settling in British Columbia and tapping into the lucrative government construction projects. He was an unabashedly ambitious man and socially connected: He was a childhood friend of Attorney General Henry Crease; his brother John was married to Governor Musgrave's sister, Zoe; his sister Caroline was married to legislative counselor Peter O'Reilly, the former gold commissioner. Trutch started his arguments with an appeal to dollars and cents, and ended them with a patriotic flourish.

First, Trutch argued that union with the United States—the only alternative to the Canadian offer—would be an economic disaster. There was no way, he said, that British Columbia could compete with Washington:

> If British Columbia were placed in the same position as Washington Territory, we should be absolutely without representation—for that Territory has one representative in Congress, it is true, but he has no vote—and all our officials would come from Washington. Annexation to the United States would also entail on us largely increased taxation, and would most materially affect an interest which the Honourable Member for Victoria told you would suffer most from Confederation. Why, Sir, under the union suggested, our farmers would be brought into direct

> competition with the farmers of Washington Territory and Oregon, and then our agricultural interests would be indeed annihilated.

Trutch also said there was no way Victoria could compete with San Francisco: "If this country were American Territory you would have the whole influence of San Francisco brought to bear against the mercantile interests of Victoria; no hope could we have of building up a port here to rival San Francisco; no, Sir, you would never see a foreign vessel in these waters."

He then implied that those arguing against joining Canada were holding out in order to profit from rich Americans. He said he had heard no advantage to joining the United States "unless it be the questionable expectation that American capital might buy up the real estate in and around Victoria, and so give the present holders the opportunity of realizing their property into money and then leave the country to its fate."[12]

Finally, Trutch sought to calm fears about the colony's place in Confederation by painting a positive and hopeful picture of an alliance with Canada: "This Colony will have its due weight and influence in the Dominion, that its representatives will be heard and listened to in the Canadian Parliament, and that this will be a favoured portion of the Confederation, when admitted, on account of its position as the outlet of Canada on the Pacific."[13]

Thomas Humphreys, the thirty-year-old representative for Lillooet, tried to speak up for the Indigenous Peoples in British Columbia, arguing that reservations would be bad for everyone: "I say the Indians are not treated fairly by us, and all they want is fair dealing from the white population. At Lillooet I was told there were upwards of sixteen thousand [Indigenous people]; and $17,000 in gold dust was purchased from Indians. Take away this trade and the towns must sink. I say, send them out to reservations and you destroy trade; and if the Indians are driven out, we had all best go too."[14]

Forty-year-old Henry Holbrook jumped in with a proposal that the terms of Confederation should specify the ability of Indigenous Peoples to occupy the land and enjoy equal protection of the law. "My motion is to ask for protection for them under the change of Government. The Indians number four to one white man, and they ought to be considered. They should receive protection."[15] The council defeated Holbrook's motion twenty to one. There was no further discussion about the Indigenous Peoples.[16]

After four weeks' debate, the resolution was passed, as Musgrave had hoped, and to no one's surprise. A delegation of three people—Trutch, Robert Carrall, and Helmcken—was sent east from the capital of British Columbia to the capital of Canada to present the terms and conditions that would seal the deal. Thirty-four-year-old Carrall, a Musgrave appointee to the Executive Council, had been a loud and loyal ally to the Confederation cause, and Musgrave knew he could be counted on to hold firm. The trio sailed south to San Francisco, then travelled east across the United States on the transcontinental railway that had been launched by President Lincoln.

That October, when the delegates had returned successfully from their diplomatic mission to Ottawa, Musgrave scheduled new elections for November. Transitioning toward a more democratic governance model, Musgrave called for a legislature that would have greater accountability to the citizens of British Columbia, with the majority of the Legislative Council members, nine out of fifteen, elected.

The new council met in January 1871, and its first order of business was to ratify the terms of union with Canada. Musgrave flattered the members as they began their business, saying, "At no time in the history of this Colony has any Legislative body... been occupied with considerations of greater moment."[17] Yet, ironically, they spent almost no time in deliberation. The resolution was passed almost immediately, with no debate.

The will of the people having thus been expressed, the Government of Canada followed through to ratify the deal in Ottawa that April. In May, the Imperial Order in Council admitting British Columbia as a new Province of Canada followed, effective July 20, 1871.

Representation in the Canadian Parliament was based on population. Thus, in 1871, when British Columbia joined the Dominion of Canada, it was granted 6 Members of Parliament out of a total of 191 (Ontario had 82, Quebec had 65, Nova Scotia had 19, New Brunswick had 15, and Manitoba had 4).[18] British Columbia received 3 seats in the Canadian Senate, out of a total of 77 (Ontario and Quebec each had 24, New Brunswick and Nova Scotia each had 12, Manitoba had 2).

Having fulfilled his task, Musgrave wasted little time in the new province. He packed his bags and left British Columbia on July 25, 1871, received a knighthood, and continued service in Colonial Offices in South Africa, South Australia, Jamaica, and finally Queensland, where he died in 1888.

Joseph Trutch was knighted and appointed BC's first lieutenant-governor in 1871. He eventually retired from government service in 1888 and moved back to England. Henry Crease was appointed a judge on the Supreme Court of British Columbia in May 1870, the month after the crucial debate concluded. He too, eventually, was knighted. Amor De Cosmos became a Member of Parliament and also British Columbia's second premier. Robert Carrall was appointed to the Canadian Senate in December 1871.

Unlike the other principal players, John Helmcken refused offers for appointments. He turned down roles as a senator, premier, and lieutenant-governor, and went back to practising medicine.

Great Britain divested itself of any further responsibility for the colony's defence, debt, funding, and laws, ceding all to the colony's new overlords in Ottawa.

In prose likely intending to convey pride, but sounding almost funereal, a July 1871 column in the *British Colonist* newspaper opined: "Today British Columbia passes peacefully... into the confederated empire of British North America."[19]

Whatever the sentiment intended or received, the United States had been stymied and "the Oregon question" was finally and irrevocably settled.

PART FOUR

Counterfactual Canada

17

NO ETCHES, NO CANADA?

WHAT GREAT Britain wanted toward the latter half of the nineteenth century was to divest itself of its responsibility for managing British North America. What the eastern colonies of British North America wanted was political, economic, and cultural security from the United States. These things were achieved first by forming a united Dominion of Canada and then by extending that Dominion's command across the prairies, over the Rocky Mountains, to the Pacific coast. All of this was possible only because British Columbia had avoided, up to 1870, being absorbed into the United States.

The single most important reason why British Columbia had remained apart from the United States until that time was the incident at Nootka involving the ships of the King George's Sound Company in the summer of 1789.

But imagine for a moment that Richard Etches had decided not to form that company, and did not send ships to the Pacific Northwest in search of fur. Or imagine that he had not had the confidence and courage to send the fateful second mission to Nootka under the leadership of Captain Colnett.

What if he had believed the naysayers in London who said the pursuit of the fur trade on the Pacific Northwest coast of America was too risky? What if he had just decided to stick with the trade in spirits and tea? Or what if he had been as unsuccessful in selling his idea to investors and patrons as William Bolts had been?

The history of British Columbia, Canada, and the United States might have played out quite differently if Richard Etches had not been so adventurous and ambitious. For the rest of this chapter, we'll examine how things might have turned out without him.

Counterfactual 1789–1821

Had Etches not formed his King George's Sound Company, the exploitation of the Pacific Northwest, triggered by Cook's voyage, would surely have continued without him. William Bolts would have tried, and failed, to launch a Pacific fur-trading enterprise, but adventurous traders and scallywags like James Hanna, James Charles Stuart Strange, and John Meares would have persisted in their efforts. They would have enjoyed the same degree of success as they did.

But without his later alliance with Etches's King George's Sound Company, Meares would have had no standing in Westminster. This alliance was critically important because the KGSC ships under command of James Colnett—the *Argonaut*, *Iphigenia*, *Princess Royal*, and *North West America*—were the only ones licensed by Britain to trade at Nootka. Without that licence, no diplomatic incident would have occurred between the British and Spanish when those ships and their cargo were confiscated at Nootka by Spanish commander

Esteban José Martínez. The Spaniard simply would have confiscated the ships and cargo, arrested James Colnett, and done everything that he did . . . but without any diplomatic consequences. In Westminster, Prime Minister Pitt would have paid no attention to Meares's complaints about the affair because it would have been an entirely private matter, and he had much bigger fish to fry.

With no licensed ships from the King George's Sound Company arriving at Nootka, Martínez's bold seizure of Nootka would have made him a hero of the Spanish Empire. The history books would record that he was responsible for building the Spanish base at Nootka and solidifying Spain's claims to the region, as sanctioned by Spanish-born Pope Alexander VI in his bull of 1493.

Having successfully established Fort San Miguel in Friendly Cove, with its ten large cannons, barracks, residences, and gardens, the colony of Santa Cruz de Nuca would have gone on to become the most northerly military base of New Spain and home to its Pacific Northwest fleet. A Catholic mission would have quickly followed, along with various commercial traders and settlers, much as had happened in previous Spanish settlements along the coast at San Diego, San Francisco, and Santa Barbara. The fort that Spain built at Neah Bay in 1792, on the southern side of the Strait of Juan de Fuca, would have proceeded and would have given Spain total control of the strait and all the riches and resources beyond. Places like Burrard Inlet, the Strait of Georgia, and Howe Sound would have retained the names given to them by Spanish naval officers: Canal de Sasamat, Gran Canal de Nuestra Señora del Rosario la Marinera, and Boca del Carmelo.

Alexander Mackenzie would have made his overland trek to Bella Coola in 1793, but with the same outcome: He would have made history as the first European to cross the continent by land, but he would still have failed to achieve any commercial advantage for the North West Company.

Despite Spain dominating the area, it is possible its Territorio de Nutca would have been included in the 1801 Treaty of Aranjuez—the deal between Spain and France that traded the Louisiana Territory for cash and other land in Europe. If that had happened, it is also possible France would have flipped it a couple of years later to the United States as part of the Louisiana Purchase of 1803. France would have received more money for the deal, it being so much larger, but the United States would have been very happy to pay the price.

Thomas Jefferson would still have sent Lewis and Clark on their overland expedition, and they would have reached the mouth of the Columbia River in 1805, asserting American claims to the newly acquired territory without question.

Simon Fraser would have failed to find the northern route to the Columbia River and taken the Fraser River to within eyesight of the Gran Canal de Nuestra Señora del Rosario la Marinera in 1808, but again with the same effect: frustration at having failed to achieve his aims, and hostility from the Musqueam People. He would have found even more evidence of Spanish trade goods among the villages of the Indigenous Peoples he encountered along the way.

After ten years of prosperity, the United States would likely have launched its unprovoked and opportunistic attack on British North America in 1812. The Americans might still have lost that war, but the Pacific Fur Company's base at Fort Astoria on the Columbia River may have been sufficiently established and fortified that it could have withstood the attack by HMS *Racoon*. In any event, the post-war negotiations culminating in the Treaty of Ghent would have likely included explicit declaration by Britain that it had no claims to the Pacific side of the continent, and would have given full recognition of the western borders identified in the Treaty of Aranjuez. The Treaty of Ghent would have succeeded in establishing the east-west border along the forty-ninth parallel to the Rocky Mountains, but the border would have ended at that point. With that taken care of, the Convention of 1818, in which the two belligerents agreed to share occupation and management of the Oregon Territory, would never have occurred. The issue would have been moot.

But even if Spain had not packaged Santa Cruz de Nuca into what became the Louisiana Purchase, it most certainly would have included the region in the 1819 Adams-Onís Treaty, in which Spain ceded Florida to the United States. That treaty also established the forty-second parallel as the northern limit to Spain's west coast claims, leaving everything north of the Columbia River—home to the thriving American settlement of Astoria—to the United States. New Spain would have dissolved completely by 1821, and the United States would be the unquestionable ruler of the entire west coast between the Rocky Mountains and the Pacific Ocean, up to the border with Alaska.

Counterfactual 1821–1870

The flow of settlers over the Oregon Trail in the wake of the Lewis and Clark expedition would have continued, but there would not have been a "54-40 or Fight" movement. Without Britain to stop them, the American settlers would have continued to come west, and to move north as well. The Oregon Treaty of 1846 would not have been necessary, so would not have happened. American settlers would have clustered around the Pacific Fur Company settlement at Astoria. From there, they would have conducted trade to San Francisco to the south, and to the old Spanish settlements of Fort San Miguel and what they probably would have called "Fort Nuca." In patriotic zeal, they likely would have renamed them Fort Washington and Fort Jefferson. The Strait of Juan de Fuca may have kept its Spanish name, but the Canal de Sasamat, Gran Canal de Nuestra Señora del Rosario la Marinera, and Boca del Carmelo would have been changed—perhaps to Liberty Inlet, Freedom Strait, and Independence Sound.

The Fraser River gold rush in 1858, hot on the heels of the California gold rush of 1849, would have attracted at least as many American prospectors as it did, and likely more. The occupation of the territory—now probably called the American North West Territory—would have been full force. More would come for the Cariboo gold rush in the following years. With them would have come thousands of Chinese merchants and labourers. A handful of Americans might have brought slave labourers to work the mines or help support their adventures, as William Clark had done on his expedition with Meriwether Lewis.

The fort town of Jefferson, located at the entry point of the Strait of Juan de Fuca, would have grown considerably. Its Chinatown would have rivalled that of San Francisco. A settlement would have been established on the mainland to provide more services and support to the prospectors, probably near the mouth of the Fraser River or near the site of present-day New Westminster. In 1851, the Americans named a city on the eastern shore of Puget's Sound after the Indigenous Chief Seattle; maybe their city on the Fraser River would also pay tribute to the people who had dominated in that area: Musqueam City.

Secretary of State Seward would have enjoyed visiting Musqueam City, Fort Jefferson, and Fort Washington on his journeys to Alaska, and would have followed through with the purchase of Alaska from Russia in 1867, giving the United States control over every inch of the Pacific coast, from San Diego to Anchorage and slightly beyond. He would have continued to lobby for a railway connection to the American North West Territory, and would have achieved it. First, he would have seen a line built connecting the Midwest to the Northwest, then a line running north from San Francisco.

Meanwhile in the east, it is likely Canadian Confederation would have continued in 1867 with the political union of Upper and Lower Canada with the Maritime colonies. Perhaps Newfoundland and Prince Edward Island would have joined at the same time as well, instead of waiting until later. Their border to the south was secure and well established, but the only thing between them and the United States to the west was the buffer territory of Rupert's Land. Canada would have continued to bargain for Rupert's Land and would have exerted whatever influence it could to persuade the Colonial Office in London to pressure the Hudson's Bay Company on their behalf. Maybe they would have been successful. But it is equally likely that the United States, fresh from buying Alaska for $7 million, may have been prepared to offer the Hudson's Bay Company $20 million—more than ten times the $1.5 million Canada had in mind.

Regardless of what happened to Rupert's Land, it is certain that by 1870, without the incident with the King George's Sound Company happening eighty years earlier, Canada would never have extended farther west than the Rocky Mountains. The terminal point of Macdonald's railway, if it were ever built, would have been Calgary.

Counterfactual Colonialism

We have established that Spain failed to retain a settlement in British Columbia only because Britain objected to Spain's treatment of the KGSC ships at Nootka in 1789. It was because of that event that Britain and Spain agreed, in the subsequent Nootka Conventions, that "neither of the said parties shall form any permanent establishment in the said port or claim any right of sovereignty or territorial dominion there to the exclusion of the other." That deal was respected right up until Britain's hand was forced by the ever-expanding Americans, in 1846, to either occupy and colonize the territory north of the forty-ninth parallel, long since abandoned by Spain, or lose it. Only then, in 1849, did Britain make Vancouver Island a colony (followed by the mainland in 1858).

For seventy years (between Cook's visit in 1778 and establishing a colony in 1849), British vessels had traded along the coast of the Pacific Northwest without establishing any settlements, and insisting that trade should be open to ships of all nations. For most of that time the sentiments of the Enlightenment, which had inspired George III's Proclamation of 1763, Lord Morton's "hints" to Cook, and John Etches's orders to commanders of the KGSC ships, governed relations between the British traders and Indigenous Peoples they encountered: If land was needed, it was to be bought, not taken; trade was to be fair and mutually advantageous; cultural and language differences were to be studied and understood. But that attitude changed significantly in the mid-1800s, with the arrival of the Victorian Age.

Old-timers like James Douglas had been able to ease the shock and pace of transition somewhat for the Indigenous Peoples living on Vancouver Island. But eventually, he and the rest of his generation were overwhelmed by unstoppable forces: the arrival overland of masses of easterners and Europeans, many transported by steam-powered ships and railways, looking for fortunes, accompanied by hundreds of engineers, merchants, bankers, lawyers, and tradesmen, all governed by a revolving door of travelling bureaucrats. After twenty years, even Britain was exhausted by the pace and complexity, and happy to see its colony become Canada's province in 1870.

Henry Crease had prophesied correctly during the Confederation debates that British Columbia was to become "a Far West into which [Canada's] rapidly increasing population may pour, instead of going to swell the bulk of the adjoining States."[1] Sure enough, the population of British Columbia exploded from 10,000 in 1871 to just under 100,000 over the next twenty years. Thirty years after Confederation, the population would skyrocket toward 200,000 and would continue at breakneck speed.

People arrived in British Columbia by the tens of thousands, the vast majority being Canadians whose families had emigrated from England, Scotland, and Ireland. Others came too, including Chinese, Americans, Japanese, and Italians.

But, again, we can ask the question: What if the King George's Sound Company had not existed? What if Martínez arrived in Nootka and established his fort at Friendly Cove, and began to colonize the area uncontested by Britain? The effect on the Nuu-chah-nulth, the Tla-o-qui-aht, and the

Makah, would have been the same as it was on the Aztecs. Spain did not make treaties with Indigenous Peoples; they conquered and converted them. This activity would have begun at Friendly Cove and radiated outward to Clayoquot Sound and then to the Olympic Peninsula. First Chief Maquinna, then Chief Wickaninnish and Chief Tatoosh would have been read a document called the Requerimiento. The document was essentially a legal text, dating back to 1510, asserting Spanish rule in the Americas and encouraging Indigenous Peoples to convert to Christianity.

Following the prepared script verbatim, as required, Martínez would have started his address by saying: "On the part of the King, Don Fernando, and of Doña Juana, his daughter, Queen of Castile and León, subduers of the barbarous nations, we their servants notify and make known to you, as best we can, that the Lord our God, Living and Eternal, created the Heaven and the Earth, and one man and one woman, of whom you and we, all the men of the world, were and are descendants..." Having provided some further explanations about the Spanish world view, and asking that his audience "acknowledge the Church as the Ruler and Superior of the whole world," he would have then read the part of the Requerimiento that asked Indigenous Peoples to consent to their conversion.

He would have then explained the pros and cons of this agreement. Starting with the pros, he would have explained:

> If you do so, you will do well, and that which you are obliged to do to their Highnesses, and we in their name shall receive you in all love and charity, and shall leave you, your wives, and your children, and your lands, free without servitude, that you may do with them and with yourselves freely that which you like and think best, and they shall

> not compel you to turn Christians, unless you yourselves, when informed of the truth, should wish to be converted to our Holy Catholic Faith, as almost all the inhabitants of the rest of the islands have done. And, besides this, their Highnesses award you many privileges and exemptions and will grant you many benefits.

Then he would have identified the consequences of resistance:

> But, if you do not do this, and maliciously make delay in it, I certify to you that, with the help of God, we shall powerfully enter into your country, and shall make war against you in all ways and manners that we can, and shall subject you to the yoke and obedience of the Church and of their Highnesses; we shall take you and your wives and your children, and shall make slaves of them, and as such shall sell and dispose of them as their Highnesses may command; and we shall take away your goods, and shall do you all the mischief and damage that we can, as to vassals who do not obey, and refuse to receive their lord, and resist and contradict him; and we protest that the deaths and losses which shall accrue from this are your fault, and not that of their Highnesses, or ours, nor of these cavaliers who come with us.[2]

As mainland settlements evolved along with the discovery of gold on the Fraser River, the Spanish authorities would have continued to read this document to the Musqueam, Kwikwetlem, Katzie, Kwantlen, Matsqui, and all the other nations encountered on their way. The Spanish language and the Catholic faith would have been expected from all subjects, and taught to them at the missions established at each settlement. Established traditions and customs would have been prohibited. Potlatch ceremonies would have been banned fifty years earlier than they later were under Canadian law.

The Indigenous Peoples living in the Spanish colony of Santa Cruz de Nuca would have experienced a second and equally disruptive cultural shock when, early in the 1800s or certainly by 1821, Spain abandoned its North American claims as the Americans moved north to replace them. The language and loyalties of the Americans would have been different from those of the Spaniards, but if the examples of Captains Salter and Thorn of the *Boston* and *Tonquin* are anything to go by, Indigenous Peoples would have continued to be subjected to physical and verbal abuse and intimidation by arrogant and ambitious newcomers.

After twenty years of Spanish rule, the political authority of Chief Maquinna and other Indigenous leaders would have been subdued, and their powers of resistance significantly diminished. The crew of the *Boston* would not have been massacred, John Jewitt and John Thompson never enslaved, and the *Tonquin* never blown up.

Settlers like Oregon lawyer Samuel Thurston, skeptical of Indigenous people and worried they would gang up with Black Americans to overwhelm white Americans and cause trouble, would have settled in the area by the hundreds. Though likely becoming a "free territory," the Santa Cruz de Nuca region—likely rebranded as the American North West Territory—might have followed Oregon's example of imposing a "Black exclusionary" law that outlawed slavery but also prohibited Black people from entering the region. Without the adamantly British presence in Oregon Territory, and without Britain constantly harping on the United States to abolish slavery in treaties, conventions, and negotiations (which would never happen in this counterfactual scenario), the odds are that slavery would have been tolerated in the American territory for many years. By law, white, Black, and Indigenous people would have lived highly segregated and unequal lives. Territorial surveyors like James Tilton, owner of Charles Mitchell, would have come to their jobs with their slaves in tow. There being no British influence in the area (or, as the *Olympia Pioneer* newspaper put it, no "philanthropic free blacks and English humanitarians"), no one would have fought for Charles's freedom.

Back in Minnesota, Senator Alexander Ramsey would have continued to lobby for a northern railway to be built from St. Paul to the American North West Territory. Ramsey, like many of his constituents, was skeptical and hostile toward Indigenous Peoples and believed that assimilation or annihilation was their only future. In 1862, he responded harshly when many starving and mistreated Dakota people, compelled by years of broken treaty promises, started raiding settlements, farms, and trading posts to reclaim, or retain, some of their land. As commander of the state militia, Ramsey sent the army to defeat the Dakota. Making his position clear in the state legislature, he said: "The Sioux Indians of Minnesota must be exterminated or driven forever beyond the borders of the State."[3] Before the year was over, more than thirty-eight Dakota men were captured and hanged. The following year, Ramsey authorized a corps of volunteer scouts to chase remaining Dakota people out of the state. The volunteers received a daily wage plus an additional $25 for each scalp they were able to provide the adjutant general's office. Ramsey also authorized individual citizens to claim up to $200 for proof that they had killed a Dakota.[4]

After Ramsey's railway arrived, the population of the American North West Territory would have exploded. The population would have matched that of Washington State, growing from about 25,000 people in 1870 to half a million by 1900—nearly 80 percent born in America, about 95 percent white.[5] To the extent any of the American-born arrivals had any ties to England, Scotland, or Ireland, they would have abandoned any sense of loyalty to British ideas and symbols and, like the many other ethnicities flooding into the country from abroad, would have quickly embraced full-blooded American values and attitudes of the era.

The Stars and Stripes would be flying proudly over British Columbia today, and no one would be visiting the Empress Hotel in Victoria for afternoon tea, if not for the unique and unpredictable set of circumstances that persuaded Spain to abandon its forts at Friendly Cove and Neah Bay, and leave its Santa Cruz de Nuca territory behind in 1794.

CONCLUSION

THE POINT of these counterfactual experiments is to consider how, but for a largely forgotten incident and overlooked personalities, the fate of British Columbia, and of Canada, might have turned out differently.

One conclusion that can be drawn from this history, and these thought experiments, is that the world is not just shaped by great leaders with lofty visions. Indeed, it is also shaped—significantly—by interesting and largely unknown people who simply encounter events and respond to them. While the origin stories of the United States and Canada are often told through stories of large personalities like George Washington and Sir John A. Macdonald, it seems unavoidably true that neither of their countries would exist as we know them today if not for people like Richard Etches and Esteban José Martínez.

Another conclusion is that social values change—almost imperceptibly—over time. The first Europeans to visit the Pacific Northwest, and the Indigenous Peoples who lived there at that time, had values that are almost entirely foreign to anyone living there today. It would be a mistake to judge those people by today's values. But if we are sincere in wishing to chart a prosperous and peaceful future, we must be equally sincere in understanding how we got to where we are. The British who arrived in the Pacific Northwest during the reign of King George III saw the world differently than those who arrived in the reign of Queen Victoria. The ideals of the Enlightenment espoused by Adam Smith and John Locke, and embraced by Cook, Etches, and Douglas, were different from those who arrived later. The same is true of the Americans who rejected colonialism in 1776 then embraced it wholeheartedly a century later. We are, today, in a new era, connected but distinct from the eras that preceded it, but it is an era that only people of the future will be able to properly define. Sometimes distance is needed to see the moment for what it is.

A final conclusion important to acknowledge is that technology plays a part in history. Like social values, it may be best seen in hindsight. The stories in the first part of this book take place in a world where most people lived near the coast and travelled by the power of wind. Until the steam engine came on the scene, that had been the way of the world since time immemorial. No one on the west coast of North America could have been prepared for the changes that would follow when the steam engine made it possible for hundreds of thousands to arrive on the scene overland, quickly, by rail. Medical science and technology improved remarkably during the twentieth century, but its state at the end of the eighteenth was such that it was not able to prevent the spread of pathogens that devastated Indigenous communities. That too was unforeseeable. Today we find ourselves adjusting to a post-pandemic world where internet technology allows many to work from home, and artificial intelligence, combined with advanced robotics, holds as yet unknown possibilities.

The King George's Sound Company and its incident with Spain at Nootka in 1789 saved British Columbia, and stopped Canada, from becoming part of the United States. We can only wonder how the political events unfolding today between the United States and Canada will shape the future of the west coast, and of Canada.

ACKNOWLEDGEMENTS

MAKING BOOKS is a team effort. The author does a good deal of researching and writing up front, but the quality and effect of the final work is shaped by several others before it gets into readers' hands.

I am grateful foremost to Lara Kordic at Heritage House Publishing for her interest in this project and for guiding a team of professionals, including Kimiko Fraser, Nandini Thaker, Monica Miller, Rachel Sargeant, and Setareh Ashrafologhalai. I am also indebted to Marial Shea for her editorial efforts, which helped me smooth the rough, trim the lengthy, clarify the opaque, and avoid the embarrassment of errors and oversights. Audrey McClellan's skillful proofreading provided an extra and much-appreciated additional layer of review.

The maritime paintings of artist Mark Myers, especially those portraying scenes of King George's Sound Company ships, have long been a fascination and inspiration to me, and I am very grateful to have received his permission to feature one of my favourites on the cover.

When I felt that new maps needed to be created, to help support the story, cartographer Eric Leinberger came to the rescue.

Together, these experts in their craft have helped me assemble the work that is now in your hands, and I thank them on my own behalf and yours.

I am also indebted to many friends, too many to name, who have entertained and encouraged my interest in this story as it developed. There is nothing more valuable to a storyteller than tolerant friends.

NOTES

Part 1: The 1700s

1. America, 1776

1 Moore, "Fun Facts: From Counties Named Liberty to $368.6M Worth of Fireworks Sold," US Census Bureau website, www.census.gov/library/stories/2019/07/july-fourth-celebrating-243-years-of-independence.html.

2 Alexander, "The Philadelphia Numbers Game."

3 Conway, "The British Army and the War of Independence," p. 185.

4 Letter from George Washington to Marie-Joseph-Paul-Yves-Roch-Gilbert du Motier, Marquis de Lafayette, November 15, 1781, *Founders Online* (National Archives), founders.archives.gov/documents/Washington/99-01-02-07408.

5 Historic UK website, www.historic-uk.com/Blog/British-Navy-Size-Over-Time/.

6 A "ship-of-the-line" is a battleship of usually no less than seventy-four guns (cannons).

7 The British Royal Navy website, www.napolun.com/mirror/napoleonistyka.atspace.com/navy.htm.

8 Scott C. Miller, "Ten Facts About the American Economy in the 18th Century," Mount Vernon website, www.mountvernon.org/george-washington/colonial-life-today/early-american-economics-facts/.

9 Holland and Sandbrook, "The American Revolution, Part 1."

10 Jesus Fernandez-Villaverde, "The Economics of the Revolution," online presentation (University of Pennsylvania), www.sas.upenn .edu/~jesusfv/PEEA_9_Economic_Costs_Revolution.pdf.
11 Letter from James Madison to Richard Henry Lee, July 7, 1785, Founders Online (National Archives), founders.archives.gov/documents/ Madison/01-08-02-0168.
12 View the full Proclamation at the Encyclopedia Virginia website, encyclopediavirginia.org/8974hpr-dfab138fa60b3d9/.
13 Black Loyalist Heritage Centre website, blackloyalist.com/about/.
14 Kolchin, *American Slavery, 1619–1877*, p. 73.
15 Black Loyalist Heritage Centre website, blackloyalist.com/about/.
16 New England Historical Society website,newenglandhistoricalsociety .com/mather-byles-bostons-witty-loyalist-even-patriots-liked/.
17 Inglis, *The True Interest of America Impartially Stated.*
18 Flick, *Loyalism In New York During the American Revolution,* p. 36.

2. Cook and the West Coast of America

1 The letter from Lord Morton can be seen and read here: nla.gov.au/nla .obj-223065583/view. Unfortunately, while Cook was a master navigator, he was neither a philosopher nor a miracle worker, and was not able to fully embrace Lord Morton's hints. In taking possession of the east coast of Australia in the name of the British Crown, Cook contradicted the advice offered by Morton. By doing so, he showed that his primary duty was to King George III and the colonial ambitions of the British government and Admiralty.
2 Weld, *A History of the Royal Society,* p. 37.
3 "Secret Instructions to Lieutenant Cook, 30 July 1768," National Archives of Australia, www.foundingdocs.gov.au/resources/ transcripts/nsw1_doc_1768.pdf.
4 James Cook, *Captain Cook's Journal During His First Voyage Round the World*, entry for January 29, 1771, en.wikisource.org/wiki/Captain_ Cook%27s_Journal_During_His_First_Voyage_Round_the_World/ Chapter_10.
5 Named after the French explorer and naval officer Louis Antoine de Bougainville.
6 There was one notable exception: a marine, Private William Greenslade, either committed suicide by jumping overboard or was

pushed overboard. This happened on March 26, 1769, as the ship was approaching Tahiti, following a conflict regarding claims of theft.

7 "Secret Instructions to Lieutenant Cook, 30 July 1768," National Archives of Australia, www.foundingdocs.gov.au/resources/transcripts/nsw1_doc_1768.pdf.

8 Bethune, "The Secret Voyage of Sir Francis Drake."

9 Cook Journals, p. 414, Princeton University Library website, libdbserver.princeton.edu/visual_materials/maps/websites/pacific/cook2/cook2.html.

10 Rickman, "Journal of Captain Cook's Last Voyage..."

11 Lindsey Flewelling, "Captain Cook's View of Hawaii," *Isles Abroad: A Group Blog of British and Irish Global History* (May 20, 2016), britishandirishhistory.wordpress.com/2016/05/20/captain-cooks-view-of-hawaii/.

12 Yes, the same fellow who "invented" the sandwich.

13 Rickman, "Journal of Captain Cook's Last Voyage...," p. 232.

14 Rickman, "Journal of Captain Cook's Last Voyage...," p. lii.

15 Rickman, "Journal of Captain Cook's Last Voyage...," p. lii.

16 Rickman, "Journal of Captain Cook's Last Voyage...," p. 233.

3. King George's Sound

1 Rickman, "Journal of Captain Cook's Last Voyage...," p. 234.

2 Berg, "Sea Otters and Iron," p. 55.

3 Rickman, "Journal of Captain Cook's Last Voyage...," p. 242.

4 Rickman, "Journal of Captain Cook's Last Voyage...," p. 234–37.

5 Frame, *The Third Voyage of James Cook*.

6 King, *A Voyage to the Pacific Ocean*, p. 3:437.

7 Berg, "Sea Otters and Iron," p. 58.

8 As reported in *The London Chronicle, St. James Chronicle, The Whitehall Evening Post,* and *The Morning Post,* September 22, 1786, web.viu.ca/black/amrc/Research/Papers/kingpaperonmeares.htm#_ednref13. Presumably, since this is reported in an English newspaper, the "l" is an eighteenth-century symbol for "pounds" of British currency. But the reference may be for Spanish dollars, or other currency. Regardless, the point is that an ambitious trader could make thirty times their initial investment or more from the west coast fur trade.

4. The King George's Sound Company

1 Etches, *Hero in the Footnotes,* p. 7.

2 John Cadman Etches [Argonaut, pseud.], *An Authentic Statement of All the Facts Relative to Nootka Sound,* p. 4.

3 Portlock, *A voyage round the world*, p. 6.

4 Etches, *Hero in the Footnotes*, p. 22.

5. Voyages of the King George's Sound Company

1 Etches, *Hero in the Footnotes*, p. 50.

2 To be precise, Frances Barkley was the first woman to sail around the world "without deception." Two other women are known to have sailed around the world before her: Jeanne Baré, disguised as a man; and Rose de Freycinet, wife of Louis de Freycinet, as a stowaway.

3 Letter from Menzies to Banks regarding the patoo patoo, July 14, 1789, in McCarthy, *Monkey Puzzle Man*, p. 66.

4 They arrived home in September 1788.

5 They arrived back in London in July 1789.

6 Etches, *An Authentic Statement* . . . , p. 12.

7 Lamb and Bartroli, "James Hanna and John Henry Cox," p. 31.

8 Lamb and Bartroli, "James Hanna and John Henry Cox," p. 32.

9 Etches, *An Authentic Statement* . . . , p. 14.

10 Etches, *An Authentic Statement* . . . p. 16.

11 Etches, *An Authentic Statement* . . . p. 25.

12 Etches, *An Authentic Statement* . . . p. 23–24.

6. The Nootka Crisis

1 This is why, to this day, Spanish is the dominant language in most of South America, with the exception of Brazil, where Portuguese dominates.

2 The papal bull *Inter Caetera*, issued by Pope Alexander VI on May 4, 1493, The Gilder Lehrman Institute of American History website, www.gilderlehrman.org/history-resources/spotlight-primary-source/doctrine-discovery-1493.

3 Likely named after Saint Rosalina because Pérez was in the area around the time of the Feast of Saint Rosalina, September 4. Seeing the peak in 1788, John Meares named it Mount Olympus, and that name has survived to this day.

4 Etches, *Hero in the Footnotes,* p. 56.
5 Meares, "Mr. Mears's [Sic] Memorial, Dated 30th April, 1790," p. 15.
6 Norris, "The Policy of the British Cabinet in the Nootka Crisis," p. 572.
7 Mills, "The Real Significance of the Nootka Sound Incident," p. 116.
8 Mills, "The Real Significance of the Nootka Sound Incident," p. 119.

7. George Vancouver, Diplomat

1 Vancouver, *A Voyage of Discovery to the North Pacific Ocean and Round the World*, pp. 67–74.
2 Howay, "Some Notes on Cook's and Vancouver's Ships," p. 269.
3 Remarkably, the *Discovery*'s Arnold chronometer still survives and can be viewed at the Maritime Museum in Vancouver, BC. Lieutenant Baker's telescope—perhaps the one he used to spy Mount Baker—is also at this museum, as is his sextant.
4 For more information about the two astronomers on *Discovery* and Arnold chronometers, see arnoldandson.com/en/john-arnold.
5 Howay, "Some Notes on Cook's and Vancouver's Ships," p. 270.
6 Cambridge-educated mathematician and astronomer William Gooch (1770–1792) had also been cut down with Hergest.
7 Menzies would later note in his journal (October 2, 1792) that "saluting was so common among the Trading Vessels that visited the Cove that there was scarcely a day past without puffings of this kind from some Vessel or other, & we too followed the example, & puffed it away as well as any of them." In Menzies, *Menzies' Journal of Vancouver's Voyage*. Other references to Menzies journal are from this book.
8 Archibald Menzies, journal entry September 22, 1792.
9 Tahsis was, as the crews of *Discovery* and *Chatham* had begun to suspect from their cruise past Point Mudge and through Johnstone's Strait, the key to an overland trade route connecting Nootka to the east coast (and other parts) of the island. Maquinna's control and oversight of the trade made him extremely important politically and economically.
10 Archibald Menzies, journal entry September 5, 1792, pp. 117–18.
11 Letter to Banks dated January 14, 1793, from Monterrey Bay. Menzies thought the island ought more rightly to have been named for the King: "It should, I think, with more propriety be named after his Majesty as the name of King George's Sound is now extinct, which Capt. Cook first named for him." legalanswers.sl.nsw.gov.au/banks/section-11/series-61/61-16-letter-received-by-banks-from-archibald.

12 Archibald Menzies, journal entry October 12, 1792, pp. 130–31.
13 Manning, *Nootka Sound Controversy*, p. 467.

Part Two: Coastal Culture and Shock

8. Coastal Contact

1 Reid, *The Sea Is My Country*, p. 8.
2 White, "Was New Spain Really First?" p. 8.
3 White, "Was New Spain Really First?" pp. 1–24.
4 White, "Was New Spain Really First?" pp. 1–24.
5 Rickman, "Journal of Captain Cook's Last Voyage," pp. 235–36.
6 Rickman, "Journal of Captain Cook's Last Voyage," p. 240.
7 Gough, *Distant Dominion*, p. 60.
8 Mr. Elliot's letter can be read in Galois, "The Voyages of James Hanna to the Northwest Coast," pp. 85–86.
9 Quotes from Taylor's notes in this section from Galois, *A Voyage to the North West Side of America*, pp. 104–18.
10 This and other versions telling the Indigenous perspective of first contact are from Galois, *A Voyage to the North West Side of America*, pp. 268–72.

9. Coastal Conflict

1 This and the following story about Wickaninnish from Reid, *The Sea Is My Country*, pp. 59–60.
2 The Requerimiento was written in 1510, based on the papal bull of 1493, discussed earlier. The text, to be read aloud, and often in Latin, demanded that Indigenous peoples accept Spanish rule and Christian preaching or risk subjugation, enslavement, and death.
3 Rickman, "Journal of Captain Cook's Last Voyage," pp. 238–39.
4 Reid, *The Sea Is My Country*, pp. 72–73.
5 Walker, *An Account of a Voyage to the N.W. Coast of America . . .*," p. 65.
6 Galois, *A Voyage to the North West Side of America*, p. 110.
7 Reid, *The Sea Is My Country*, p. 73.
8 Boit and Gray, *The John Boit Log and Captain Gray's Log of the Ship Columbia*, pp. 299–303.
9 In 2005, William Twombly, a descendant of Robert Gray, met with five Hereditary Chiefs and about one hundred band members of the Tla-o-qui-aht to apologize for the destruction of Opitsaht.

10 Archibald Menzies, journal entry, August 12, 1793.
11 Vancouver, *A Voyage of Discovery*, p. 179.
12 Archibald Menzies, journal entry, August 12, 1793.
13 Vancouver, *A Voyage of Discovery*, p. 172.
14 Vancouver, *A Voyage of Discovery*, p. 174. Whether any of the Tlingit were killed is unknown, but Vancouver wrote: "To what degree our firing did execution, was not ascertained. Some of the natives were seen to fall, as if killed or severely wounded; and great lamentations were heard after they had gained their retreat in the woods, from whence they showed no disposition to renew their attack."
15 Vancouver, *A Voyage of Discovery*, pp. 175–76.
16 Vancouver, *A Voyage of Discovery*, p. 180.
17 John R. Jewitt, *The Adventures and Sufferings of John R. Jewitt*, pp. 27–28.
18 "Wa-cosh" is thought to be a word of salutation. Perhaps "Farewell, Maquinnah" or "Adieu, Maquinnah."
19 Howay, "An Early Account of the Loss of the *Boston* in 1803."

Part Three: The 1800s

10. The British East Goes West

1 Canadian Encyclopedia, Immigration Timeline, www.thecanadian encyclopedia.ca/en/timeline/immigration.
2 Also known as the Canada Act.
3 The Act of 1791 also gave women who owned property in Lower Canada the right to vote.
4 Mackenzie journal quotes from Mackenzie's *Voyages from Montreal on the River St. Laurence*, pp. 383–436, dx.doi.org/10.14288/1.0364258.
5 The Scottish pronunciation of the surname Menzies is "Mengis"; the English pronunciation is often closer to "Mensis," which could easily sound like "Bensins" when heard for the first time.
6 Fraser journal quotes from Lamb and Gnarowski, *The Letters and Journals of Simon Fraser, 1806–1808*, pp. 124–28.

11. War, Treaty, and Convention

1 The Bastille was stormed on the same day that HMS *Discovery* arrived back at the River Thames.
2 Prom, "The U.S. Navy in the War of 1812."

3 Prom, "The U.S. Navy in the War of 1812."

4 The Treaty of Ghent was not officially ratified by the US Senate until February 1815.

5 The full text of the Proclamation can be found at this Government of Canada website: www.rcaanc-cirnac.gc.ca/eng/1370355181092/1607905122267#a6.

6 Parsons, "'A Perpetual Harrow upon My Feelings,'" p. 340.

7 This was not entirely without criticism on the British side. The *London Times* called the Treaty of Ghent "a premature and inglorious peace," and many argued then and since that Britain had the upper hand in 1814. Napoleon was no longer a bother and the US was close to financial ruin. A little more effort and Britain could have crushed the American Republic entirely by 1815 or shortly thereafter.

8 Americans would indeed argue that Gray was first to sail up the Columbia River; however, Broughton held the view that Gray had only entered the bay near the mouth of the river, not the river itself. Broughton's charts named the bay "Hezeta's Inlet" after the Spanish captain Bruno de Heceta, who first identified the river (in 1775) and named it Entrada de Ceta. From this perspective, Gray was the second to enter the bay and Broughton was truly the first to explore the Columbia River.

9 The Pacific Fur Company was a subsidiary of the American Fur Company (est. 1808), owned by John Astor.

10 Franchère, *Narrative of a Voyage to the Northwest Coast of America*, pp. 200–201.

12. The Americans Go West

1 The deal has since been recognized as one of the greatest land bargains in US history, working out to a cost of less than three cents per acre for 2,144,520 square kilometres (828,000 square miles). The purchase doubled the size of the United States.

2 To Thomas Jefferson from Lacépède, May 13, 1803, *Founders Online* (National Archives), founders.archives.gov/documents/Jefferson/01-40-02-0275. (Original source: Oberg, *The Papers of Thomas Jefferson*, pp. 367–70.)

3 Jefferson, "President Thomas Jefferson's Confidential Message to Congress," catalog.archives.gov/id/306698.

4 York would become the first Black American to reach the Pacific by land from the east and was a full participant in the expedition. However, unlike the army employees (each of whom received 320 acres), he received no pay or land in return for his services. He would eventually, however, receive his freedom. In a January 2001 presentation in the White House, President Bill Clinton gave York, posthumously, an honorary promotion to the rank of sergeant in the US Army. At the same event, Indigenous guide Sacagawea was also made an honorary sergeant.

5 Lewis and Clark, *Journals of the Lewis and Clark Expedition.*

6 Many of the place names assigned by Lewis and Clark met the same fate as those named by Broughton. When homesteaders arrived from the east they changed the names again. Fanny Island is now Crims Island (named after James Crim) and Canoe Island is now Hayden Island (named after Gay Hayden).

7 From Thomas Jefferson to John Jacob Astor, April 13, 1808, *Founders Online* (National Archives), founders.archives.gov/documents/Jefferson/99-01-02-7829.

8 Franchère, *Narrative of a Voyage to the Northwest Coast of America*, p. 48.

9 Franchère, *Narrative of a Voyage to the Northwest Coast of America*, p. 86.

10 Haeger, *John Jacob Astor,* chapter 6.

11 Franchère, *Narrative of a Voyage to the Northwest Coast of America*, p. 193.

12 We should shed no tears for Astor. He failed at this grand vision of the Pacific Fur Company but went on to make millions of dollars in Manhattan real estate, and was worth about twenty million dollars when he died in 1848.

13 The use of the term "manifest destiny" originated in 1845, when journalist John Louis O'Sullivan wrote that it was America's "manifest destiny to overspread and to possess the whole of the continent which Providence has given us for the development of the great experiment of liberty and federated self-government entrusted to us." John O'Sullivan, "Annexation," *United States Magazine and Democratic Review*, 17, no. 1 (August 1845), pdcrodas.webs.ull.es/anglo/OSullivan Annexation.pdf.

14 Another part of the agreement was that the United States would recognize Spain's sovereignty over Texas. This did not last long.

13. The Oregon Territory

1 Miles, "'Fifty-Four Forty or Fight,'" p. 293.
2 Miles, "'Fifty-Four Forty or Fight,'" p. 294.
3 Shi, "Seward's Attempt to Annex British Columbia, 1865–1869," p. 218.
4 McLagan, "A Peculiar Paradise," p. 30.

14. The Columbia District

1 Pethick, *James Douglas*, p. 31.
2 The first governor, Richard Blanshard, was appointed to that role in July 1849 but did not arrive from England until March 1850; he resigned in frustration and left the island in September 1851.
3 The decision was named after an enslaved Black man named Dred Scott and his wife, Harriet, who had sued for their freedom in St. Louis Circuit Court. They claimed that they were free due to their residence in a free territory where slavery was prohibited. They lost the case, but the decision was eventually overturned, after the Civil War, by the 13th and 14th amendments (1865 and 1868 respectively) to the Constitution, which abolished slavery and declared all persons born in the United States to be citizens of the United States.
4 McConaghy and Bentley, "Wrongfully Detained," pp. 45–50.
5 Seattle Times staff, "The tale of a slave from Olympia," *Seattle Times,* February 13, 2013, www.seattletimes.com/pacific-nw-magazine/the-tale-of-a-slave-from-olympia/.
6 Pethick, *James Douglas,* pp. 77–78.
7 Pethick, *James Douglas,* p. 145.
8 Pethick, *James Douglas,* p. 151.
9 Pethick, *James Douglas,* pp. 159–60.
10 The buildings established in this area of Victoria would lay the groundwork for what would later be the business and cultural centre of Canada's first Chinatown.
11 When Fort Victoria officially became the City of Victoria, in 1862, its population of 5,000 included 300 Chinese people. Twenty years later the national census of 1881 would show the number had doubled to reach 693 (in comparison, the eastern cities of Toronto and Montreal recorded 8 and 7 Chinese people, respectively).
12 Pethick, *James Douglas*, p. 219.

13 Nevertheless, in a move reminiscent of those undertaken by the British governors and naval officers in the Revolutionary War and in the War of 1812, Douglas oversaw the establishment of the Victoria Pioneer Rifle Corps, a militia unit of Black volunteers eager to protect the colony and, if called, to attack the United States.

14 Sage, "The Critical Period of British Columbia History," p. 427.

15 "Responsible government" means an executive or cabinet that depends on the support of an elected assembly for its legitimacy to govern. In responsible government, the political leaders are accountable to the people (the people with voting power, anyway); this differed from the system where the appointed colonial governors were accountable to colonial ministers and officials in Britain.

15. Two Suitors

1 Canada established its Royal Military College for army officer training in 1876, but would not establish its own navy until 1910. The Royal Canadian Air Force was created in 1924. The three services were united in the Canadian Armed Forces in 1968.

2 Section 146 of the British North America Act of 1867.

3 Shi, "Seward's Attempt to Annex British Columbia," p. 223.

4 Lincoln rewarded Seward for his loyalty and made him secretary of state in 1861. So closely was Seward associated with Lincoln's administration that he was, like Lincoln, targeted for assassination on the night of April 14, 1865. He survived the attack after his assassin's gun jammed and his knife attack failed to deliver a fatal blow. Undeterred by the distraction of civil war and assassination attempts, Seward remained convinced that the United States was destined for greatness—including territorial expansion.

5 Seward, *Works of William H. Seward*, p. 333.

6 Shi, "Seward's Attempt to Annex British Columbia," p. 222.

7 Shi, "Seward's Attempt to Annex British Columbia," p. 232.

8 Shi, "Seward's Attempt to Annex British Columbia," p. 234.

9 An initial petition of forty-three signatories was supplemented by a list of sixty-one additional signatories, bringing the total to just over one hundred. Considering that the non-Indigenous population of Victoria at this time was about four thousand, and the non-Indigenous population of British Columbia was somewhere between ten and fifteen

thousand, one hundred signatories does not seem particularly large. But the document was significant. The petitioners were sincere in their concerns and expressed them frankly; and the US president received the petition with interest. The Colonial Office in London was also aware of the petition and, ironically, may have been motivated by it to promote Confederation more vigorously.

10 Ireland, "The Annexation Petition of 1869."

11 Shi, "Seward's Attempt to Annex British Columbia," p. 236.

12 *London Daily News*, January 2, 1868.

13 Shi, "Seward's Attempt to Annex British Columbia," p. 227.

14 Seward put his signature on the Alaska deal just one day before Queen Victoria put hers on the British North America Act.

16. Falling for Canada

1 Blakey-Smith, *The Reminiscences of Doctor John Sebastian Helmcken*, p. 252.

2 Pethick, "The Confederation Debate," p. 169.

3 Pethick, "The Confederation Debate," p. 170.

4 Pethick, "The Confederation Debate," p. 182.

5 Sage, "The Critical Period of British Columbia History," p. 441.

6 Pethick, "The Confederation Debate," p. 171.

7 Pethick, "The Confederation Debate," p. 171.

8 *London Daily News*, January 2, 1868.

9 Pethick, "The Confederation Debate," p. 170.

10 British Columbia Confederation Debates, March 10, 1870.

11 British Columbia Confederation Debates, March 10, 1870.

12 British Columbia Confederation Debates, March 10, 1870.

13 Pethick, "The Confederation Debate of 1870," p. 175.

14 British Columbia Confederation Debates, March 10, 1870

15 British Columbia Confederation Debates, March 11, 1870.

16 A few years after British Columbia joined Canada, in 1876, Ottawa passed the Indian Act—a one-size-fits-all policy approach for managing the "Indians" of Canada. Patronizing and infantilizing, the Act assigned all of the Indigenous land, property, and people to the custodianship of the federal government—civil servants and policy-makers who had no experience with or understanding of the traditions and customs of the coastal tribes, or of any of the mainland tribes west of the Rockies. While Indigenous Peoples were estimated to comprise

80 percent of the British Columbia population in 1870, they would account for just 6 percent by 1900. Today, the Indigenous population of British Columbia, numbering about 270,000 people, is still just 6 percent of total population.

17 B. Smith, "The Confederation Delegation," p. 213.

18 The province of Manitoba was created by Canada on July 15, 1870, after British Columbia had concluded its debates but before it had been formally admitted into Confederation.

19 B. Smith, "The Confederation Delegation," p. 216.

Part Four: Counterfactual Canada

17. No Etches, No Canada?

1 Pethick, "The Confederation Debate," p. 170.

2 The full English translation of the Requerimiento can be found online at nationalhumanitiescenter.org/pds/amerbegin/contact/text7/requirement.pdf.

3 See the Alexander Ramsey House website: www.mnhs.org/ramseyhouse.

4 The bounty orders remained in effect until at least 1868, when their constitutionality was questioned by the Minnesota Supreme Court in State v. Gut. Bounty laws had also existed in the States of Arizona and California.

5 According to the US Census, the population of Washington State in 1870 was 23,955. In 1890 it was 357,232; in 1900 it was 518,103 (including 2,531 Indigenous people on reservations). According to the University of Washington's Center for the Study of the Pacific Northwest, smallpox and other diseases such as influenza and malaria reduced the northwestern Indigenous population by 65 to 95 percent by 1840. Had Spain kept and developed its colony at Nootka, and had it sold its rights to the region we now call British Columbia to the Americans in the early half of the nineteenth century, the effects of European pathogens would have started earlier and likely had more devastating effect.

BIBLIOGRAPHY

Alexander, John K. "The Philadelphia Numbers Game: An Analysis of Philadelphia's Eighteenth-Century Population." *The Pennsylvania Magazine of History and Biography* 98, no. 3 (1974): 314–24. http://www.jstor.org/stable/20090869.

Bartroli, Tomas. "The Spanish Establishment at Nootka Sound (1789–1792)." Master's thesis. Retrospective Theses and Dissertations, 1919–2007. University of British Columbia, 1960. dx.doi.org/10.14288/1.0105930.

Bawlf, Samuel. *The Secret Voyage of Sir Francis Drake: 1577–1580*. Douglas & McIntyre, 2003.

Bennett, Linda. *Captain Cook at Nootka Sound: A daily account of Captain Cook's stay at Nootka Sound, compiled from Cook's and other's [sic] journals, for the days March 7 to April 26, 1778*. Vancouver School Board, 1978.

Berg, Maxine. "Sea Otters and Iron: A Global Microhistory of Value and Exchange at Nootka Sound, 1774–1792." *Past and Present*, Vol. 242, Issue Supplement_14, November 2019, pp. 50–82. doi.org/10.1093/pastj/gtz038.

Bethune, Brian. "Book Review: The Secret Voyage of Sir Francis Drake." First published in *Maclean's* magazine, October 15, 2003. *The Canadian Encyclopedia*. Historica Canada. Last edited December 16, 2013. www.thecanadianencyclopedia.ca/en/article/book-review-the-secret-voyage-of-sir-francis-drake

Blegen, Theodore C. "Campaigning with Seward in 1860." *Minnesota History* 8, no. 2 (1927): pp. 150–71. www.jstor.org/stable/20160659.

Boit, John, and Edmond S. Meany. "A New Log of the Columbia." *The Washington Historical Quarterly* 12, no. 1 (1921): 3–50. http://www.jstor.org/stable/40473782.

Boit, John, and Robert Gray. *The John Boit Log and Captain Gray's Log of the Ship Columbia*. Ivy Press, 1921.

Botting, Ellen Hunt. "From revolutionary Paris to Nootka Sound to Saint-Domingue: The international politics and prejudice behind Wollstonecraft's theory of the rights of humanity, 1789–91." *Journal of International Political Theory*, 18:1, pp. 46–65. doi.org/10.1177/1755088220978432.

Broughton, William Robert. *A Voyage of Discovery to the North Pacific Ocean*. BC Historical Books. London: T. Cadell and W. Davies, 1804. dx.doi.org/10.14288/1.0222637.

Cain, P. J., and A. G. Hopkins. "The Political Economy of British Expansion Overseas, 1750–1914." *The Economic History Review* 33, no. 4 (1980): 463–90. doi.org/10.2307/2594798.

Captain Cook Society. www.captaincooksociety.com.

Chandler, Thomas Bradbury and Myles Cooper. *A friendly address to all reasonable Americans, on the subject of our political confusions: in which the necessary consequences of violently opposing the King's troops, and of a general non-importation are fairly stated*. New York: 1774. www.canadiana.ca/view/oocihm.20462.

Conway, Stephen. "The British Army and the War of Independence" in *The Oxford Handbook of the American Revolution*, edited by Jane Kamensky and Edward G. Gray, 2012. doi.org/10.1093/oxfordhb/9780199746705.013.0011.

Cook, James. *The Journals of Captain James Cook on His Voyages of Discovery*. Edited by J. C. Beaglehole. Hakluyt Society, Extra series, no. 34–37. Cambridge University Press (for the Hakluyt Society), 1955. British Library Shelfmark: Open Access Manuscripts Reading Room MSL 912.09.

———. *The Journals of Captain James Cook On His Voyages of Discovery*. Edited by J. C. Beaglehole. Cambridge University Press (for the Hakluyt Society), 1974.

Coote, Jeremy. "Joseph Banks's Forty Brass Patus." *Journal of Museum Ethnography*, no. 20, 2008. www.jstor.org/stable/40793870.

Cornwall, Claudia. "The Suicide Bomber of Clayoquot Sound, Revived." *The Tyee*, March 14, 2008. thetyee.ca/Life/2008/03/14/SuicideIn1811/.

Crawford, Kilian. *Go Do Some Great Thing: The Black Pioneers of British Columbia*, 3rd ed. With a foreword by Adam Rudder. Harbour Publishing, 2020.

Dugard, Martin. *Farther than Any Man: The Rise and Fall of Captain James Cook*. Allen & Unwin, 2003.

Elliott, T. C. "The Log of H.M.S. 'Chatham.'" *The Quarterly of the Oregon Historical Society* 18, no. 4 (1917): 231–43. www.jstor.org/stable/20610082.

Etches, John Cadman [Argonaut, pseud.]. *An Authentic Statement of All the Facts Relative to Nootka Sound: its discovery, history, settlement, trade, and the probable advantages to be derived from it : in an address to the King.* London: Printed for J. Debret, 1790.

Etches, Michael. *Hero in the Footnotes: The Life and Times of Richard Cadman Etches, Entrepreneur and British Spy.* AuthorHouse UK, 2021.

Fanning, Edmund. *Voyages Round the World: With Selected Sketches of Voyages to the South Seas, North and South Pacific Oceans, China, etc.* New York: Collins & Hannay, 1833. https://hdl.handle.net/2027/mdp.39015021581171.

Flick, Alexander Clarence. *Loyalism In New York During the American Revolution.* Columbia University Press, 1901.

Frame, William, and Laura Walker. "The Third Voyage (1776–80)." In *James Cook: The Voyages.* McGill-Queen's University Press, 2018.

Franchère, Gabriel. *Narrative of a voyage to the Northwest coast of America, in the years 1811, 1812, 1813, and 1814 or the first American settlement on the Pacific.* New York: Redfield, 1854. dx.doi.org/10.14288/1.0222788.

Fraser, Simon. *The Letters and Journals of Simon Fraser, 1806–1808.* Edited by W. Kaye Lamb. Foreword by Michael Gnarowski. Dundurn Press, 2007.

French, Christopher J. "'Crowded with Traders and a Great Commerce': London's Domination of English Overseas Trade, 1700–1775." *The London Journal* 17 (1): 27–35, 1992. doi.org/10.1179/ldn.1992.17.1.27.

Galois, Robert M. "The Voyages of James Hanna to the Northwest Coast: Two Documents." *BC Studies*, no. 103, fall 1994. doi.org/10.14288/bcs.v0i103.932.

Galois, Robert M., ed. *A Voyage to the Northwest Side of America: The Journals of James Colnett, 1786–89.* UBC Press, 2003.

Gilbert, Bill. "The Dying Tecumseh and the Birth of a Legend." *Smithsonian Magazine,* July 1995. www.smithsonianmag.com/history/the-dying-tecumseh-97830806/.

Gough, Barry. *Britannia's Navy on the West Coast, 1812–1914.* Heritage House, 2016.

——. *Distant Dominion: Britain and the Northwest Coast of North America, 1579–1809.* UBC Press, 1980.

——. *Gunboat Frontier: British Maritime Authority and Northwest Coast Indians, 1846–1890.* UBC Press, 1984.

——. *The Northwest Coast: British Navigation, Trade, and Discoveries to 1812.* UBC Press, 1992.

Gray, Edward G. "Visions of Another Empire: John Ledyard, an American Traveler across the Russian Empire, 1787–1788." *Journal of the Early Republic* 24, no. 3 (2004): 347–80. www.jstor.org/stable/4141438.

Haeger, John Denis. *John Jacob Astor: Business and Finance in the Early Republic*, illust. ed. Wayne State University Press, 2017.

Helmcken, John Sebastian. *The Reminiscences of Doctor John Sebastian Helmcken*. Edited by Dorothy Blakey-Smith. University of British Columbia, 1975.

Hewitt, Bernard. "Minutes of the Proceedings at Quebec,1864." In *Confederation: Being a Series of Hitherto Unpublished Documents Bearing on the British North America Act*. Edited by Joseph Pope. Carswell Co. Ltd., Law Publishers, 1895: 1–38. primarydocuments.ca/confederation-being-a-series-of-hitherto-unpublished-documents-bearing-on-the-british-north-america-act/.

Holland, Tom, and Dominic Sandbrook, hosts. "The American Revolution, Part 1." *The Rest is History* podcast. July 2, 2023. podcasts.apple.com/gb/podcast/the-american-revolution-part-1/id1537788786?i=1000619057107.

Howay, F. W. "An Early Account of the Loss of the Boston in 1803." *The Washington Historical Quarterly* 17, no. 4 (1926): 280–88. www.jstor.org/stable/40475046.

——. "Some Notes on Cook's and Vancouver's Ships, 1776–80, 1791–95." *The Washington Historical Quarterly* 21, no. 4 (1930): 268–70. www.jstor.org/stable/40475364.

Inglis, Charles. *The True Interest of America Impartially Stated, in Certain Strictures on a Pamphlet Intitled Common Sense: By an American*. 2nd ed. James Humphreys, Jr., 1776. www.vlib.us/amdocs/texts/inglis.html.

Ireland, Willard E. "The Annexation Petition of 1869." *BC Historical Quarterly*, vol. IV, no. 4 (October 1940): 267–87. open.library.ubc.ca/collections/bcbooks/items/1.0416601.

Janis, M. W. "Jeremy Bentham and the Fashioning of 'International Law.'" *The American Journal of International Law* 78, no. 2 (1984): 405–18. www.jstor.org/stable/2202284.

Jefferson, Thomas. *The Papers of Thomas Jefferson*, vol. 40, March to July 1803. Edited by Barbara B. Oberg. Princeton University Press, 2013. doi.org/10.2307/j.ctv301hcq.

——. "President Thomas Jefferson's Confidential Message to Congress Concerning Relations with the Indians and Proposing an Expedition to Explore Across the Continent to the Western Ocean." January 18, 1803. US National Archives Catalogue. catalog.archives.gov/id/306698.

Jewitt, John R. *The Adventures and Sufferings of John R. Jewitt, Captive Among the Nootka, 1803–1805*. Edited by Derek G. Smith. McGill-Queen's University Press, 1974.

King, James. *A Voyage to the Pacific Ocean*. Vol. 3. W. and A. Strahan, 1784. https://lccn.loc.gov/05034847

King, Robert J. "John Meares: Dubliner, Naval Officer, Fur Trader and would-be Colonizer." Presented at Shamrock in the Bush, August 6, 2010. In *Journal of Australian Naval History*, vol. 8, no.1 (March 2011): 32–62. web.viu.ca/black/amrc/Research/Papers/kingpaperonmeares.htm.

Kolchin, Peter. *American Slavery, 1619–1877*. Hill and Wang, 1994.

Lamb, W. Kaye, and Tomas Bartroli. "James Hanna and John Henry Cox: The First Maritime Fur Trader and His Sponsor." *BC Studies*, no 84 (Winter 1989–1990): 3–36. https://doi.org/10.14288/bcs.v0i84.1333

Lewis, Meriwether, and William Clark. *Journals of the Lewis and Clark Expedition* Online. University of Nebraska Press. lewisandclarkjournals.unl.edu/.

———. *Journals of Lewis and Clark, 1804–1806*. American Philosophical Society; Project Gutenberg e-book edition: 2005. https://www.gutenberg.org/ebooks/8419.

Lynch, John. "British Policy and Spanish America, 1783–1808." *Journal of Latin American Studies* 1, no. 1 (1969): 1–30. www.jstor.org/stable/156483.

Mackenzie, Alexander. *Voyages from Montreal on the River St. Laurence through the Continent of North America to the Frozen and Pacific Oceans in the Years 1789 and 1793 with a Preliminary Account of the Rise, Progress, and Present State of the Fur Trade of That Country*. Raddisson Society of Canada: 1927. dx.doi.org/10.14288/1.0364258.

Manby, Thomas. John Crosse research collection, Great Britain, Public Record Office, 1977. *Journals and Logs of the His Majesty's Ships HMS Dover (1819–1824) and HM Sloop Discovery (1790–1795)*. London: The National Archives.

Manning, William Ray. *The Nootka Sound Controversy: A Dissertation*: US Government Printing Office, 1905. dx.doi.org/10.14288/1.0224029.

Mattson, Linda. Northern Gateway Pipelines Project: Gitxaala Nation—Written Evidence. Affidavit, December 15, 2011. File OF-Fac-Oil-N304-2020-01. apps.cer-rec.gc.ca/REGDOCS/Search/Index/?sr=1&loc=773564&srt=0&isc=FalsE&Iscd=TruE&Filter=Attr_12186_7&pt=18.

McCarthy, James. *Monkey Puzzle Man: Archibald Menzies, Plant Hunter*. Whittles Publishing, 2008.

McConaghy, Lorraine, and Judy Bentley. "Wrongfully Detained." In *Free Boy: A True Story of Slave and Master*, 45–50. University of Washington Press, 2013. www.jstor.org/stable/j.ctvcwn39f.9.

McLagan, Elizabeth. *A Peculiar Paradise: A History of Blacks in Oregon, 1788–1940*, 2nd ed. Oregon State University Press, 2022.

Meares, John. "Mr. Mears's Memorial, Dated 30th April 1790 (14 Inclosures): To the Right Honourable William Wyndham Grenville, one of His Majesty's principal Secretaries of State." 1790. dx.doi.org/10.14288/1.0308168.

———. *Voyages Made in the Years 1788 and 1789 from China to the North West Coast of America*. Logographic Press, 1790. dx.doi.org/10.14288/1.0315360.

Menzies, Archibald. *Menzies' Journal of Vancouver's Voyage, April to October, 1792*. Edited by C.F. Newcombe. William H. Cullen, King's Printer, 1923. dx.doi.org/10.14288/1.0226118.

Menzies, Charles. "Report on Gitxaała Use and Occupancy of the Area Now Known as Prince Rupert Harbour with specific reference to the site of the Prince Rupert Container Port Development." University of British Columbia, 2008. blogs.ubc.ca/ecoknow/files/2009/04/Port_Sept19_2008.pdf.

Miles, Edwin A. "'Fifty-Four Forty or Fight'—An American Political Legend." *Journal of American History*, vol. 44, iss. 2 (September 1957). doi.org/10.2307/1887191.

Miller, Holly and Michael Reese. *"Indians and Europeans on the Northwest Coast, 1774–1812": A Curriculum Project for Washington Schools*. Center for the Study of the Pacific Northwest, University of Washington. sites.uw.edu/cspn/indians-and-europeans.

Millett, Nathaniel. *The Maroons of Prospect Bluff and Their Quest for Freedom in the Atlantic World*. University Press of Florida, 2013. doi.org/10.2307/j.ctvx06xn9.

Mills, Lennox. "The Real Significance of the Nootka Sound Incident." *The Canadian Historical Review* 6, no. 2 (1925): 110–22. doi.org/10.3138/chr-06-02-02.

Mockford, Jim. "Before Lewis and Clark, Lt. Broughton's River of Names: The Columbia River Exploration of 1792." *Oregon Historical Quarterly* 106, no. 4 (2005): 542–67. www.jstor.org/stable/20615586.

Norris, John M. "The Policy of the British Cabinet in the Nootka Crisis." *The English Historical Review* 70, no. 277 (1955): 262–80. www.jstor.org/stable/558040.

O'Brian, Patrick. *Joseph Banks: A Life*. Harvill Press, 1987.

Orchiston, Wayne. "Cook, Green, Maskelyne and the 1769 Transit of Venus: The Legacy of the Tahitian Observations." *Journal of Astronomical History and Heritage* 20, no. 1 (2017): 35–68.

Parsons, Lynn Hudson. "'A Perpetual Harrow upon My Feelings': John Quincy Adams and the American Indian." *The New England Quarterly* 46, no. 3 (1973): 339–79. doi.org/10.2307/364198.

Peckham, Howard H., ed. *The Toll of Independence: Engagements and Battle Casualties of the American Revolution*. University of Chicago Press, 1974.

Pethick, Derek. *The Confederation Debate of 1870: British Columbia and Confederation*. University of Victoria, 1967.

——. *James Douglas: Servant of Two Empires*. Mitchell Press Limited, 1967.

Portlock, Nathaniel. *A voyage round the world: but more particularly to the north-west coast of America performed in 1785, 1786, 1787, and 1788, in the King George and Queen Charlotte, Captains Portlock and Dixon*. John Stockdale and George Goulding, 1789. dx.doi.org/10.14288/1.0305880.

Preusch, Matthew. "Old anchor or new chapter in Washington Irving tale?" *Taipei Times*, September 22, 2003. www.taipeitimes.com/News/feat/archives/2003/09/22/2003068853.

Prom, William J. "The U.S. Navy in the war of 1812: Winning the battle but losing the War, Part One." Center for International Maritime Security, 2019. cimsec.org/the-u-s-navy-in-the-war-of-1812-winning-thebattle-but-losing-the-war-pt-1/.

Reid, Joshua L. "The Power of Wickaninnish Ends Here." In *The Sea Is My Country: The Maritime World of the Makahs*. Online edition. Yale Scholarship Online, 2016. doi.org/10.12987/yale/9780300209907.003.0001.

——. *The Sea Is My Country: The Maritime World of the Makahs*. Yale University Press, 2015.

Rickman, John. "Journal of Captain Cook's Last Voyage to the Pacific Ocean on Discovery: Performed in the Years 1776, 1777, 1778, 1779." E. Newbery, 1781. dx.doi.org/10.14288/1.0305031.

Routel, Colette. "Minnesota Bounties On Dakota Men During The U.S.–Dakota War." *William Mitchell Law Review* 40 (2013): 260. https://dx.doi.org/10.2139/ssrn.2334923.

Roy, Patricia E. "The Interests of Confederation Demanded it: British Columbia and Confederation." In *Reconsidering Confederation: Canada's Founding Debates, 1864–1999*. Edited by Daniel Heidt. 171–92. University of Calgary Press, 2018. https://doi.org/10.2307/j.ctv8jp067.11.

Sage, Walter N. "The Critical Period of British Columbia History, 1866–1871." *Pacific Historical Review* 1, no. 4 (1932): 424–43. doi.org/10.2307/3633112.

——. "Spanish Explorers of the British Columbian Coast." *The Canadian Historical Review* 12, no. 4 (1931): 390–406. muse.jhu.edu/article/625684/summary.

Seward, William H. *Works of William H. Seward*. Vol. IV. Edited by George E. Baker. Houghton, Mifflin and Company, 1884.

Shi, David E. "Seward's Attempt to Annex British Columbia, 1865–1869." *Pacific Historical Review* 47, no. 2 (1978): 217–38. doi.org/10.2307/3637972.

Smith, Brian. "The Confederation Delegation. British Columbia and Confederation." In *British Columbia and Confederation*. Edited by W. George Shelton. University of Victoria, 1967.

——. "The Barbeau Archives at the Canadian Museum of Civilization: Some Current Research Problems." *Anthropologica* 43, no. 2 (2001). doi.org/10.2307/25606034.

Thurman, Michael E. *The Naval Department of San Blas: New Spain's Bastion for Alta California and Nootka, 1767 to 1798*. A. H. Clark Co., 1967.

Tolstoy, Nikolai. *The Half-Mad Lord: Thomas Pitt, 2nd Baron Camelford (1775–1804)*. J. Cape, 1978.

University of Victoria Humanities Computing and Media Centre. British Columbia Confederation Debates, March 10, 1870, *Legislative Council: Debates on the Subject of Confederation with Canada*. hcmc.uvic.ca/confederation/en/lgBCLC_1870-03-10.html.

Vancouver, George, and John Vancouver. *A Voyage of Discovery to the North Pacific Ocean and Round the World; in Which the Coast of North-West America Has Been Carefully Examined and Accurately Surveyed : Undertaken by His Majesty's Command, Principally with a View to Ascertain the Existence of Any Navigable Communication between the North Pacific and North Atlantic Oceans; and Performed in the Years 1790, 1791, 1792, 1793, 1794 and 1795, in the Discovery Sloop of War, and Armed Tender Chatham, under the Command of Captain George Vancouver.* London: 1798. dx.doi.org/10.14288/1.0368509.

Walker, Alexander. *An Account of a Voyage to the N.W. Coast of America in 1785 and 1786*. Edited by Robin Fisher and J.M. Bumstead. Douglas and McIntyre, 1983.

Watt, James. *The Voyage of Captain George Vancouver 1791–95: The Interplay of Physical and Psychological Pressures*. Canadian Bulleting of Medical History 4, no. 1 (1987): 33–51. https://doi.org/10.3138/cbmh.4.1.33.

Weld, Charles Richard. *A History of the Royal Society, with Memoirs of the Presidents*, vol. 2. London: John W. Parker, 1848.

White, Frederick H. "Was New Spain Really First?: Rereading Juan Perez's 1774 Expedition to Haida Gwaii." *The Canadian Journal of Native Studies* 26, no. 1 (2006): 1–24. https://cjns.brandonu.ca/online-issues/vol-26-no-1-2006/.

Young, George. *The Life and Voyages of Captain James Cook*. Whittaker, Treacher & Co., 1836. dx.doi.org/10.14288/1.0368731.

INDEX

Page numbers in *italics* indicate images. Page numbers in the form 262n3 indicate an endnote; in this case, note 3 on page 262. Abbreviations: BC = British Columbia; BNA = British North America; HBC = Hudson's Bay Company; KGSC = King George's Sound Company; NWC = North West Company; OR = Oregon; US = United States; WA = Washington State

ABOUT THE AUTHOR

BAIRD MENZIES

GRAEME MENZIES is a writer, researcher, storyteller, and international marketing and communications professional with a natural curiosity that informs his writing and fuels his passion for sharing stories with an audience of like-minded readers. He is the author of the historical biography *Bones: The Life and Adventures of Doctor Archibald Menzies* and co-author (with Dave Doroghy) of several books in the 111 Places series of guidebooks, including *111 Places in Victoria That You Must Not Miss*, *111 Places in Whistler That You Must Not Miss*, and *111 Places in Vancouver That You Must Not Miss*. He is an Associate Fellow of the Royal Historical Society.